Christopher Hilton has covered motor sport for the *Daily Express* for several years, particularly Grand Prix racing. He has written extensively on other sports and covered four Olympic Games. He has had four novels published, also *Nigel Mansell* (a Corgi paperback), and *Conquest of Formula 1*. Christopher Hilton lives in Hertfordshire.

'Hilton reveals more about the Brazilian sensation than the driver will want us to know' – Jim Dunn, *Scotsman*

'A unique and in-depth work' – Peter Dick, *Formula* magazine, Toronto

D0367352

Also by Christopher Hilton

NIGEL MANSELL

and published by Corgi Books

AYRTON SENNA

The Hard Edge of Genius

Christopher Hilton

Photographs by Keith Sutton

CORGI BOOKS

AYRTON SENNA: THE HARD EDGE OF GENIUS
A CORGI BOOK 0 552 13754 5

Originally published in Great Britain by
Patrick Stephens Ltd

PRINTING HISTORY
Patrick Stephens edition published 1990
Corgi edition with additional material published 1991

This book is set in 10/12 Meridien Medium
by Falcon Typographic Art Ltd

Corgi Books are published by Transworld Publishers Ltd.,
61-63 Uxbridge Road, Ealing, London W5 5SA, in Australia
by Transworld Publishers (Australia) Pty Ltd, 15-23 Helles
Avenue, Moorebank, NSW 2170, and in New Zealand by
Transworld Publishers (NZ) Ltd, Cnr Moselle and Waipareira
Avenues, Henderson, Auckland.

Made and printed in Great Britain by
Cox & Wyman Ltd, Reading, Berks.

Contents

CHAPTER ONE

The Hall of Mirrors

Autumn was the coldest season, autumn was frozen into images so cold they carried frostbite within them. Sunday 21 October 1990, the Suzuka circuit Japan, one o'clock local time. An official stood motionless for a moment on the rim of the track, waiting. With a theatrical flourish he drew the flag in front of him, hoisted it high in his right hand and sprinted across the rear of the grid in bouncy-bouncy bounds, waving it to signal that all twenty-five were at rest. The red light came on.

It flicked to green faster than the blink of an eye.

Way up there at the front of the grid Ayrton Senna, heading the right-hand column of cars, was feeding the power into his Marlboro McLaren Honda. Alain Prost, heading the left-hand column, was feeding the power into his Ferrari. Senna's power was so enormous, so sudden that the McLaren moved towards the centre of the track under its impetus. Already Prost had nosed his way ahead. It was less than two seconds into the Japanese Grand Prix. At six seconds Prost was completely in front, Senna directly behind him. At seven seconds Prost had the Ferrari positioned mid-track but angling into the first corner which was coming at him in a great rush: an unfolding right. At eight seconds Senna had thrust the McLaren towards the inside of Prost. At nine seconds Senna's front wheels were alongside the flank of the Ferrari but never further than the Ferrari's rear wheels – and that for no more than a milli-second. Prost was still turning into the corner, still turning across Senna . . .

1

They touched, the Ferrari's rear wing was wrenched off and flung savagely away like debris on to the track, the McLaren's front left wheel was wrenched clean off and both cars were engulfed in a vast rolling ball of dust as they went off across the broad run-off area and this ball was rolling at frantic speed exactly like a dust-storm driven on some terrible wind. The two cars ploughed on all unseen somewhere within it. At sixteen seconds they struck the tyre-wall at the far side of the run-off area, sending a short, sharp tremor through it. A single white tyre was wrenched from it and bounced lazily away, then settled. The two cars were beached at angles to each other perhaps ten yards apart, perhaps a little closer. At eighteen seconds Prost had already unclipped his seat belts and was elbowing himself out of the Ferrari; and the images became ethereal, almost surreal as the dust thinned and drifted and ebbed away, rubbing itself, as an autumnal mist would have done, against Prost. For an instinctive instant he stood beside the carcass of what eight seconds before had been a beautiful, prehensile racing machine costing several million dollars; as Prost stood Senna began to elbow himself out of the McLaren and just enough of the mist remained to wreathe him, just enough to render him an apparition rather than a medium-sized man in a yellow crash helmet and blood-red flameproof overalls.

Ayrton Senna da Silva was World Champion. Prost had had to beat him across the full 53 laps, the full 192.953 miles of the Grand Prix to prevent it, then perhaps become Champion himself in the final race at Adelaide. Now this.

'He did it on purpose,' Prost would say. 'He knew he had no chance of winning the race if I got ahead so he pushed me off. If this is the way the Championship is going to be concluded then the sport is dead. Whatever he may think about me, I can't understand how he is prepared to risk his

2

own safety going into the first corner. I never expected him to do this. I thought he was a member of the human race, that he was hard but always fair. If there is no change in the regulations, if it is not possible to apply sanctions to this sort of driving then it may not be possible for me to continue in racing. I'm not ready to fight against irresponsible people on the track who are not afraid to die.'

'I don't give a damn what he says,' Senna would respond. 'I can't be responsible for his actions. He moved over on me. He has tried to destroy me in the past but he will not succeed.'

Was it only a year before, deep into another autumnal chill, that Prost had said: 'Ayrton has a small problem. He thinks he can't kill himself because he believes in God and I think that's very dangerous for the other drivers'? Was it only a year before that FISA, motor sport's governing body, had reprimanded Senna for being a driver who 'endangers the safety of others' and fined him $100,000? Only a year before that Senna himself said after a crash with Nigel Mansell at Portugal: 'What happened could have had a terrible ending. A disastrous ending. Mansell put in danger the life of another person. When we went off the track I managed to stop in 200 metres. There was a barrier. I could have lost my life'?

In 1989 and 1990 one impossibly talented driver's obsession reached a conclusion which with hindsight it was always going to reach: a conclusion impelled by an all-pervading logic. The obsession was by turns magnificent and meagre and all manner of other adjectives suited it. The whole world of sport had seen nothing like this and few faced directly with it had the remotest idea how to cope. Forgive them. There were no precedents. And behind it all stood a bemusing, bemused Brazilian who was shy, awkward, charming, savagely subjecting himself to a single idea, a World Champion in a merciless activity, and all

3

manner of adjectives suited him as well as his obsession. This is a book about that and we need to confront the problem head-on, we need, in a certain sense, to have a car crash with him because Ayrton Senna is elusive prey. He lives his professional life in front of the global audience, his often mournful pasty-complexioned face is as familiar in São Paulo as it is in Suzuka, Sydney and Spa but except at rare, impromptu moments it is always the same face, always screwed down under the weight of what he judges The Face should portray. Invariably that is – nothing.

He knows the language of minimal communication, he'll go round Monaco so fast even obtuse observers shake their heads, and then he'll talk of tyres and grip and traffic and the rest of it almost as if somebody else had done the lap. In a sense, somebody else had. Another Ayrton Senna. The prudent course, perhaps the only course is to see him through his own eyes and the eyes of others who have been touched by him and the obsession along the way. This method will bear us forward on a strange journey.

'He's worked out that whatever he says could be misconstrued so he confines himself to the obvious. When you get to know him better he is a very interesting person, someone whom I like very much. When you're one-on-one with him he's humorous, there's a Latin warmth, it's just that the public never sees it.' – Steve Nichols, former McLaren designer.

He can also, when he chooses, be quite remarkably candid and eloquent in English and Italian as well as Portuguese and, deep into the chill of 1989, so candid that his press conferences became events, confessionals. The one he gave at Adelaide lasted almost an hour and a half, his eyes hooded by sadness and what he considered injustice.

He is shy and doesn't talk to strangers, they say. Maybe.

I used to phone him in 1983 when I was a total stranger and painfully, as if he was stepping over sharp stones, he'd urge his limited English to try and tell me what he was doing in Formula Three. I have never known him be anything less than exquisitely polite except when he was tired, mobbed or harassed at the wrong moment. Others have had other experiences but they're not writing this book.

'Since my childhood, I have been taught that it is not honourable to ignore people and therefore when journalists come up to me I try to answer their questions.' – Ayrton Senna.

He is arrogant and insensitive, they say. It's not that. He's living in another dimension where ordinary values do not obtain. It is the other side of money, the other side of what passes as fame, it is the whole of one life consciously consecrated and condensed to one end and nothing else. Think about that. Think about the obsession, and the cold autumns it brought to him and to so many others who were touched very hard indeed by it.

'He is the most dedicated person to anything I have ever come across. I don't think he can be knocked for that. People look from the outside and say he's arrogant but I didn't find him at all like that. He was forever tying my shoelaces together when I was asleep.'– Kenny Andrews, former team mate.

Along the way the intensity opened up tensions in others, put enormous strains on all manner of different human beings who became caught up in it. Again, few could cope – long before '90 – because it had never happened to them before, probably never would again and always it happened fast, fast, fast. There is violence in this book – long before '90 – many tears, there is blazing anger against Senna and equally the stoutest defences of Senna as well as awe and adulation. There is loneliness, the part so rarely mentioned.

'At least twenty-four hours most days he concentrates on races and when he comes back to himself as a human being he feels around himself emptiness.' – Paulo Casseb, a friend.

'Perhaps it is a professional tic, but I can't do anything without thinking of technical things. Mere speed, or even victory, have little meaning to me in themselves.' – Ayrton Senna.

He is not popular within Formula One. It does not interest him and is beyond him anyway. He's not that kind. To be popular you have to be one of the lads or at least know how to meet the lads on their level. The practical jokes he plays are not the same thing at all. The jokes aside, you get a slow-burning smile or, more likely, The Face again.

A random example. Spa '89, the dying moments of the Saturday session for the grid. Alain Prost has covered the 6.940 kilometres in 1 minute 51.463 seconds. Senna is deep within the pit and now The Face is not recognizing anything. People flit by, cars pass on the track, photographers peer through their lenses clicking and clicking, there is the strident brouhaha of activity, engines shrieking, engines gurgling and dying nearby as they're turned off, but he has completely withdrawn. He's somewhere else. He is already in Eau Rouge, the fearsome downhill-uphill kink where, as he will say 'you can only believe so much', he's out at Stavelot and he's watching a film of himself out there, too. He slips into the car, it's fired up and he does go out. The rest? The lap didn't look fast, he didn't rattle the kerbs, didn't pitch the car at all; it was smoothed, softened, damn near sensuous: the whole power of Honda, the whole technology of McLaren brought to its natural climax.

One minute 50.867.

Nichols, like a foot soldier in his Marlboro uniform, was moving down the concrete staircase from the paddock to the motorhome immediately afterwards. I ventured that Senna would have found another second if he'd had to – well, two seconds if Prost had gone out again and equalled that.

'Yeah.'

Senna thought the lap was good but not more. Under more persistent questioning he thought it was among his best pole positions and he did now have thirty-seven to choose from. The Face was fashioned in stone, not paste, when he said it and we're back where we began. With the elusive prey.

'You must think of everything in the enormous turmoil at the start of a race. You must not look at all at the other people around you. It is wrong to recognize people, except your mechanics, perhaps. People always think the start is something terrible, that your heart beats like mad, that your brain is about to explode but it's a totally unreal moment, it is like a dream, like entering another world. Your spirit goes and the body sets itself free.' – Ayrton Senna.

They changed Spa, incidentally, years ago and comparisons aren't valid with The Old Days so, confining ourselves to the modern era, no driver had gone round faster than that pole lap. To Senna this is a familiar feeling, a birthright, and what's all the fuss about?

Another random example. 'We were at Donington one day in 1982 and Ayrton said we could get to Snetterton to see Mauricio Gugelmin race in an hour and a half's time. I said it took two and a half hours. He said: "We can make it. I'll drive." I had a Mazda and I sat in the front passenger seat. Fortunately I had a book with me which I put in front of my eyes because I really didn't want to see some of the things that were happening. I understood then that the guy had a belief in his own ability – that he was blessed from above, if you like – that, say, no tractor could come out.

We reached Snetterton in just over one and a half hours, a time that could not be done.'– Dennis Rushen, FF 2000 team manager.

The fuss is about so many people truly trying to cope with genius. There are chilling words, too, in this book about that, words from the heart, words from the pit of the stomach, and they all struggle in the search to explain it, accommodate it, rationalize it. 'He was certainly the first driver since Ronnie Peterson to have people as excited about some of the things he could do with a race car – you know, things you just couldn't believe.' This is the mature reflection of Peter Warr, former team Lotus manager, who, speaking two years after Senna left, remains awkwardly in awe of not only what he could do but what he did do and is still trying to believe it. And Warr was deep on the inside, he knew better than almost everybody else the limitations of the Lotus cars Senna drove.

John Watson wasn't simply in awe, that doesn't do it justice at all. John Watson was thunderstruck. As he recounted this to me, the timbre of his voice vibrated with excitement as if, absurdly and amazingly, he was a child again rediscovering the intoxication of speed. 'Round Dingle Dell corner at Brands Hatch I saw this car coming very quickly behind me. Just at the bottom of the dip Ayrton came through on the inside – I'd left him room – and I witnessed visually and audibly something I had not seen anyone do before in a racing car. It was as if he had four hands and four legs. He was braking, changing down, steering, pumping the throttle and the car appeared on that knife edge of being in control and out of control. He made his commitment to the corner, the car was pitched in with an arrogance which made my eyes open wider. Then – hard on the throttle. I mean, it was a master controlling a machine.'

That was '85. A year earlier Senna had had precisely the same effect on a group of people.

'The first time we ran on Michelin tyres I went to the test. By agreement with them we would run their previous year's tyres which, by their own acknowledgement, were uncompetitive. Ayrton was able to keep improving the car. It amazed even the Michelin technicians.' – Alex Hawkridge, former Toleman boss.

And the elusive prey himself? In the end it was all balance and counterbalance, all Yin and Yang; the shriek in your head to win, win, win versus the voice in your mind making diagnoses about how you could do it. Sometimes the shriek was louder but, as Senna got older, less frequently. That this still happened made it nerve-stretching because you didn't always know what was round the next corner and, as it seemed, neither did he, never had, really. And that was what created the cold autumns.

It had always been the same, however far back you care to go.

'He was throwing the kart about too much going into the corners, he was going too fast, he was losing speed because the kart was too much sideways.' – Terry Fullerton, kart racer.

By 1990 he was arguably (and it is a very contentious argument) the best driver since Jim Clark, killed twenty-two years earlier. He was certainly the fastest. He had established a reign of something approaching terror: in qualifying people scampered out of his way whenever they glimpsed that yellow helmet moving from the horizon towards them. Nobody wanted the global audience to see them blocking him. It was the same in the races. Even René Arnoux once ceded rites of passage at Monaco, an event as momentous as the Second Coming and just as difficult to believe.

It all tempts Peter Warr to say: 'For people of a certain age – my age! – Clark was the best there was by a long way and Senna is the only driver you can mention in the same breath. A question: would Clark have been as good in the Senna era and vice versa? The answer: Senna would have been as good then as he is now because he could have handled the cars no problem at all, and I think Clark would have been as good as Senna in the hi-tech era of having to read the fuel, adjust the boost button, radio to the pits and so on.'

Senna redefined the possibilities of the hi-tech car. That is what he has done in his era and of course he is a prisoner of it just as Clark was of his or Juan Manuel Fangio before Clark. You can only drive the car they give you to drive. It is hard to believe any man could have driven faster than Senna; with more skill perhaps, more style perhaps, more tactical awareness perhaps, but not faster; and speed is really what it's all about because you have to go faster than the man directly behind you to win.

It is certain that the more cars are planned and built by computers, the less scope there is for style. People remember Clark's consummate ability to drift the Lotus 49 but a Formula One car circa 1990 won't drift at all. It sticks. And, as Warr has said, there are all those other things in the cockpit now, something Senna explains like this: 'I go through a sort of check list like a pilot, except we have nothing on paper. Everything must be in your head. It's a kind of mental radiographic control.' This does not diminish Clark, but it sure as hell doesn't diminish Senna either.

In trying to catch the elusive prey I am indebted to the man himself for years of courtesy, for reading the manuscript so carefully and adding his own insights. He also said 'well done, good job, best regards' and excuse me if I say it touched me. I hope the book touches you. I thank, too, the people who have helped me with their memories, insights and opinions or just plain information: Reginaldo Leme, Paulo Casseb, Wagner Gonzalez,

Keith Fullerton, Peter Koene, Martin Hines, Rick Morris, Malcolm Pullen, Ralph Firmin, Dennis Rushen, Calvin Fish, Kenny Andrews, Eddie Jordan, Dick Bennetts, Martin Brundle, Alex Hawkridge, Chris Witty, Herbie Blash, Peter Gethin, Johnny Dumfries, Peter Warr, Nigel Stepney, Steve Hallam, Lee Gaug, Barry Griffin, Francine Chatelain, Kaspar Arnet, Eric Silbermann, Caroline Horsman, Chuck Nicholson, Martin Pass, Mike Hill, John Watson, The Rev. Ian Tomlinson, Henri Pescarolo, Derek Bell, Jackie Stewart, Derick Allsop, Russell Bulgin, Phil Collins, Maurizio Sala, Samantha Harris (BBC) and Keith Sutton who took the pictures and also reminisced so vividly. McLaren International were magnificent, and thanks particularly to Ron Dennis, Peter Stayner and Juliane White.

Frequently I have quoted people virtually verbatim; I have let them speak for themselves because that is more authentically them, just as I hope the result is more authentically Senna. For that reason many say the same sort of words, often exactly the same words, and you will recognize them soon enough: unbelievable ... incredible ... single-minded ... intensity ... dedication ...

The stark fact that he struck so many people in the same way is central to the story; the repetition from so many mouths stands as confirmation of who he is and who he has always been, because many who weren't close to him saw him through different mirrors and perhaps what they saw was distorted, perhaps not. I have quoted at length those who were close so that you can make up your own mind.

Incidentally, we need too to look at Senna's nomenclature. In karting he would be called Silva; in Formula Ford 1600 da Silva although also he would be given the nickname 'Harry'; in Formula Three he would decide to use only 'Ayrton Senna'. ('There are a lot of da Silvas in Brazil, not many Sennas,' he will say, smiling naughty as an urchin.) For convenience I call him Senna all the way through. Otherwise if you were fast-reading the book you might imagine we are talking of a clutch of relatives rather than one and the same person.

I am deeply in the debt of *Autosport*. The scope and sympathy of the magazine's reporting is quite extraordinary and I thank Simon Taylor for permission to quote from it. I have leant heavily on the famous *Autocourse Annual* and the *Marlboro Grand Prix Guide*, both pillars in their different ways, *Karting* magazine for invaluable descriptions of their World Championships, *Cars and Car Conversions* for a portrait of what happened in mid-Wales. A videotape, Senna the Champ (VSR International) was extremely illuminating.

And before we begin, one last quotation, this time from a man utterly remote from motor racing, the German philosopher Hermann Hesse. 'The life of every man is a way to himself, an attempt at a way, the suggestion of a path. No man has utterly been himself, yet each man strives to be so, the dull, the intelligent, each one as best he can.'

This, then, is Ayrton Senna's path to himself.

CHAPTER TWO

Horses and Karts

Geography is important but not decisive in motor racing. If you want it badly enough you can go for it from any starting point, as Keke Rosberg from frozen Finland proved; but an established starting point helps and Brazil is that. People in the sport speak of a Brazilian 'mafia', meaning Brazilians who help Brazilians who help Brazilians to get on. Brazil is a rich-poor country (no contradiction) and if you're among those immediately in front of the hyphen that helps, too. It is also, incidentally, the same size as Australia; and that's the end of the geography.

Ayrton Senna da Silva was born in São Paulo on 21 March 1960 to Milton and Neide. They already had a daughter Viviane who is now a psychologist. Another son, Leonardo, would follow. Milton had a successful car components business as well as farms. 'The factory had about 750 employees,' Senna says, 'and my father started from nothing. There were about *ten* [Senna's italics] farms and a total of 400,000 hectares with well over 10,000 head of cattle.' The family lived, as you might expect, in a large house. It was in a northern suburb called Santana. They were, as you might expect, a close family and an Anglo-Saxon mind like mine has to stretch itself to imagine what a haven and a bastion that remains in Latin and Hispanic lands. The family does not close ranks in time of trouble: the family closes ranks all the time.

Senna now has a pad in Monte Carlo – which is almost obligatory for Formula One drivers and some not even in Formula One – but this is not home. Home is where it has always been, the big house in São Paulo, home is where you go back to whenever you can. 'Homesickness, evidently I have that. My heart is over there, it's my country and it contains my family, my friends, the people I know, my hobbies. Here in Europe I work, that's all. The other drivers, the Europeans, don't suffer from this uprooting, they can get home in an hour or two as soon as they have a day off. For us it's different and I miss Brazil. My family misses me, I am very attached to my family, my friends, my girlfriend who works there six days out of seven. It's hard but I don't complain. I chose this life, I knew the inherent sacrifices and I accepted them but in the future I will try and organize my calendar to go back to Brazil as often as possible. It's very difficult because during the season we have testing every week.'

Alain Prost – after the great Marlboro McLaren rift of '89 which appeared on the Richter scale – may or may not have been accurate when he complained that Senna was back in Brazil with 'Mommy and Daddy' instead of sharing the burden of testing, but in another sense Prost had missed the point: home is not where you escape to, not where you take refuge in, home is where your existence is. Prost having long decamped France for Switzerland and conducting a lively, sometimes loveless lament with many of those who professionally ought to have been nearest and dearest to him – French journalists – had become effectively international, at ease anywhere on Mother Earth. Senna remained Brazilian, only Brazilian juices flowed in him and one evening, when I tackled him about how you can live amongst so much poverty he mounted a defence lively enough for the man from *The Times* to feel the need to step in, conciliating and mediating in that Foreign Office way you'd expect from a *Times*man.

Casseb, the friend, makes this judgement: 'Ayrton is familiar, very familiar. It means he likes to be all the time near his family. His father is very quiet. It's very hard to explain because he has a strong personality but he's such a fine person that if you come to talk to him for two minutes you feel like you've known him for ten years. Ayrton was a normal child, but ever since he was a little kid he liked to drive a lot. When Ayrton was four his father made his first handmade kart for him. He played in it in the back yard and in public parks.' It had one horsepower. Senna ruminates among his memories to remember that. 'I was just doing it for myself, for my own feelings. I hardly knew who I was.'

This feeling of power is a very basic one to human beings. You have only to press an accelerator and you are travelling at speed. Consider it: no man has been recorded as running faster than twenty-five miles an hour, and this − you'd better believe it − for a short, lung-busting distance; no horseperson (man or woman) can make a horse go faster than forty miles an hour. A family saloon driven by an unfit obesity will do a ton and more, effortlessly, all day and night.

Casseb gives us the very first example of amazement. 'I recount something which happened when Ayrton was seven. His father had a jeep at the farm, looked after by the man who looked after the farm, and he was very good friends with Ayrton (and therefore presumably allowed it to happen). One day Ayrton drove the jeep by himself. Nobody had ever taught him to drive and he was changing the gears without the clutch. His father didn't believe what he was seeing, it was so amazing. Ayrton didn't hurt the jeep. Because it was a very old engine it would have been necessary to push the clutch hard and so Ayrton was going first, second, third and fourth without it.' There is coincidence here with Jim Clark who wrote of his early years: 'I remember being interested in mechanical things like most boys, although I was not particularly attracted to motor sport. I believe I was first drawn to driving and motor vehicles by an interest in their engines rather than their capacity for speed. As a small boy I was quick to take any chance of jumping upon a tractor and going for a little spin. Because of this almost insatiable mechanical curiosity I probably knew as much about our tractors as the farm workers who drove them.'

At ten Senna had a more powerful kart but legally could not race it until he was thirteen, so each weekend he drove at a track called the Parque Anhembi. The first race was in 1973 at Interlagos. Casseb: 'It's at São Paulo, a nationally-recognized kart track near where they had the Formula One Grands Prix before they moved to Rio [in 1978]. He won, he won, he won. Since he was a kid the only taste he knew was victory. His father sponsored him because his father was in the car components business anyway. I must say that of all the tracks in Brazil that Ayrton was ever on he's breaking all records. Till now the records haven't been beaten.'

At that first race he met another ambitious youngster called Maurizio Sala. 'Ayrton had been testing without racing. He was a really shy boy, not many friends but a lot of determination. I was a guy who could communicate, I could mix with people no problem, he was the opposite of me. Anyway, I was the new up-and-coming man in karts and I'd won the last few races. At Interlagos he beat me . . .'

For the record, as they say, Emerson Fittipaldi won the Grand Prix at Interlagos that year of '73, a season in which Emerson's brother Wilson also competed. This, then, was a living tradition, one which could be followed and inevitably it is easier for those who follow. The pathfinders have already been there.

'In São Paulo my life was about racing,' Sala says. 'The first word I spoke was not "Mama" or "Papa" but "car". When I was a little older I would drive about at great speed with my sister in our parents' old Fiat. I could not reach the pedals so my sister had to do that while I steered the thing. After going to a kart school I started to race them myself. My father said "I make kart for you." I wait one year, two years – nothing, so I buy one myself. The first year I spent racing with my own small team against Ayrton da Silva. He was always first, me second. Every race da Silva and I blam, blam, blam but Ayrton was just a little bit quicker in those days. I used to have to think a lot to stay with him. Da Silva, then, was spectacular and a bit wild – he did not need to think about his driving so much . . .

'I had an old Volkswagen [his mother's] and I used to put the kart on the top of it and go to the races. Ayrton was from a different background, he got his first kart because his father gave it to him. He had – well, not an easy life but a better life because of the money. His father was very rich but please understand that that never changed Ayrton's character, it was only that he never had to worry about money. He had his own van with a chauffeur to look after him. He was his own mechanic, him and the chauffeur. He was taking it very professionally, always he did. (The van had a workshop in it.) He had the right equipment, the right engine, the right everything.'

The ordinary racers built their own engines at the workshops of a Spaniard who was known as Tche, but Senna didn't. Tche built his engines and folklore has it that whenever the phone rang Senna answered, explained politely that Tche couldn't take the call, he was too involved in working on an engine. He was, and the engine belonged to Senna.

'I thought,' Sala says, 'he was really good, aggressive and on the track he was like he is now: everything or nothing. He started to win races but he never made a lot of friends. His determination was his main thing. We crashed many times because I was competitive, he was

17

competitive, I didn't want to give way and he didn't want to give way.'

And a memory of Interlagos, a track, grass beyond it and two karts locked in combat, the first bearing the number 27, its tiny front wheels pointing straight towards you, its (slightly) larger rear wheels pointing left, left, left and a helmeted head dipped over a big steering wheel.

Senna.

Just behind, another kart, another helmet, another visor, like equipment for a lunar landing, and the four wheels all pointing a different way.

Sala.

The third kart, whoever that might have been, is a long, long way behind.

I've reconstructed this from a photograph, taken at a random moment at a random race circa 1976 and I've reconstructed it because it captures something. I don't want to belabour the point but there it is, beautiful in its innocence, the urge of combat, one young man leading another and both working the steering wheels so hard. Before we leave it, another thought: the position of Senna's wheels suggest something you can't do at all. You used to be able to do it long ago when Jim Clark worked quite other steering wheels in quite other circumstances. Four-wheel-drift. A ridiculous notion at Interlagos circa '76 in a suction-orientated kart.

Isn't it?

'Power comes from my education which, you would say, was privileged,' Senna says. 'I was privileged to grow up in a healthy environment. My family gave me this opportunity and have always been behind me. When I have some problem, some question, I have people whom I trust to go back to. I know a lot has been said about my sister's role in my career [she is a psychologist, don't forget] but in fact it's my whole family which plays a big role. I am

18

close to my parents, my brother and my sister. My sister has three children, which is the most beautiful thing that can happen to you in life.'

Senna moved to the 100cc international category and in 1977 won the South American Championship in Uruguay. He was also Brazilian champion, of course, and would be so four times. Casseb remembers the flavour of those days: 'He had a lot of support because everybody liked him. He would always talk, he never refused reporters. He was promoting the sport. He was very, very serious as a boy, I think too much serious. He seemed like a child who was thirty years old.'

Sala remembers, too. 'In those days I was a close friend of his – no, not close but we used to go out together, he used to come to my house. Conversation wasn't difficult but it wasn't deep. We never talked about motor racing. He couldn't relax when there were a lot of people around. He went out with my sister Carolina but he was dedicated in his career and she wanted something different.'

In 1978 he came to Europe, perhaps unconsciously following a certain logic because Europe would be the place he'd have to come to eventually. Europe is pivotal to all forms of international motor sport except the secular North American championships. He would contest the World Kart Championships at Le Mans in deepest France. There he met a complete set of new people, among them a lively Londoner called Terry Fullerton, who recalls his first impressions of Senna:

'He'd been racing karts in Brazil and for whatever reason he got in touch with the DAP factory in Milan – which was the factory I was driving for at the time – and said he wanted to do the World Championships and how much would it cost? They gave him a price and he arrived in Italy two or three weeks before and did some testing. He was immediately quick but as a driver he looked a bit raw and obviously not very polished. He did, however, have natural ability. The testing was at Parma, a good kart track, a proper international kart track about an hour and a half from Milan. We used to do a lot of testing there. He came down with us, just someone over from Brazil who nobody had heard of and who was paying. People would do that from far-flung places, they'd be reasonably good but you wouldn't think of getting a result out of them. It happened frequently and it still does. But this guy was quick.

'I remember that day. He asked me about his driving and what I thought he was doing wrong. That's quite amusing looking back. He was throwing the kart about too much going into the corners, he was losing speed because the kart was sideways too much. His English was not very good. He used to speak to the factory in some sort of broken Italian-Portuguese and his English was fairly monosyllabic.'

A Dutchman, Peter Koene, was also a DAP driver and was also at Parma that day. 'He was very fast. He wasn't racing, he was playing in the car. By that I mean he was driving so easily. For him it was easy to drive, you understand. He was a nice man but not very open. Later on, when I used to speak to him more, it was better. Of course we had to speak in English and that was not very good. We managed.'

Motor racing people always do, but you must see the isolation of this, however temporary (until you learn English properly). You are on another continent, Brazil and the big house are the width of the Atlantic away, you're surrounded by strangers and you don't even know what they're saying, about you or anything else. And you're seventeen. It is nowhere near manhood, whatever seventeen-year-olds think. Perhaps a degree of isolation was born at anonymous Parma, at an anonymous test session, and perhaps it has never completely gone away. In time, of course, he would master the language and become comfortably fluent in it, but that would take another seven years. It was by its very nature a long seven years and after his divorce – and apart from another Brazilian, Mauricio Gugelmin and Gugelmin's wife Stella – he had only one constant companion. Himself. You can find yourself in loneliness and lose a part of yourself, too: but it hardens the resolve, strips away all distractions, concentrates you upon your primary purpose, and no person I have ever met mistook Senna's primary purpose. None of them (including myself) takes any credit for this. Even if you tried you couldn't miss it. It was as all-pervading as a car crash, wham, everything all at once and whatever else you care to think, you've been in the crash.

Gugelmin met Senna 'through kart racing. The Brazilian championship is very competitive and we travelled around the country to many different circuits. He was just about to enter his first World Championship. I had a sponsor with a big lorry and Ayrton couldn't keep his kart safe in the back of his road car so we arranged to put it in my transporter. He was racing in a different category and we became friends then.'

Senna didn't win the World Championships at Le Mans. Another Englishman, Martin Hines: 'At Le Mans there is a kart club and they have their own circuit. It's not very far from the pits of the big twenty-four-hour sports car race; it's a proper tarmac surface.'

Despite the custom-built track the event was chaotic. The French officials couldn't cope and at several moments it became a theatre of farce in the proper sense of that word. (A pretty girl in a bikini tried to force entry into the paddock wearing an accreditation pass which bore the photograph of a bearded man and nearly made it.) Although this is no place to examine the full extent of the chaos, it did at least prepare Senna for the years to come, where he would meet other forms of chaos and other forms of officialdom.

Karting magazine described him as 'extremely rapid' and (in a caption) 'sensational'. He won a couple of the early heats, broke down once – although the officials assumed he'd been punted off by the leader, an Austrian called Anton Zoeserl, and prepared to black-flag him, not Senna. Once Senna's kart had been examined, officials found the engine had seized and there had been no collision at all. During this Championship there were precious fragments of Senna.

'It was a nice clean start and the Brazilian rapidly disappeared into the distance, never to be challenged.'

'At one stage the Brazilian drew alongside Lake Speed [an American] and gained about three inches only for Lake to coolly shut the door at the next corner.'

'Perhaps it was a tactical error, but as Mickey Allen [an Englishman] challenged the Brazilian so he appeared to be unable to match the adhesion of the other and the resultant collision put them both on the grass.'

That was the second of three races which constituted the final. Senna had been seventh in the first, would be sixth in the third and sixth overall.

'In 1979 he came over again and did much more of a season,' Fullerton says. 'He was at a big meeting which they held at Jesolo [a resort on the Gulf of Venice] every May. It was the biggest race after the World Championships. By this time he was recognized as being very good. He was very single-minded about his racing although in international terms he didn't have that much experience. For example, testing. The way to test is not to go for the fastest time. You try six or seven engines with tyres which will stay consistent so that you get a proper comparison between the engines and you know which one is best. Then, when you've sorted that out, you put them to one side and test the chassis. He wouldn't do that, he wasn't tuned in to doing that. Once he and his mechanics had found a good engine they'd want to put that on, go out and try to get a time.'

You might be tempted to dismiss this as the exuberance of youth. Senna was still only nineteen. You'd be wrong. It was a primitive impulse, something far within the depths of the teenager, something he could never shed or even moderate without altering who he was and who he fully intended to be. It would run like a strand through the years all the way to Formula One and would never cease to astonish people who witnessed it for the first or umpteenth time. In Formula One he was true to what he had always been. Certainly at the outset in Formula One he felt he had to be quickest at every test session, every untimed session, every qualifying session, every Sunday morning warm-up, every race. It's actually – don't listen to the critics – the most telling description of a racing driver you can get. 'I have never changed my motivation, I have always wanted to win, I always want to be the first. It is the best way to thrive in this business – if not the only way.'

'Very often in unofficial practice he'd do very good times,' Fullerton says, 'then in official practice he'd be surprised when I beat him. I'm sure it was inside him that he had to be the quickest. He kept making that mistake: to be quickest when it doesn't matter and, because of that attitude, you're not quickest when it does matter. I think he learned that over a period of a couple of years. [Author's note: I don't, but I wasn't there.] It perplexed him – because he was tackling it the wrong way. He used to come over to the tent where I kept my times to compare them with what he'd done. I said: "Why do you keep coming over looking at my book?" "You don't want me to?" "No, not really, I don't." That was it. I never saw him in my tent again.'

Hines reflects that, 'Senna was a dedicated racing man but most people are like that, really. Selfish. They want to go out and win for themselves and because they want to win they keep their secrets to themselves. They're not being nasty but they're not going to divulge things they've learnt. I've always been under the impression that people are not born to be absolutely naturally talented drivers. Perhaps what happens is that you're driven (no pun intended) towards motor sport because that's in your blood, but once you get there it's the sort of person you are which determines how successful you will be: at the end of the day it's an absolute gut feeling that you've got to win no matter what the others do. All winners are selfish.'

If Ayrton Senna did not know that already, he did the moment he left Terry Fullerton's tent for the last time at Jesolo in May 1979. He would not forget the lesson. It did not, of course, affect the primary purpose and we can illustrate that with his own words which, although spoken five years later, capture it exactly. 'Physically I was at the end after the Spanish Grand Prix but because I had won I recovered quickly. Winning is the best medicine to regain strength. In the evening I had fully recovered and I drove the race again in my mind. I wanted to enjoy my victory once more that way.'

Fullerton explores those early days of the obsession. 'I've seen him do silly things when he wasn't quickest. At Jesolo for the Champions Cup: at that stage I'd won it every year for about four years and he wanted to win it very badly, that and the World Championship. He wasn't quite quick enough and he still didn't have the experience to know quite what was going on. The track at Jesolo used to get grippier by the half-hour during testing. Unless you altered the kart to cope with that you wouldn't go fast enough and it was dangerous because the kart would lift on to two wheels.

'I remember the last test session. The track had got grippier, he hadn't adjusted his kart, he was too eager to get out on to the track, he went up on two wheels on a fast corner – right by where I was standing so I could see he didn't lift off – the kart went over and he had an enormous accident. He went into the fence flat out. It was an horrendous moment. The run-off area was so short, then there was an iron fence. He'd have been doing sixty, seventy miles an hour. He hit the barrier first with the kart behind him. He was very badly winded.

'That was inexperience. It really messed him up, he obviously didn't do a good time after that and in the race he had another horrendous moment. He was over-trying, trying too hard. He dived up the inside of some-one and got catapulted out of the kart. The kid was loaded with ability but he didn't have any fear, which kids of that age tend not to have. That was the year he was married to a Brazilian girl. She had an hour-glass figure . . .'

'Terry Fullerton was rated as the best kart driver in the world for many years,' Hines says, 'and the only driver I ever heard Terry have a good word for was Senna. He was the only one that he really did rate. He was brilliant, at the end of the day he was brilliant.'

The World Championships were at Estoril, '79. Like Jesolo it is an agreeable seaside resort, not always as sun-kissed as the travel brochures insist but no bad place to spend a weekend, in a kart or out of one. 'In practice he had a big crash,' Hines says. 'He and another driver were absolutely neck-and-neck alongside each other in every corner and eventually they touched. It was a major accident. Senna was lucky to get away with it.' Senna himself takes

25

it up. 'The accident was in the third semi-final where I only needed second place to take pole position for the first final. So I stayed in second place, chasing, right on the tail of the leader and suddenly his engine seized, I hit him and rolled over. I restarted and finished eleventh. The leader was . . . Fullerton! That accident eventually cost me the title. The Championship was eventually decided on places in the semi-finals.'

And now we have a further strand to interweave with that of always being quickest: not backing off. It too would run through the years all the way to Formula One and, again, would never cease to astonish people who witnessed it for the first or umpteenth time, like Suzuka 1990. Senna would find himself alongside many people down many straights and into many corners, and wouldn't back off except on rare occasions when force majeure demanded absolutely that he did, and even then he didn't always. It terrified some drivers, enraged others who were pitched off themselves; made yet others fearful for Senna's safety; but it was there, another primitive impulse and somehow not negotiable.

Now – Estoril. He was eighth after the opening heats.

Like Le Mans the final was spread over three races. In the first Senna took the lead 'to a roar from the crowd' – who were Portuguese, of course, and connected to Brazil by an umbilical cord, as it were – but he fell back to fifth. In the second, 'in characteristic flamboyant style, the Brazilian took them one by one until he was behind the leader – the master blocker [Dutchman Peter de Bruyn].' Bruyn's hand shot up to signify he was in trouble – he had a broken chain – and Silva inherited the lead. With three laps left Koene got past Silva 'without an entanglement'. In the third race Senna led to 'a tremendous roar of appreciation' and 'responding to the encouragement of the public and mechanics waving anything that bore the DAP

26

name Silva adopted a dashing driving style, with rapid flicks and swoops, in the twilight.' He won.

'Of the three finals he won one, I won one and we had the same points,' Koene says. 'To win all I had to do was finish in front of another Dutchman [Bruyn], that was all. I did it but Senna thought he was World Champion. About five minutes after the end of the race everybody knew it was me. He was very disappointed. I can't remember if he spoke to me. I didn't know him well. That began the next year, 1980.' Senna says that 'it was the year the rules were changed. Previously, if it was still a tie it was decided on your results in the third final. Now it was decided on the semi-final results.'

That next year Senna contested the Champions Cup at Jesolo again. 'By halfway through the race I realized I was reeling him in,' Fullerton says. 'I could see that he was looking across the hairpin at me getting closer and closer. Then I got this feeling I was going to be sick. Maybe it was the physical exertion, the adrenalin, but when your mind is tuned into something like that everything else seems secondary.' Fullerton did catch him, they touched wheels, Fullerton (literally) held on and won. They were by the swimming pool next day but Senna 'just sat in a deckchair not joining in the fun. All of a sudden he jumped out of his seat and pushed me into the pool. After that the smile came back to his face.'

The World Championships were at Nivelles, Belgium. Senna went off in one heat, won the next, was third in the third and overall second, just as he had been at Estoril. It was the closest he would get to something he did want so badly; but Nivelles was also the meeting where Koene thought he saw levitation at the corner – 'it seemed as if he lifted the kart, turned it in midair and then took the corner. I knew then that he was very, very special.'

He was twenty. It was time to make the decision: to go

upwards, stay in karts or get out of the whole thing. There were no other options. Many people assume this is a natural and inevitable decision because most kids start in karts, it's relatively cheap, it's (literally) thumping good fun as well as a valid way to find out if you are any good. Actually karting was not and is not a kiddies' playground – in the late 70s one driver a year was being killed – nor was it a playground in another sense, which was why Fullerton was testing six or seven engines before turning a knowing eye to the chassis. Most Formula One drivers started exactly here and I won't bore you with the list except to say that between 1978 and 1980 Senna had raced against Stefano Modena, Ivan Capelli, Stefan Bellof and Corrado Fabi.

Karts can be, if you wish, an end in themselves, a complete world; the next step is on to a ladder and in 1980 the ladder had specific rungs: Formula Ford 1600 leading to Formula Ford 2000 leading to Formula Three leading to Formula One. The air gets more rarefied and harder to breathe the further up you get. A lot of kart people stay contented kart people, like Martin Hines; few, entering single-seater cars in Formula Ford 1600, intend to stay there except for the minimum time, which is one season. They're already gazing up the ladder towards interesting commodities like fame, fortune and immortality – as well as, on one rung or another, finding out how good they really are, how high they can climb.

The ladder is why the decision is so big. You are very probably committing the next decade of your life to it and this is not something to be done lightly. For a start it's going to cost a packet and you might end up broke very quickly (which is what happened to Nigel Mansell), although that was one factor Senna didn't need to worry about.

Hines remembers Milton da Silva as 'very, very rich, like mega rich' and setting aside Hines's natural ebullience with words we can safely conclude that Milton was eminently able to finance a season of Formula Ford 1600 for his son if he chose so to do. And this is 1980 going on 1981, before Latin America ran headlong into the devastation of total debt; before the Bolivian peso – to take a potent example – moved from 44 to the dollar to 45,000 to the dollar and inflation moved to 34,000 per cent and bank robberies became self-defeating because robbers couldn't lift enough banknotes; before Uruguay – where Senna had won in those steady, prosperous yesterdays – was swamped by Argentinian flight capital and Argentina went completely bust in any recognizable sense and there they were, Brazil's immediate neighbours to the south and the south-west. Brazil itself got into a 100-billion-dollar debt, a figure so large that like inter-stellar distance no sane person can envisage it; but that was not the point. The rich in all those countries stayed rich, as they always tend to do. I repeat: Milton da Silva was eminently able to finance the season of '81.

Sala thinks, 'Ayrton started in karts [only] because his father gave him one and the kart took him towards motor racing. I don't think that in those early days he wanted to be a Formula One driver or if he did he never let us know. But he was determined to do things perfectly and that's what he did in karts. He won everything in South America.'

Soon enough a shy, quiet, polite, self-contained young man would present himself on the doorstep of an office at Snetterton circuit, a most modest place in the quiet and rural county of Norfolk, and ask for a Formula Ford 1600 drive. His wife with the hour-glass figure would be a sensation, no less, in such parts.

Reginaldo Leme is a TV commentator based in São Paulo: 'For the first year in England it was at least fifty per cent of his father's money.'

'Ayrton went to college in São Paulo (business studies),'

Casseb says. 'His father wanted him to stop racing and help him in the factory so Ayrton went there in order not to disappoint his father. But his father felt he was really unhappy so he decided to give Ayrton another push.' We shall hear Senna's own revealing account of what happened at a later moment, and it is not at all as it has been publicly portrayed before; and before we reach the doorstep at Snetterton we need to listen to the three karters we've already met because, in retrospect, each has something of significance to say.

Hines: 'A kart reacts so quickly because it is so small and light.'

Koene: 'If somebody handles a kart well they can handle a Formula One car. I thought he would end up in Formula One, yes. I thought that was his intention. He was as good as that. When I got to know him better he was still very close, he didn't speak before the races, only during qualifying, that's all. I saw him years later when he was driving Formula One at Zandvoort and I spoke with him and he was very nice, very normal, you understand.' (What else would he be?)

Fullerton: 'The last time I spoke to him was one day at Silverstone in '83. He looked quiet, confident but he hadn't changed that much. I think he'd grown up a bit. He'd had a good feel for a kart. I'd sensed he was going to go on with this as a career. When I heard he'd started to do cars I was sure he'd get to the top.'

It was a sentiment shared by someone else. Ayrton Senna.

CHAPTER THREE

Twitchy Little Tyrants

A small, functional office butting on to a factory near the London to Norwich road. Across the road, a view of a modest racing circuit. It had the feel of a rural, pastoral place and in that it reflected its setting: East Anglia is a labyrinth of lost lanes where through tall hedgerows you can glimpse old barns or thatched cottages nestled into the sleep of centuries. You're much more likely to hear the churn of a combine harvester racing to finish the harvest than the shriek of a racing car itself, unless you go to the place in the fields beside the London road. It is called Snetterton.

Early spring '81. The young man standing before Ralph Firmin seemed confident. However far he'd travelled to be at Snetterton – half the world – Firmin scarcely felt he was a stranger even at this first meeting; felt, in fact, that he knew him already.

Firmin, a stocky man of great presence, was in charge of Van Diemen, a highly successful works team in junior formulae. If you want to launch a career, here is the best place to begin. 'We ran Chico Serra [a Brazilian] in 1977 and we maintained a good contact with him. He talked a lot about a driver called Senna and he kept saying: "He's coming, he's coming." For whatever reason it took him two years to come. I'd not seen him until he walked into my office but I did feel I knew him because Chico had been telling me how good he was.'

That very, very first impression: he's confident.

31

'We had dinner at a restaurant, The Doric, in Attleborough, a nice restaurant, English-stroke-Italian.' Attleborough is typically Norfolk, a market town moving at its own pace and The Doric one of a row of venerable houses facing a small green. It had a feel of quality about it: a pleasant bar and beyond that tables in a stately wood-panelled dining room. 'His English was very poor but I'd got used to that kind of thing, particularly with Brazilians.' Serra apart, Firmin had run Carlos Pace, Roberto Moreno and Raul Boesel. 'We sat there and we did a deal. Like any driver with Van Diemen he settled in Norfolk, rented a house. We always arranged things like that for new drivers. It was a nice little two-bedroom bungalow just south of Norwich.'

Another impression was gathering in that dining room in Attleborough: Senna knew precisely what he wished to do, and that was win motor races. Not compete in them, you understand. Win them.

He would contest – or, more accurately taste – three 1600 championships scheduled to go on simultaneously during the season: the P & O, sponsored by the shipping company, the Townsend Thoresen, another shipping sponsor, and the RAC, the Royal Automobile Club, guardian angel of domestic motor sport.

He would meet many new circuits although they soon became familiar. There is a reason. There are many meetings but few circuits so you find yourself returning and returning. Between 1 March and 29 September – the span of the season – Senna would drive Brands Hatch five times, Mallory Park four times, Snetterton three . . .

This is of enormous benefit to the young driver because once he becomes familiar with Brands Hatch he can forget about simply finding his way round and start on the more important business of refining himself immediately prior to exploiting himself; and, just as important, familiarity becomes an equalization. All the kids know their way round so direct comparisons between them become valid, especially since they all have the same power 'lump', the Ford 1600 engine.

The cars are twitchy little tyrants and, with all that fearless, youthful ambition fuelling them, the races often move from Armageddon to Götterdämmerung and back again. Derek Warwick, then an established Formula One driver, once said: 'I don't know how we did it in 1600, I don't know how we steered them in straight lines, I don't know how we dared.' Firmin himself says: 'Put it this way, they are difficult to handle and go quickly with.'

As I've said, Senna was known by his proper surname, da Silva, although the factory quickly nicknamed him 'Harry' because firstly Ayrton Senna da Silva does not roll effortlessly off many an English tongue and, of a subtler significance, acquiring a nickname always implies acceptance in England.

He was now into another world and a complex one, a world with several clearly defined elements which interlock. An example. In Firmin's office, and quite by chance, Senna would meet a Norfolk man whom he would meet again and again. He was called Calvin Fish. 'He knew of me. I was at the factory one day – I was driving a Van Diemen engine. This was before he ever drove a car for Ralph. Ralph said: "I've got this Brazilian over, he's called da Silva, he knows your name well." Ayrton had obviously read about me. He was extremely polite. It's difficult because you're not a Brazilian and there was a language barrier. We used to laugh about it a little bit. I think he spoke more English than sometimes he'd let on but if the situation demanded it he'd suddenly say: "I don't understand what you're saying."'

At this moment Van Diemen did not have their '81 car ready. A mechanic, Malcolm (Puddy) Pullen explains that 'I think we were short of parts or something. We decided to put him out in the last year's model just so he could learn to drive.' Pullen's thought processes were as you might expect, and understandably so: Senna was 'just another foreign driver, you know, like you get'. This did not survive Senna's first session in the car at Snetterton. 'He had something about him and it's hard to put your finger on exactly what. It was something. He had this very professional approach, he was very precise about everything. He'd come in and say: "The car does this, the car does that and so on."'

Firmin was watching closely, too. 'You find some people who come out of karts — which have got a fair power-to-weight ratio and quite grippy tyres — and take to it straight away, others take longer.' That first time, on a quiet day against the rural, pastoral backdrop? 'It was obvious he was very, very good. I could see he was going to be an excellent driver. You can tell by the way a driver handles the car, by the way he controls it. He was fairly quick from the word go. He started in a less-than-perfect car (the '80) and, like many drivers, he was too keen to go quickly too soon but I had no doubt the guy was going to win races. He was self-assured, calm, he was very hard and demanding but not in an unpleasant way. He was very sure, which I think he's always been. He's a perfectionist, isn't he? That is Senna. He is a perfectionist at his trade. He hadn't been in the car much before the first race.'

We must not pass over Snetterton itself too quickly. It is — and I am not being unkind — a place to dream, perhaps, but not a place to make your dreams come true. That will have to be done elsewhere, on the great and famous circuits. It is flat, almost treeless and has a rudimentary atmosphere about it. The entrance was once a runway for United States bombers. The stands for spectators are small, almost humble. On a weekday there is a drone of cars going round and you can glimpse them wheeling and turning on the flatland, surging under the narrow bridge which leads to the pits. Behind the pits there is a very British institution: a café. It is a proper café, Formica tables, plain chairs, a menu designed for lorry drivers – sausage, beans and chips, that kind of fare. Solid nutrition, of the strength and hue that does not exist beyond the territorial waters of the United Kingdom. I bet the tea was just as strong and colourful, but I didn't have a cup. At the end of the room, next to the door to the toilets, the games machines stand like challenges to your dexterity and, as an irony, the day I went (autumn, '89) someone was playing one of those infernal computer race circuits where the track flows wildly at you and you caress the lever wrongly and you hit an obstacle like a pine forest or a tower block. The someone was making what looked suspiciously like a Marlboro McLaren spin and spin helplessly all across the screen in rodeo rotations.

Nor must we pass over the café itself so quickly. Senna would come here, would become an inhabitant of it as much as all the other people who habitually used Snetterton, would taste one aspect of real England, would see mechanics hunched over the solid nutrition, their jaws making joyless chewing motions, and inescapably this was not Brazil; it was several cultures away but it was where he would have to begin if the dreams were to come true. You might imagine that such a man would be pretty hot at the games machines: sureness of touch, vision, concentration; in fact the kind who'd show the boys a thing or two. We shall have some interesting evidence of self-denial about that soon enough. But first the racing.

Senna reflects on this. 'For sure the karting enabled me to go fast. It is much, much easier than FF 1600 where, apart from the basic car control, you cannot use the experience you get from a kart because they are so slow; there is no grip.' This is not a contradiction. Karts are twitchy little tyrants, too, and a wonderful place to learn the delicate nuances of control; the lessons remain valid in FF 1600 where, as Firmin has said, handling and speed are an elusive combination; and we shall have the evidence of another drive to corroborate that, too, soon enough.

1 March 1981. The club circuit at Brands Hatch – a round of the P & O Championship and the only one Senna would contest, thereafter concentrating on the TT and RAC. Brands, an awkward place to begin. All downhill-uphill loops and corners, adverse cambers and an alarming rush along the start-finish straight to a drop at Paddock Hill so sharp you can leave your stomach behind. He qualified in mid-field, behind the other two Van Diemen works drivers, Enrique (Queque) Mansilla and Alfred Toledano; and behind, also, a crisp, neat businessman running a Nelson-Royale more as a love affair than a career. He was called Rick Morris.

'In the race he drove very aggressively and very wildly and I thought: Oh, it's another Brazilian. We'd had a trail of people like that, Chico Serra and Roberto Moreno and so on. He was wild at Clearways. I have a distant impression of that.'

This is an unfolding right-hand corner from the club circuit on to the Grand Prix circuit, but so wide that it permits several permutations as you feel for the apex; once you're familiar, you find the apex every time. When you're unfamiliar . . .

'Obviously he was wild,' Firmin says defensively, 'but he matured, both as a person living in England and as a driver.'

Pullen, on the pit-lane wall watching as the small cars – capable of 125 miles an hour – darted by during the twelve laps of the race, found himself making a different kind of judgement. 'I felt he was working his way into the racing without making a fool of himself, I felt he was building himself up.' He was fifth.

Enrique Mansilla (Van Diemen) 10 minutes 18.1 seconds

Rick Morris (Royale – Nelson) 10m 19.5

Dave Coyne (Van Diemen) 10m 20.4

Alfie Toledano (Van Diemen) 10m 24.6

Ayrton da Silva (Van Diemen) 10m 26.1

The British magazine *Autosport,* which must be one of the most comprehensive and well-informed of its kind in the world, carried this astonishing paragraph constructed by a journalist who can't have seen Senna before and constructed only on the evidence of that fifth place eight seconds behind the winner: 'Making an impressive FF 1600 debut at Brands Hatch was Brazilian 100cc kart star Ayerton [sic] da Silva. Undoubtedly we shall hear more of this young man.' If the journalist hasn't demanded a pay rise on the strength of the paragraph in the intervening years he ought to do so now.

A week later Senna was at Thruxton – another rural place but in Hampshire – for the first round of the TT Championship and *Autosport* reported: 'All eyes were on Ayerton [sic, again] da Silva who engaged and got the better of Mansilla in a thrilling all-angles tussle.' Morris won, Senna third.

At that meeting a diffident young photographer moved quite by chance into his life. His work you see throughout this book but in 1981 he was as Senna was: making his way into his profession. He was called Keith Sutton. 'I was working for a Brazilian magazine and they asked me to take pictures of Brazilian drivers racing in England. At Thruxton I did a lot of shots of him, portraits, action, everything. Liliane, his wife, was extremely attractive, you know. A Brazilian girl. She spoke very little English. At Thruxton she'd walk through the paddock and everyone would stop what they were doing. She had the Brazilian shape, the Brazilian bum. She was very nice.'

A week after that he was back at Brands (you see the circuits returning already, and this time you know all about the mysteries of turning into Clearways). It was the second round of the TT Championship. Pullen guards emotional memories of that. 'The new car was finished and he had that. It was a wet race and he just drove away into the distance. You could see he was going to be a winner. I mean, he was a winner. At Brands he was overjoyed – like I was. There is no feeling on earth like winning for the first time. As he went over the line Liliane nearly picked me up off the ground. She was ecstatic, I mean she was nearly in tears.'

Keith Sutton had gone to Brands and 'Ayrton recognized me from Thruxton, remembered I'd been taking pictures there. He said: "Are you a professional photographer?" "Yes, of course." "I need pictures doing. Can you help me out?" "Yes, of course." He won his heat, then he won the race and there I was on top of the rostrum doing the shots – fantastic light, him and his wife. Brilliant. [Photographers talk like this.] Basically that was it. I tried to get to as many Formula Ford races as possible, doing shots for him. He paid me for the pictures. I was just doing prints from the negatives.'

Senna was establishing himself. It had taken exactly two weeks. He was already thinking ahead, far, far ahead. He needed the pictures to publicize himself in Brazil so that, one distant day when he might be looking for sponsorship and his father was no longer paying the fifty per cent, getting it would be much easier. He sensed that in 1981 Moreno and Boesel in Formula Three and Nelson Piquet in Formula One would command most of the column inches in the Brazilian press and so he'd have to push himself in. If you've been dallying with the notion that he wanted the pictures for reasons of vanity or to put in a scrapbook, forget it. He intended to make history, not record it.

Already, too, he had begun to wreathe a kind of mythology around himself. He'd go to the pub with the boys but rarely speak. Many found him shy although that ceased as soon as he was in a car. 'We'd go testing and he'd do a particular time, say 1 minute 30 seconds,' Pullen says. 'Ayrton would then reason: "I can go two-tenths quicker there, three-tenths quicker at that corner but there's no point because we're only testing. When we are qualifying for the race I'll go five-tenths quicker." He always would. That amazed me. He would never put everything on the absolute limit in testing because, as he pointed out, you might go off and once you go off that's the end of your testing for the day. He always knew how much quicker he could go. Instinctive talent? That's right.'

Liliane was endearing herself to the team, too. 'She used to bake these amazing banana cakes,' Pullen says, 'and bring them down to the workshop for the mechanics. I'd never eaten anything like them – delicious. It was a treat for us. I think it must have been a Brazilian recipe.'

Ayrton Senna would prove a treat for them, too, although not in his fourth race, Mallory Park.

He took pole. *Autosport*: 'Mansilla made a storming start from row two and drove all the way around the outside line at Gerrard's to take the lead in opportunistic style, while da Silva held off Ricardo Valerio, Toledano and then the works Royale of Morris. Valerio and da Silva swopped positions a couple of times in the opening laps before the Mexican dropped back to fourth on lap 4 and left da Silva in second place ahead of Toledano. Over the next few laps da Silva homed in on the leader, cutting a lead of several seconds to just a length by lap eleven. On the last lap da Silva made a faster exit to Gerrard's than Mansilla. He came up alongside but was unceremoniously edged off onto the grass by the

Argentinian and angrily had to settle for second place with Toledano right on his tail.'

What followed is still recounted in hushed tones, as if the witnesses wished they had not been witnesses. One of them – who forbade me to use his name – says 'their tempers began to bubble'. The two drivers had to be forcibly pulled apart, someone arm-locking Senna round the neck to do it. Keith Sutton found something thrust over his camera lens so he couldn't take more than a couple of pictures.

In the years to come Senna would be involved in much heating of the blood, both his own and other people's. This is the only instance when he seemed to lose control of himself. He would know great anger but he would never come this close again.

(You could dismiss it as no more than Latin temperament, which many people would be inclined to do; after all, only a year later, Piquet sprang out of his Brabham at Hockenheim and kicked and punched Eliseo Salazar, a Chilean, after they'd both gone off; but that year, too, at Dijon, Brian Henton squared up to Mansell and it was Mansell who got hold of Senna at Spa in 1987, not vice versa – and I defy you to name two men (Henton, Mansell) further removed from so called Latin temperament. When anybody gets supercharged, sweet reason is no longer guiding them on their actions.)

Senna was second again at Mallory, this time behind Morris who 'nipped' through near the end and won by 0.1 of a second after a frantic race; the pace was so 'fantastic' that the lap record, which had stood secure since 1974, was broken by Toledano who did 49.40 and clipped 0.2 of a second off it.

And then there was Snetterton, wind dragging rain over the flatlands, where Senna squeezed out a small but commanding lead and held it from Morris. During that race an affable Formula Ford 2000 team manager was 'walking along the grass not really paying much attention. I saw this little black and yellow car in the lead but only by a few yards. It was Senna, just another Brazilian, people were saying. It started to rain and I looked on the next lap and he was half a lap ahead. Everyone else had slowed down and he hadn't. I thought: My God. I walked up to him afterwards and said "I'm Dennis Rushen." His wife was there, the lady with the hour-glass figure who used to wear jump suits. I said that I ran a two-litre Van Diemen team and "if you want to do two-litre in 1982 you can have the whole British and European season for £10,000." I plucked that figure off the top of my head. It was a really cheap deal but, I mean, anyone who can do that in the wet is special. Very, very special. I hardly spoke to him any more throughout the season.'

And then there was Oulton Park. 'I was on pole by quite a margin,' Morris says, 'half a second or something and up the hill to the double-apex right-hander Senna came up the inside of me and literally banged me out of the way. We'd have been doing about ninety miles an hour, third gear. You come up, you brake, you turn in. It's not an accepted overtaking place, especially on the first lap. But he did it. His front wheel was to the side of my car, I was already moving out of the way and he put me onto the grass. Two things are very characteristic of his driving: aggression and force. But everyone drives aggressively in Formula Ford 1600. The trick is to get away with it, to be skilful enough to get away with it.'

As Morris has already said, 'We'd had a trail of people like Serra and Moreno and I always got on well with those guys. Ayrton was the first Brazilian I didn't really click with in the way I had with all the others. I mean, we used to have a laugh but he wasn't a laugher, he was very serious, he seemed introverted, he seemed unsure and I never knew whether it was an arrogance or an introversion.

41

People behave soberly for various reasons and I couldn't make up my mind. We got on well, there was friendship but that was later, in 1982 not 1981.'

This is interesting because in the course of this book others will say it too: there was no friendship while you were in direct competition with him because he did not wish friendship then. He wished to beat you and any form of sentiment might dilute that. If he did like you – and he seems to have liked most people – he pressed that far down within himself and ignored it. It made for loneliness. He accepted that it would. In this sense, he was not an ordinary person at all. And he was only twenty-one . . .

And then there was Mallory Park on 25 May – a good start, a six-second lead held comfortably to the end.

Firmin is not a man given to extravagant words but he is insistent about this: 'From about the middle of the season I thought he was going to be World Champion. It wasn't any particular moment, it was a gathering impression.' Funny. Pullen felt that, too.

And then there was Silverstone, at the *Daily Express* International Trophy meeting and as Morris recounts with particular relish: 'That 1600 race is a legend of Silverstone, quite amazing. He got away and I was stuck in the pack. I caught up with him with about four laps to go and we were towing round together. He was very quick into the corners – another characteristic of his driving, quick to the apex, sort out the consequences afterwards – but I was coming out quicker. My style was slow in, quick out because in 1600 you can scrub off the speed if you're not careful. I went to overtake him on the back straight on the last lap, going into Stowe corner. I went to the inside, he moved to the inside, I moved to the outside with him alongside me and we were at full bore, at 125 miles an hour. He had me on the grass – not an uncommon thing in 1600 – halfway down the straight. I had two wheels on the grass.

I backed off, I followed him and we came under the *Daily Express* Bridge towards the chicane.'

The whole approach has been changed now: you flick left-right under the Bridge and are faced by a graceful curve to the start-finish line. In 1981 it was radically different: you came under the Bridge and flowed straight ahead to the chicane about 300 yards away. The chicane was like a circular traffic island and tight, tight, tight. It was the eye of a needle and positioning was all-important. Once you got the inside line, logic insisted that you had it all to yourself. There wasn't room for two. And you must picture a couple of small rockets hammering towards it. 'I went to the right, to the inside,' Morris says, 'he blocked me there and he thought he'd won the race.'

Picture, now, the rockets nose to tail, Senna positioned to snake through, the right-hand line feeding him directly into the chicane. Morris again: 'I went to the outside and I waited until he braked and then I came right across his bows from the outside. I went straight across the chicane' – the kerbing formed a hump and the whole car bounced – 'but inside the yellow penalty line.'

Morris won.

'Ayrton was unbearable. Apparently he went past the pits going like this [shaking his fist], he was shouting at Ralph [Firmin] when he got back, there was talk of protests; but, you know, I'd got the corner. I was so wound up about the incident on the straight. Outside line at the chicane on the last lap isn't exactly a healthy thing to try. Perhaps that's why I got away with it – because he wasn't expecting it. I didn't speak to him that day but we talked about it later. We laughed about it later.'

The race report is just as intriguing. Senna did take a clear lead and Morris had caught him by lap 5 – it was a ten-lap race. 'Morris spent the rest of the race working out where and how he could pass the Brazilian. On the second last lap Morris scrabbled through on the inside but then coolly let da Silva past again as they braked for Woodcote. All the way round the final lap da Silva doggedly clung to the inside line and this left Morris with only one option: to try the outside line into Woodcote. Morris gave it a go, whereupon da Silva left his braking as late as he dared and left Morris with seemingly nowhere to go. Did he give up? Not a bit of it! Rick used every bit of his Formula Ford experience to bounce his Royale over the chicane kerbs . . .'

Morris 17 minutes 1.85 seconds, Senna 17 minutes 2.72.

We are now ten races into the season and the sequence is worth setting down. Senna had been fifth, third, first, second, second, second, first, first, first, second. Firmin understood perfectly what was happening. 'Why he won so many races is because he did it on the first lap. Pole position. Soon as the lights go, bang, he's away. He pulled ten, fifteen, twenty yards clear. In two or three laps you'd find other drivers circulating as quickly but they'd lost the race. They'd never get the gap back. That's the sign of a driver: a man who can just do it from the word go.'

This is another theme which will run through the remainder of the book. It became a strategy, a tactic, call it what you will, and it also became a constant. It imposed enormous strains on the drivers trying to pull the gaps back. because, as they were forced to conclude, they had to stay with him on those crucial first and second laps. But to do that they had to pit their nerve and skill against his nerve and skill in the most direct way, and he had lots and lots of both; so much, in fact, that even now nobody is truly sure how much.

There is another way of looking at it, and this may help to penetrate the mythology which clings to Senna like a shroud. You get pole, you take the first corner first, you feed your skill into the circuit while the others are sorting themselves out, bedding in their tyres, getting their brains in gear, you pull away and they can't catch you. You win. Why doesn't everybody do this? Because they can't. Of course it doesn't always work – we've just seen Morris catch and overtake him, although it required extreme risk to do it; but often enough it does work, in a Van Diemen or a Marlboro McLaren Honda.

And then there was Donington. 'I'd always thought he was fairly good,' Morris says. 'At Donington I got fastest lap although a typical thing happened, I'd got stuck in the pack after the start. I was fourth or fifth or whatever. Ayrton did have the ability to put in the most amazing first lap – unbelievably good starts, tremendous opening laps. I started reeling him in, reeling him in, reeling him in. I got to within ten feet of him and I watched him through the corners. I was impressed. He was kicking up dust every time he came out of Coppice, he was using not only the track but the rumble-strips and two or three inches of dirt beyond them – and not on one lap, on every lap. That was unusual because one of the hardest things to do in Formula Ford 1600 is drive consistently. They are pig-awful things to drive. And lap after lap after lap off the track by two or three inches . . .

'I was using the rumble-strip and I might have used the dirt every once in four or five laps if I went too fast but he was doing it deliberately.

'He got very annoyed with me at that meeting for mucking up his practice. I had a problem and I was going to come into the pits. I don't know whether I hadn't seen him or whatever. I'd moved over to the right with my hand up, slowing down, I moved into the first part of the chicane as Ayrton was coming round. Obviously I spoilt his line, however unintentionally I'd done it. He came to me. He said: "Rick, you spoil my lap." I said: "Sorry, Ayrton, I didn't mean it."'

I am haunted, in reconstructing these episodes, by the words of an English author who wrote: 'Biographers are driven to invent, like Frank Harris on Oscar Wilde, or to rewrite, like Guedella on Wellington and Rosebery on Napoleon. There is another method, the research on the trivial, which is very much esteemed in the United States. It consists in squeezing a little dust from a subject which was long ago milked dry, and then arranging the particles over many hundreds of folios. We are gravely informed that the Christian name of Wordsworth's cook was not, as supposed, Maria, but Clementine; that Dickens preferred haddock to plaice.' (*46 Not Out*, by R.C.Robertson-Glasgow, pub. Hollis and Chater.)

I am haunted because I have tried to do more than avoid all this. What happened in the races is not, I hope, spreading particles of dry dust but revealing the man through his chosen medium, racing a car. Part of the man is why he raced at all, another part is what he did when he got there. You cannot, I insist, appreciate either without the little mosaic of episodes at tracks which are, often enough, former Air Force bases where the faithful gather to watch kids. And further, I insist, that – like Ralph Firmin himself – you will be forming a gathering impression by this mid-season of '81. The boy could play.

And then there was Brands Hatch again, on 12 July. *Autosport*: 'The RAC 1600 men gave their all in one of the most hectic 15 lappers seen all year. Setting up problems in practice confined series leader da Silva to the third row whereas his team-mates Mansilla and Toledano shared the front rank. A truly sensational start by da Silva saw his yellow car arrive at Paddock alongside Mansilla's blue one, Ayrton having displaced four cars instantly, seemingly without contact! The Argentine gave not one inch at the notorious right-hander [the stomach-churning drop, remember] but he had to relent at the hairpin [Druids], da Silva forging ahead immediately. The brilliance of the former karter once free was a joy to behold. Deft flicks of opposite lock through Paddock – such elegant car control can only be natural talent – took him further out of reach until dramatically the Van Diemen slewed sideways beyond instantaneous recall at Clearways with three laps remaining. Ayrton resumed fourth with a water hose adrift.'

There you are, you see. No dry dusty particles at all. In fact, a little water.

Senna now began a cascading, imperious run of six straight victories: at Oulton on 25 July (plus fastest lap), the same at Mallory on the following day; at Brands on 2 August he made a 'storming start', completed lap 1 six lengths in front and stayed there (although Toledano set fastest lap); at Snetterton on 9 August he faced the penultimate round of the RAC Championship and by then only he, Mansilla, Toledano or Morris could still win it. Halfway through, it rained. Senna, 'tip-toeing', looked 'master of difficult conditions'.

Here is another theme, and it too will run through. His car control was so sensitive that others might flounder amidst the waves which cars churn; he never. It would lead directly to a performance, in a storm at Monaco, so consummate in its bravery and touch that people still speak of it, but that was four years away, another at Estoril but that was five years away; another at Montreal but that was eight years away.

Now, at Snetterton, others proved the depth of the risk in the wet, and that set what Senna did in its true context. Half a dozen of them plunged off 'like a bomb had burst'. Senna won by a couple of seconds from Mansilla; and set fastest lap, of course. He had 105 points, Morris 95, Mansilla 75. He could not be caught. He was champion.

At Donington in the TT Championship on 15 August he beat Morris by almost a couple of seconds; at Thruxton on 31 August he was in full control by the third lap and that – the final victory of the six – gave him the Townsend Thoresen title. One race of that championship remained, at Brands Hatch. He was second to Morris.

Keith Sutton was to receive a short, sharp shock. 'Brian Jones [the suave on-circuit commentator who also did the interviews on the rostrum afterwards] said to him: "Well, Ayrton, you've done very well in Formula Ford 1600, you must be looking forward to Formula Three next year." [It would have been an acceptable step up the ladder, missing the Formula Ford 2000 rung.] Ayrton said: "No, I finish with racing, I'm going back to Brazil." I'm stood there and I just couldn't believe it. He was a bit disillusioned because to continue he needed sponsorship and his father needed help on the farm and that was it.'

'When I left I was unhappy for a number of reasons,' Senna says. 'I was very disappointed. One of the main reasons was that, as you know, in order to find a sponsor you need good publicity. That is especially important in Brazil because it is so far away. Of all the Brazilians who have come to England I was the first to win two championships in the first year, the RAC and the TT. I won twelve races; I qualified on pole position fourteen or fifteen times – in eighteen races. These were very good results but I couldn't get good press in Brazil and without that I couldn't find a sponsor. I knew that I needed a sponsor before I could move into Formula Three and I tried very, very hard. I was competing for space in the newspapers with Moreno and Boesel, who were winning in Formula Three, and also Nelson Piquet was winning the World Championship. After all that there was no room for FF 1600.'

Nor much for karting and another attempt to win the

World Championship, held at Parma. 'I was one of the favourites and I was in a good position to win. But then the material I got was no good; the engine and the frame. They changed the regulations to allow 135cc engines and my frame was not strong enough for the engine. I could finish only fourth. I was very upset.' The opening time trial told him the worst. He was only sixth quickest. In the heats he was third three times. In the final he was fourth twice, taking him to that fourth place overall.

He did go home, missing the famous (and notorious) Formula Ford Festival at Brands Hatch which is traditionally a chance – if you win it – to reach a larger audience within the world of motor sport. Small wonder. It attracted an entry of nearly 250 FF 1600 cars.

'He had completed his two championships and for whatever reason he decided he had to go back to Brazil,' Firmin says. 'His father wanted him to go back, his father had only given him the one year, that's right. We had no contract to do the Festival. Having said that, he did say he would let me know whether he could do the Festival or not. In the meantime young Tommy Byrne [an affable Irishman currently with Van Diemen in FF 2000] had come up and said "I will definitely do it for you." To be fair, Ayrton phoned me from Brazil and said he would do it but I declined. I couldn't really mess Tommy around when he had committed himself.'

'So Ayrton missed the Festival, which I am sure he would have won,' Sutton says. 'The guy who took over his car, Byrne, did win it. Ayrton sent me a letter saying thanks for all your help. His English was still really poor.'

So it was over, finished, done with. He'd be remembered as a talented kid who went away. Rick Morris puts that into its context. 'Fernando Riberio, for example, was very introverted and got God and when I beat him he threatened God would kill us all. At Hockenheim he'd been thrown out of his team and we were sitting there after practice sipping beers and he hadn't got a car to drive because Royale had taken it away, and the Lord was coming and we were all going to be killed. At the start of the race he had his overalls on and his helmet in his hand, still convinced the Lord would provide him with a car.

'At the end of 1981 Alfie [Toledano] gave me a great big Mexican hat, Queque [Mansilla] gave me a present – I can't remember what it was now – but Ayrton wasn't on that level. Ayrton was much more remote, much less friendly. You'd go up to the Van Diemen pits after practice and ask how it went, you'd talk to the drivers. Some were very emotional afterwards, others would go away and hide in the truck. Riberio would sit in the truck and play a flute. Ayrton would just sit. He was always insular, a little bit lost maybe, certainly not gregarious.

'Raul Boesel – because of his German stock – was more straight-back-on-the-horse-with-leather-boots, Roberto Moreno was more of a monkey-on-a-stick, Ayrton was more calm, controlled, authoritative, slightly arrogant. I think it was a combination of different country, loneliness and dedication. He was always very dedicated, much more than the other two [Mansilla and Toledano].

'I remember when he got his first Mercedes – 1983 or 1984 – a black Mercedes, and his showing it to me at Brands Hatch. He was inordinately proud of it. He said: "Come and have a look at my car!"' This wasn't vanity, any more than Sutton's photographs had been. After all, a Mercedes carries a certain cachet but a Ferrari it ain't. No, it was something more profound. Son of a rich father, he had earned the Mercedes himself. It is entirely possible, if not inevitable, that whatever he had done in a racing car – an extremely masculine and independent activity – he regarded the Mercedes, gained by his own talent, as representing his true manhood, his true independence.

And another memory from Morris. 'It happened in the paddock at Brands. I had my new son Stevie with me on my shoulders and Ayrton was very attentive, "How are you, Stevie?" and so on. He was always happy to talk, he just wasn't smiling-talking.'

But we're still in October '81. 'I decided to buy a house so I never had the determination to be a full-time racing driver,' Morris says. 'I was quite happy driving what anybody would put in front of me.' The implication is clear: he'd have spent the money on such a career, not a house, if he did have the determination. Senna himself obviously didn't have the determination either, because he'd gone.

It was quite natural he'd been so attentive to Stevie, quite natural for a family-loving South American; and that was ironic in its way. As Ayrton and Liliane da Silva boarded their Varig flight for Brazil that late autumn, all was not well with them as a couple.

CHAPTER FOUR

Return of the Prodigal Son

The plane had lifted off from a place called Foz do Iguacu, famous for its waterfall and kart track, 500 miles from São Paulo. Ayrton Senna had been there as a celebrity guest for the Brazilian Championships. He didn't take part and neither did Sala, who was looking for sponsorship to get to England. (Mauricio Gugelmin won.) Now, on the plane, Senna and Sala sat together. 'He said to me he had retired and he was working for his father's company. I could feel he wasn't happy, that he wanted to be in racing again. I think in his mind he said: I dreamed of England, I went, now I want to go back.'

Dennis Rushen remembers that 'there was a lot of pressure from his father, who didn't want him to race and said this is silly and so on. Over the winter Ralph Firmin and I discussed someone to replace Tommy Byrne in Formula Ford 2000 and Senna was the man to have. Ralph did more than I did to get him back. Ralph used to ring him and say: "It's great over here."'

'When we'd decided to go into 2000 in 1981 we'd contacted Rushen Green to run our works car,' Firmin says. 'Now, in 1982, Ayrton decided he did want to compete in it. He rang me up . . .'

Rushen remembers the meeting. 'We sat down in the office, him, myself and Ralph and he said: "Yes, OK, but Dennis told me I could do the lot for £10,000." Ralph went mad. "What?!" Ralph said. But Senna hadn't forgotten what I'd said to him that day at Snetterton and we had to do it for that figure. He had some Brazilian

53

money from Banerj and he still had the car in yellow and black.'

'My father simply made me free to decide what I wanted to do,' Senna says, 'and after I decided we agreed together (Father, myself, the family) that this was simply *Go* and we would not look back any more, just look ahead. That happened after my first season – 1981 – after I got back to Brazil. At the end of 1981 I had tried to help my father in his business, from that October to February 1982. That month I made my mind up and again together we decided to go for it. For sure without my father's help life would have been a lot more difficult, but we also agreed as a matter of principle that the day I was in a position to, I would pay back all the investment. That happened when I got to Formula One.' At the time, 1982, he'd said he was 'very excited' to be back.

He had come back alone. We must approach his marriage in one context and one context only: how it materially affects a proper portrait of the man.

Liliane has already moved in the background like a mute bit-part player, gorgeous to behold but, to us, a total stranger.

I propose to offer you the words of four men and then leave it alone until the fleeting words of a fifth later on, and dwell on it no more.

The first is Brazilian, and will remain anonymous. 'She was from a very good family, accustomed to servants, she was completely unprepared for being a housewife in a house in Norfolk.'

The second is Keith Sutton. 'I think he had a few problems with his wife at the time. He'd only been married since the February before. She was very nervous. I could see that. She seemed to be very nervous about his racing. I don't think he could cope with that kind of pressure. I mean, he was totally dedicated to being in racing. I think he realized he had made a big mistake and he came back without her.'

The third is Sala. 'I met Liliane only once. I think Liliane was his first love and when he decided to come to Europe he was a little bit afraid to come by himself and he took her with him to have support, but in the end he didn't have the support he wanted from her.'

The fourth is Calvin Fish. 'His wife was good looking and that's just another sacrifice he made to get where he's got. She seemed very friendly. You'd see them at the track. He'd be in the car testing, she'd be watching. Even back then I always believed that his goal was to be Formula One World Champion. He really believed he could do that and when you're racing against a guy, you don't know the depth of his feeling. It was like this was the one goal. I felt it even then, I really did.'

Liliane has remarried now, has two children. She does not give interviews. It is somehow all as if it never happened, although they remain, in the time-honoured phrase, on good terms.

Senna himself talked motor racing, rationing out his thinking, his priorities, how he was reasoning what he had come back to do. 'Last year I won many races in FF 1600. If I am lucky I can do the same this year in two litre. Then I don't need to do Formula Three this year. If I was to do Formula Three then I must win to get good publicity, because people will be looking to next year and I must keep the sponsors happy. To win in Formula Three you must do many miles of testing in the car – that is for sure – but really there is not enough time.'

There was the option, perhaps, of Formula Two. Please listen to a man of twenty-one talking: 'It is true that a Swiss man contacted me by phone and he said that Maurer were interested in me for F2. He said that he had a sponsor and that there would be no problem with the money, but he

55

changed his tune by the second time that we spoke and I knew then that there was no security, no real chance. I don't really want to do F2 anyhow, because I think to do well depends too much on what tyres or what engine or what chassis you have. I think that in Formula Three it is much more even. There are only little differences between the cars and the engines; the tyres are the same. It is much more up to the driver. I hope that if I can go well and win races in Formula Three then I will be able to jump straight into Formula One – like Raul Boesel. I think that if you can be competitive in 1600, in 2000 and maybe Formula Three, why not in Formula One?'

'He didn't come over until the start of the season,' Rushen says. 'I can't even remember him testing. The first race was at Brands Hatch. He jumped in and I gave him a crash course in what wings and slicks were all about. I said: "This is a wing . . ."'

He won by fourteen seconds, beating – among others – Fish. 'He creates this mystique about himself, not letting people get too close to him. It's strange because obviously you reflect on how you raced against him and how his career has gone since. You admire the guy now for what he's achieved and what he's achieving but when you're competing against a guy, you don't admire him, you respect him. You don't sit back and say: "Well, this guy is great" because if you do you won't be able to race against him.

'What stands out in his character is his single-mindedness about racing, the incredible intensity of it. I wonder whether he really enjoyed it at the time. I wonder if the intensity takes away the enjoyment. He comes from a different culture and I don't know how they express themselves. They may do it in a different manner – but I never really felt he was enjoying himself.'

What he did was win: at Brands on 7 March, at Oulton on 27 March. Keith Sutton was at Oulton and 'I saw him there. I said: "Look, you've got the talent to make it, we're both on the same level in our different careers, we both want to do well, why don't we get people to know you by doing press releases and sending them to all the Grand Prix managers? I work for a lot of foreign magazines. I can send them the releases and pictures and obviously if you're doing well they'll print them." He said it was a good idea and we came to an arrangement. He was paying me. It had never been done before – press releases to Grand Prix managers, Bernie Ecclestone, Frank Williams, Peter Warr and everybody else and he was only running in Formula Ford 2000. I had headed notepaper done for him with his helmet in all the colours. I wasn't a journalist or a writer or anything, I just wanted to help him because I saw the talent and I thought it might help me.'

He took pole, battered the two-year-old lap record after 'rocketing away' at the start, set fastest lap and beat Fish by ten seconds.

He won at Silverstone on 28 March, at Donington on 4 April. 'Ayrton's closest friends were Mauricio Gugelmin and his wife Stella,' Rushen says. 'He lived with them and Stella was like a mum to him, if you like. So we were at Donington and Mauricio was in Formula Ford 1600 at Snetterton. I also ran a man who worked for Mazda and he got me a Mazda. Ayrton won the race and he came walking over with the garland around his neck and he said: "We can get to Snetterton to see Mauricio in his race. It's going to be in a hour and a half's time. We can make it." I said: "But it's two and a half hours between here and Snetterton." He said: "I'll drive." So I sat in the front passenger seat and Spider the mechanic sat in the back seat and we got from Donington to Snetterton in just over one and a half hours – a time that could not be done. Fortunately I had a book with me which I put up in front of my eyes because I really didn't want to see some of the things that were happening.

57

'I understood then that the guy had a belief in his own ability – that he was blessed from above, if you like – that, say, no tractor could come out in front of him. He'd overtake and there would be something coming the other way and you'd think: this can't be done. He'd go at roundabouts flat out and he'd sort it out when he got to them. Spider was pure white and he was nearly sick. When we got to Snetterton Spider said: "I'll never drive with you again." I just went into a corner out of the way.'

He won at Snetterton on 9 April.

It is worth dwelling on this race. Several cars at the back of the grid tumbled into a *carambolage* on the first corner. By then Senna had long gone, and as he crossed the line to complete lap one Kenny Andrews, Senna's young team mate, was fractionally behind him, Fish fifth. They all moved through the debris of the *carambolage*. Almost immediately after that Senna slowed. Rushen was understandably puzzled. 'Ayrton came round first, then he came round seventh, the lap after that he slowed down as if he was coming into the pits but didn't. Then he started picking people off.'

Andrews was equally puzzled. 'I was leading the race by about fifteen seconds and I saw him in my mirrors. He was a long way away and I thought: this is it, I'm going to win, I've got this one sewn up. He caught me very quickly and overtook me.'

Rushen will never forget the end of that race. 'Ayrton won but he didn't stop after the line, he stopped about 300 metres down the road. He got out and said: "I've got no [expletive] brakes." We looked and a flint had come up and sheared his front brakes, so he'd driven the whole race with only rear brakes.' (This was why he'd slowed earlier.)

'Afterwards we were having a discussion in the office,' Andrews says. 'I asked Ayrton: "Where do you think I'm going wrong?" He said: "You brake too early for the esses,

I was braking later than you and I only had the rear brakes . . ."'

He won at Silverstone again on 12 April and that was six pole positions, six fastest laps, six victories. Rushen summarizes it simply. 'We had Nelson engines and one of them was brilliant so we had not only overkill in the shape of the best driver but we had the best engine. We were winning the races by up to seventeen seconds. It was quite amazing. But at that time he hated being away from Brazil, he hated England and he would not drive the car until his gloves and balaclava had been laid on the radiator to warm them up. He couldn't take the cold, hated it. He wouldn't test in the mornings because he didn't want to get out of bed — but, I mean, all Brazilians are like that. They don't want to get up.

'We had Dunlop tyres and by Dunlop's own admission it was a bad tyre. You could grain it in about six laps. When we tested, all we did was have a huge stack of tyres to see if we could find a good set. If we did, that could be worth a second, a second and a half over everyone else.

'We found out very early Senna's testing ability. He could be on his own lap record at Snetterton within four or five laps and he was so accurate that it was pretty obvious driving the car was the easy bit. He had so much time to tell you the left rear tyre was doing such and such on such and such a corner — and that was absolutely unbelievable. It's obvious now he's good but if you worked with him then you could already see how good he was.

'I'll give you an example. One day Ayrton was testing at Snetterton — you know, to find a good set of tyres — and Gary Evans, then a young driver, was there in a Formula Ford 1600 car. Gary came in and said the car didn't feel right, the engine didn't feel right and he was painfully slow. I said to Ayrton: "Would you mind just hopping in this and see what's happening?" He goes out and he needs no time to adjust. He'd just been on wings and slicks and now he isn't. The third or fourth lap out he was as quick as Gugelmin who was also there, in the works Van Diemen – and they're always the best cars. He just did it. Unbelievable. Then he came in and said: "Yes, the car is awful." I've never seen anybody else be able to do things like that.'

Fish sensed, and then saw, that Senna 'was susceptible to pressure. I think he's overcome it and he understands that on a certain day another car will be in better shape and he won't be able to beat it. But in 1982 when you were challenging him – and when I say challenging I mean wheel to wheel, overtaking him or leading him (sitting at five car's length behind him was a different deal altogether) – it was as if he shouldn't be put in that position. He personally felt he was head and shoulders above everyone else and simply shouldn't be in that situation. He felt as if he was in a different league to everyone else. When it came to "I may get beaten today" he didn't know how to handle it. He'd either put you off the track or maybe crash trying to overtake you. It was very strange. Maybe it was a phase he was going through. Whenever it got to that point, it was panic, he'd go completely to the nth degree to get back in front.'

On 18 April he contested the European 2000 at Zolder. He took pole by a clear second, led, but the engine gave way on lap 3. At Mallory Park on 3 May he didn't take pole but he won. And he went back to Zolder – on 9 May – for another round of the European Championship.

'We were at Zolder and it was the weekend when Villeneuve was killed,' Rushen says. 'We got there in the morning and Ayrton said he'd been offered a contract by Toleman and one by McLaren. "I want to go over and introduce myself to Nelson Piquet." He wandered off on his own and he came back really crestfallen. I said: "What's the matter?" "He just snubbed me. I'll beat the bastard one day." He could let things like that get really inside himself, to some-where bitter and intense. That hurt him a lot, it really did.

'I had the only [road] car and he wanted to go and see this girl somewhere. I said: "Right, if you win, you can take the car and I'll find my own way back to the hotel, but if you lose you've got to drive me all the way back." He said "Yes, fine, yes." He was thirteen seconds in the lead and the next lap he didn't come round. He walked back holding his helmet and as he went past me (he'd spun off) he said "Sorry." I made him drive me back to the hotel . . .'

Toleman did make an approach. Alex Hawkridge was running the team then. 'I'd seen him win Formula Ford 1600 races in 1981 like it was just an everyday event. He dominated it in a fashion I hadn't seen since Geoff Lees in 1975 and he was clearly an outstanding natural talent. We approached him and asked him if he was interested in a sponsored Formula Three drive – and he wasn't particu-larly. Chris Witty, who was our sponsorship man, made the approach . . .'

'I went up to him and spoke to him,' Witty says. 'That was the initial approach. I knew that, at the same time, Ron Dennis was sort of sniffing.'

Hawkridge takes it up again. 'We arranged a meeting. At that point he'd already been speaking with others in Grand Prix racing. He got introduced through the Brazilian machine, as it were, but it was all very long term, nothing immediate and of course he hadn't done Formula Three at this point. He turned down our offer of a sponsored drive. Then the rules were changed and he had to qualify for Formula One through results in a lower formula and Formula Three was stipulated as the minimum entry level. The "Superlicence" had just been established. We said: "Look, Ayrton, you can handle Formula One no problem," because we thought he could. "All we've got to do is get this definition of a Superlicence out of the way in half a dozen

Formula Three races and then you can come and be our Formula One driver." He turned that down cold on the basis that he needed more experience, he wanted to learn about racing and in his view there were no short cuts to that.'

Witty vividly remembers Hawkridge saying: '"Look, if you sign an option form we will sponsor you in Formula Three, we will give you a Formula Three budget" – because we reckoned he was worth it. He said: "No, no, no, I can cope with finding my own money." We kept working on him. I mean, I used to meet him in his Alfasud at the Hangar Lane gyratory system [infamous roundabout on London's North Circular road] and pass pieces of paper to him . . .'

'He took the view,' Hawkridge says, 'that the car determines your performance so much in Formula One whereas in the junior formulae, where the engines and tyres and chassis and power are so similar, individual performance makes you shine. He wanted to prove himself the best – and he was desperately anxious to prove that point to himself as well as everybody else. It was kind of ridiculous because he stood out so far as being the exceptional talent of the decade to anybody who bothered to look: and he wasn't just occasionally that, he was systematically that. He qualified fastest, he got the jump at the flag, he got the first corner, he automatically won the race. Since I'd watched Jim Clark in my childhood nobody had dominated motor racing in the way that he did.

'Along the way we spoke to people who were involved with him, Ralph Firmin, Dennis Rushen – Dennis was an old friend of mine and he told me just how amazing the guy was. It wasn't an aspiration to ever get into Formula One, it was an ambition to dominate Formula One. That's all he contemplated. It wasn't "I want to get into Formula One, I want to be a Formula One driver and now I've made it," he never thought in those terms. So when it came to actually trying to negotiate with him it was against a background where you were interviewing a candidate who only wanted to be considered by a team which had a Formula One World Championship winning car. The negotiations with Ayrton were difficult . . .'

Senna expresses this sentiment, or compulsion, in a single sentence. 'I could never be just another Formula One driver.'

Hawkridge pauses as if the enormity of it still lives with him. 'When he was in Formula 2000 he was not interested in getting any toe on the Formula One ladder at all. That was a constant right through the negotiating. I respect Ayrton for this: he made no secret of the fact that he's completely self-centred and it was an overwhelming ambition to be World Champion. I think he will change as a consequence of being World Champion, I think he'll be a more contented individual. I don't think he'll be any less competitive because I don't think he can be any other way. He will be someone who will be more pleasant to be with, less unnerving to be in conversation with.

'Anyway, he turned down an option to get paid for a Formula Three drive and said no, if he couldn't do it on merit he wouldn't do it at all. I said: "Well, this is merit because you're good enough." He said: "Ah, but there are conditions attached, I've got to drive for you, I want a choice if I win the Formula Three Championship. I think I'll have a choice." He was not wrong, he was completely right and he had the self-confidence to do it. He had the self-confidence all the way through the piece to know that that would happen. He was never likely to rush into anything.'

I have quoted Alex Hawkridge at length and in doing so interrupted the flow of the narrative because the whole episode is so instructive, startling and very likely unique. Every driver you meet who is on the edge of Formula One is actively hustling to get into it but the last rung is the hardest of all and, of course, the highest. Those with vertigo need not apply. As Hawkridge has hinted indirectly, the normal route is to get in anywhere you can – grab what any small team offers, raise money yourself and pay the team for the privilege of having you in it; then establish yourself, make a favourable impression, move to a middle-ranking team, start getting points (not necessarily easy) and confirm the favourable impression; then the door to Aladdin's cave magically opens and you're negotiating a multi-million dollar contract with a winning team and Marlboro in Lausanne (who pay the multi millions). There are many variations on this theme but the theoretical progression is still valid. At any given moment, some drivers are moving up through it and some down through it and some staying put. But you do not under any circumstances anticipate that you will go straight into a team which is poised to make you World Champion.

Senna did.

And please remember we are still at Zolder in May 1982, he still hadn't even driven a Formula Three car. He would, though, within a few weeks, courtesy of another affable Irishman, Eddie Jordan, an ex-driver now running his own team.

The next race was Oulton, 30 May. Fish was leading, Senna in second place and Andrews third. Andrews remembers it as if the enormity of this still lives with him. 'We were up each other's gearboxes, within inches of them. Cascades is the flat left-hander going down the hill, it's very tricky and on about the third lap Senna's rear right tyre exploded. He was flat in fourth gear, doing 125 miles an hour and the car snapped sideways. He was broadside on a negative camber corner – and there is no way you can get out of that. I lifted immediately because I thought this was going to be a big shunt. I thought I wouldn't be able to miss it. Then I saw his ability. He controlled the car until it was pointing forwards again. I was in awe of that control.

He went through the next corner on three wheels and the corner after that and then he pulled over and let me by. I'd have gone off, Calvin Fish would have gone off . . .'

Rushen is smiling about it now. 'He came into the pits with just bits of rubber hanging off the wheel and he said: "I've got a puncture . . ."'

At that Oulton meeting Fish had pole (and shaved 0.1 seconds off the lap record). Senna took part in a Sunbeam Ti celebrity race and there were two seasoned drivers among those against him, John Brindley and Chuck Nicholson. 'I don't think I even spoke to him,' Nicholson says. 'He had one of the faster cars – they weren't all the same – but that made no difference to what happened. I remember he made a perfect start and quite literally we didn't see him again at all. He made no semblance of a mistake, obviously. Just vanished into the distance. He broke the lap record! It was a 7-lap race and he did it in 9 minutes 50.2 seconds, Brindley, who was second, in 9 minutes 57.3 seconds. So Senna was pulling out a second a lap, that's a great deal round Oulton, and Brindley was known as a very, very fast driver. Of course at that stage Senna was only regarded as a promising newcomer but I said to somebody afterwards: "Promising? This man is going to make it."'

'Initially in 1982 we were in a very close-knit community,' Fish says. 'I had my own team but we were both based at Snetterton. At midday everyone would go down to Reg's Café and have lunch, we'd be eating table to table and then on a Thursday afternoon we'd be on the same racetrack. When we'd go to Europe the transporter trucks would leave at the same time, we were constantly in each other's presence but he always felt it was necessary to detach himself a little bit. One of my best friends is Tommy Byrne but when it comes to race day we go at it as hard as we can. After the race we go and have a beer. But Ayrton didn't feel – rightly or wrongly – that he should be doing that. Basically, underneath, Ayrton is a nice guy but he had to put on this front which didn't let anyone get too close. Now and again he'd join in when we were playing the video games – the mechanics would be there, too – but more often he'd leave and do something else. Underneath he wanted to play the video games but he had this plan and the plan said that that wasn't the way it was done. He felt that if he let you too close to him he would lose that little edge he thought he had. He was taking it incredibly seriously.

'My car was a match for his but that wasn't enough. You had to do your job right, you had to qualify on the front row, you had to have a great start, and Ayrton would take tremendous chances – well, not chances but he'd go for it on the first lap when the tyres weren't up to temperature and the car could get out of shape. He'd put in a dynamite lap. Gradually, when I was finishing second to him so many times – and we were trying to beat the guy to the championship – we started looking at the lap times and they were basically similar. What he was doing was taking that chance when the tyres were cold, pulling out a lead of maybe a second (and we're only talking about 10- or 12-lap races) and I'd run the rest of the race sitting exactly one second behind him. I don't think he was controlling the races. It was the advantage that he'd pulled out immediately.'

Sutton knew Senna's career was gathering significant momentum. 'He was winning every race and by the middle of the season people started to take notice. Frank Williams was contacting him, Toleman were contacting him. I got home from somewhere one day and my mother said: "There's been a telephone call for you. Bernie Ecclestone's been on the phone." I couldn't believe it. I said: "What does he want?" "He wants to talk to you about Ayrton." Then I had a letter from Peter Warr at Lotus, and one from Frank and I put them in contact with Ayrton.'

It was certainly time for Senna to step into a Formula Three car, where he would meet Eddie Jordan. 'It was at Silverstone on the Club circuit in midsummer,' Jordan recalls. 'He was clean-sweeping in two-litre and I rang him up one day. I had started the team at the end of 1981 and '82 was my first full season. I was running James Weaver and we were having big difficulties getting money together. I wanted to get into driver-management and I was looking for young talent. I rang up several of the top promising young guys to give them a test, although Senna was one of the few I did it for free for. Normally I wasn't likely to do things like that in those days.

'He said his father had just come across from Brazil and he was driving for Rushen Green and he needed to get permission. Could he come on a Wednesday afternoon because he'd be at Mallory Park doing a couple of laps in the morning? I said OK, and he came down.

'Weaver had done a pole position time the previous weekend which was, I think, 54.2 seconds (in the morning qualifying). Ayrton arrived and he did twenty laps and he looked amazingly good. It was in the afternoon, please remember, and in the crisp morning air Formula Three cars always go that bit quicker. The warmer it gets, the more the barometric pressure increases and the engine suffers a bit. So to equal the time set in a morning represents a slightly quicker time.

'He came in, made a couple of adjustments to the car – it was driver-tuning, really, he wanted to tune it for himself. It had some slight understeer and he moved it just ever so slightly, he didn't change anything seriously. We had set the car up exactly as Weaver had raced it. He didn't do anything with tyres. He went back out again and after another ten laps he equalled the time we had been on pole with. After another ten laps – it was his first time in a Formula Three car, don't forget – he became one of the first drivers to get into the 53 seconds on the Silverstone Club circuit. That was astonishing, absolutely amazing. Whatever adjustments he had made we kept and Weaver went on to win three races very soon after that. We won with Senna's adjustments at Donington, Jerez and Nogaro.

'As a person I think he lacks something. He would never have driven for me because, to be honest, I think he was keen on the Ron Dennis thing. Perhaps I didn't have the pedigree. I would say that even then he was looking as far ahead as Ron. The inkling was there. But I have nothing but the highest regard for the boy. What he did in our car was a joy and I was thrilled. I feel honoured that he did it.'

On 31 May Senna won at Brands Hatch. Fish, who had a new car, took pole but Senna beat him to Paddock and, as a contemporary account says, 'Fish lost part of his nose-cone as a result.' Senna set fastest lap and won by a couple of seconds. He won on 6 June at Mallory, on 13 June at Brands again. The next round of the European Championship was Hockenheim. Reginaldo Leme met him for the first time. 'I work for the big newspaper in São Paulo and TV Globo. He introduced himself to me in a hotel in Heidelberg [favoured haunt of the Formula One fraternity and a comfortable drive from the circuit]. "I'm Ayrton Senna, I'm planning to race until Formula One," he said. I felt in him very big ambitions. I knew his name very well but I didn't know him personally. We went to dinner together and he talked a little bit about racing, about his plans. I remember that after this I felt his talent was so good, that his plans were so good, his objectives so good that I introduced him to the journalists I knew well, British, French, Italian. I said to them: "For sure we'll see him in Formula One." He appreciated that. Sometimes he asked me to do that.'

This is a nice point, and an important one. Contrary to what you might think, racing journalists tend to specialize. Even if a Formula One reporter wished to cover other formulae he lacks the time. A very, very good Formula Ford 2000 driver will almost certainly be a stranger to them. The power of the press (except in a revelatory, destructive sense) is much overrated but if the press are raving about you, others will become curious – if they're not already. Senna would now become a person to the Formula One reporters, rather than a name which was winning races.

Actually, he took pole at Hockenheim, 'cooked' his clutch on the start line and then became sucked helplessly into mayhem at the first chicane when a driver called Cor Euser, in the lead, overdid it and barrel-rolled.

He won at Oulton on 26 June, overtaking Andrews on the first lap, won at Zandvoort on 3 July despite missing the first practice with clutch problems. He hadn't been to the circuit before and now had only thirty minutes to feel his way round. He took pole. At the start he missed second gear and was second. He stayed there for a lap, out-braked the leader, Jaap Van Silf Hoat, at the corner called Tarzan and won – from Fish. He was – wait for it, wait for it – only second at Snetterton on 4 July. It was his first defeat in a race he had finished. He won at Castle Combe on 10 July and they were at Snetterton again. Senna's balance went into counterbalance.

'He had me off,' Fish says. 'We were the local racers, it was a big local race, all our friends were there, we were both on the front row. The strange thing is that when you race with Ayrton at that level he almost takes you away from the rest of the field. It was him and me – I'm not putting the other guys down – but it really was him and me and then a gap and then the rest. That's what he brings out of you: the best. You have to squeeze yourself to find that last little bit and when you look in the mirror the rest of the field has disappeared. It makes you wonder if that's happening even now with Prost [in 1989]. Everyone says it's the superiority of the McLarens, but maybe they are pulling further and further away from the rest of the field because they are pulling so much out of themselves. Maybe Prost doesn't even realize it's happening.

'Anyway, Ayrton took the lead at Snetterton, my team was "hooked up" a little bit better and about six laps into the race going down the back straight I was fastest and I moved out of his slipstream to go by him. He moved over and kept pushing and pushing and pushing.' (He had already firmly blocked Fish past the pits.) A contemporary account describes them both 'weaving back and forth' across the straight. Fish: 'I was alongside the guy and he pushed me right on to the dirt. I went off the track. We were both young, we were both going for it and what I should have done was lift off, tuck back in behind him and had a go somewhere else – but at that age you keep your foot down. It wasn't as if he left me a car's width at the end of the straight. I'll try and intimidate someone to the point where they lift off but I won't push them off. I don't think he'd do it today, but back then it was "this guy can't be passing me!" – it was like that all the way across the track.

'I bounced ten feet up, it was all very spectacular and everyone was watching. I landed OK but I had to retire because the clutch was full of dirt. It was a time when I had started to close a little bit on him in the Championship and it was important to get every point I could. Of course it gave him twenty points and I didn't score any and it was a big deal. Everyone said: "Hey, you need to do something about that" and the marshals' reports said that number eleven pushed number seventy-four off the track and we put the protest in and it was one of the biggest splits Ayrton and I had.

'After that he was very angry with me. He felt that I should have gone and had a word with him. I don't think it would have made much difference, I don't think he really would have listened. Well, he would have stood there and listened but it wouldn't have made any difference. We felt that if something official was done and if the same situation arose he wouldn't do it again.'

Rushen is candid, despite his enormous affection for Senna. 'Ayrton put Fish on the grass and kept him there all the way to the esses. It was down to the stewards and this, that and the other and Ayrton said: "They pick on me because I'm Brazilian." But I mean he was well out of order. But he was so intense, he wanted it so much.'

Fish is candid, too. 'He was angry that we went through the official channels. He got fined something like £25 – typical RAC – and then we went to another tribunal and they upped it to £200 but they let him keep his points so it didn't help us at all. It changed the relationship between us because we then went off to Europe on a three-week trip and we stayed in the same hotels, and their mechanics and I used to get on really well but Ayrton was still angry and didn't want to be around any more than he had to be. That put more strain on it.

'He put racing on such a level – in the way he went about things – that I'm really not sure he was enjoying himself. He may sit down today and say: "Hey, I had a great time," but from the outside you wondered about that. He was very solemn, you know, and the people who were associated with me used to look at him and say: "He's not really a happy kind of guy." But on certain occasions he would come out and he could be funny, actually. He had a good sense of humour – when he let it come out.'

This is confirmed by Keith Sutton. 'He did the race at Snetterton and I went up to spend the weekend with him. That was good fun, him and Mauricio Gugelmin in the house at Norwich.'

The three-week trip took in Hockenheim (again), Austria and Denmark. 'When we went to Europe we travelled in the car, just him and me together,' Rushen says. 'We got very close. We'd talk about many things. He was very shy and didn't want to talk to people much but the people he liked – for example Spider his mechanic, and myself – he had all the time in the world for. He pushed other people out of the way to come and talk to us . . . because he felt comfortable with us.'

He took pole at Hockenheim, set fastest lap, won the race. He and Rushen drove on to Austria and the Österreichring. During the journey he said to Rushen: 'Who do you think is the best, me, Chico Serra or Nelson Piquet?'

Rushen: 'I dunno really.'

Senna: 'Well, I've got a big advantage over them. I've been driving karts from four years old.'

'He was,' Rushen says, 'really honest like that. He's got a lot of talent plus the fact that he was lucky enough to have been driving for so long. That makes a big difference.'

In Austria Senna took pole with a 'staggering' lap and vanished into the distance. He beat Fish by *24 seconds*. This meant that in the next race (Jyllandsring, Denmark) he could clinch the European Championship. He said to Keith Sutton: 'I'd like you to come, I'll pay for your air fare and your hotel.' Sutton comments: 'That was pretty decent of him. I flew out to Denmark. That was just a superb weekend. It was also a very fraught weekend, there was a lot of tension.'

Rushen reflects that 'there was something magical about that event. We had already won the British Championship and this European one meant a lot. I remember sitting on the grass in the paddock discussing with Senna whether we should put half a degree of rear wing on or not and it became an obsession. Should we, shouldn't we? Suddenly I said: Hang on, we don't normally act like this, we're getting all twitchy about this.'

You know the story. Pole. Fastest lap. He beat Fish by

$2^1/2$ seconds over the 25 laps. 'He was crying,' Rushen says, 'Ayrton was crying. He told me that: he was crying on the last lap. He went a bit wild afterwards.'

'We went out for a meal and he was thrilled,' Sutton says.

'It was the first time Ayrton got drunk – on two vodka and tonics. There was a motor cycle in the street and he got on it and did wheelies,' says Rushen.

'It's hard to explain to the average person how close you are, living in the same hotels and so on. After he'd won the Championship he did come out and it was the first time anyone had seen him drunk. It was fun, it was good to see him let his hair down. We were all in a bar and we all had a few drinks and obviously that was difficult for a Brazilian who was used to being a Coca-Cola man. It was nice: there was camaraderie now that it was over, we'd done our best, the Championship was settled. I don't have any bitterness. He took away a lot of the glory that some of us others might have had and there's a fine line in this sport between really achieving success and being one of several people who do a good job,' says Fish.

Domestically, he won at Thruxton on 30 August and Fish is illuminating about that. 'He's very shrewd, he's extremely clever even if you forget about the fact of how quick he is. He thinks way ahead of time. At Thruxton I was leading by a couple of seconds and we came up to lap the back markers at the complex. I decided the gap between me and him wasn't big enough to sit back and follow them through so I went inside on the first corner, the guy in front didn't see me, blocked me and I did have to follow them through. I lost a bunch of time through all three corners. Ayrton read it perfectly. As we came out of the complex he swept by and beat me. It was a day when he had one of his biggest smiles after the race because he knew he shouldn't have won but he still managed to do it.'

He won at Silverstone on 5 September – joint pole with Fish, a small lead which he built on. He won at Mondello Park on 12 September. The last race of the season was at Brands Hatch. Rushen won't ever forget that, either. 'Just before Brands he went off to do the World Kart thing [the World Championship in Kalmar, southern Sweden] and it was a disaster. He finished fourteenth and it was rubbish, everything was wrong. He came back and you could see his attitude was bad.'

At the very start of the season Senna had confided that 'I have already been to Italy and DAP have built a brand new frame. It is completely different. The engine is still not too good yet but we know where the problem is and the new parts will be ready soon.' Clearly there were other problems but Senna had still hungered for the kart championship. *Karting* magazine reported that 'timed practice began at 9.30 on Saturday morning with the air temperature on the low side under a ten-tenths cloud cover. All went well until da Silva stopped on his first lap with a flat tyre and was not allowed a re-run as he had passed the start flag.' And then there were the heats.

'A rolling lap for the second heat saw a comedy-like situation as a driver from Monaco halted and his supporting mechanic tripped in his anxiety to help.' Ten drivers spun out at the first corner and 'overshadowing the efforts of the front-runners ... was the meteoric progress of da Silva, his engine smoking copiously as he carved forwards from the very back of the grid to gain twenty-two places by race end. The young Brazilian remains as unassuming as ever, despite his successes in Formula 2000, and continued to affirm that it is karting that represents the great challenge.'

In the third heat 'da Silva performed yet another of his miracles, once again climbing no less than twenty-three places on his long-suffering DAP.' In the sixth da Silva

74

'again made up a tremendous amount of ground'. In the final itself 'the amazing Mr Silva made up half a lap deficit and then got all the way up to fourteenth.' And no higher. It was the last time he would contest the karting Championship; he was deeply disappointed and, as Rushen says, his attitude was bad for the last Formula 2000 at Brands Hatch.

'It all became a story of the front wings,' Rushen says. 'I said: "That's where we want the front wing." He disagreed. The qualifying session lasted twenty minutes and he came in three times to fanny around with this front wing. He didn't normally do that and he'd hardly done any laps. The fastest time was 46.5 seconds but three people were on that and he did it last so he started on the second row (Victor Rosso and Fish were the others) and halfway through the race he broke the lap record but it was too late to catch Fish. We had an argument – the only time we ever fell out. I said [expletive expletive] what was that about? He said: "You [expletive expletive]." That was the only race where his attitude was wrong.'

So what did happen? 'He decided,' Rushen says, 'that he was in a race and all of a sudden he wanted to win it. You could visibly see him speed up.'

Rick Morris was there as an interested spectator. 'I distinctly remember Ayrton and Calvin Fish going into Paddock that time Fish beat him. Fish had a better engine but – going into Paddock – the difference between the two drivers was noticeable, how Senna would catch up on pure skill . . .'

And before we leave 1982, we ought to glimpse briefly back to savour and appreciate. He had raced twenty-eight times and won every one except six – and of those, four times he didn't finish (engine failure, spun off, puncture, crash). In other words, he was only actually beaten twice – at Snetterton and that final 2000 at Brands.

'He was always on a roll,' Fish says. 'When people start winning it's hard to get them out of the habit. There's no such thing as luck. You make your own and if ever there was a situation like that – I'm thinking of the complex at Thruxton when I was blocked – Ayrton would make his own. When you race against somebody you don't analyse them strongly, you analyse how you can beat them. You don't get into their abilities because if you do you're beaten before the race starts. Looking at it now, he had tremendous car control, tremendous natural ability and the ability to find things which could be turned into his favour. He was extremely intelligent in manipulating his own destiny – always being with the right teams, having the right equipment and having some control over all of that.'

'When I raced with him I thought a lot of people didn't understand him,' Andrews says. 'He was very shy and people got the impression that he was a difficult person. The thing was, when he was at a racetrack or driving the car he was absolutely dedicated. Away from the racetrack he was great fun, he was as good fun as anybody. He is the most dedicated person to anything I have ever come across. I don't think he can be knocked for that but people look from the outside and say he's arrogant. I didn't find him at all like that. There were a lot of practical jokes. He was forever tying my shoe laces together when I was asleep. But when people were talking he couldn't answer because he didn't understand the English language brilliantly. The guy is straight. If you ask him a question you get a straight answer, no nonsense. He was helpful to me, he was a good team mate.'

It wasn't the end of '82. One race remained, at Thruxton and for a man and a team we haven't encountered. The man: Dick Bennetts. The team: West Surrey Racing. The event: a televised Formula Three meeting.

CHAPTER FIVE

Starlet Wars

The tall man has a face which is almost florid. Down at the end of the transporter, beyond the tools and the workbenches, a small modern office has been created and he sits within it, hands resting on the table in front of him. He has a becalmed presence but eyes which, from time to time, are surveying you in small bird-like darts. Dick Bennetts wields words in a phlegmatic way, as most team managers do, and he discusses the calms and storms of motor racing dispassionately. To you it may be heady, hedonistic, exotic, nakedly exciting, a cocktail of extremes. To him it's a job and all the incidents merely factors in his big equation.

'I'd met Ayrton Senna in the middle of 1982,' he will say, his voice still carrying the lingering traces of a New Zealand accent. 'It was quite a laugh. The year before he'd driven with Mansilla – the young Argentinian – and he didn't rate him very highly. We had taken a few races in 1982 to get Mansilla into the winner's circle and we almost got the Formula Three championship. Ayrton's reasoning was that if he didn't rate Mansilla and we could make Mansilla a winner we must be a pretty good team.

'We did the non-Championship Formula Three race at Thruxton at the end of 1982 and Ayrton drove in Mansilla's car. He got into it and virtually without touching it he was flying. He said the car felt very, very good and he just wanted one small adjustment because it had a little bit too much understeer for him. He put it on pole by a mile, won by thirteen seconds. We reached a verbal agreement after the race and he signed in January.'

'At the beginning of the year,' Senna said that October day at Thruxton, 'the most important thing for me was Formula Ford 2000. I didn't think it would be possible for me to race this year with a good team in Formula Three but by the beginning of September I had already clinched the 2000 championship so I decided it was a possibility for me to do this televised F3 race. I went home to Brazil in order to enjoy a little bit of the summer, the sunshine and also to meet my sponsors and talk about this race and about next season. I arrived back in England two weeks before the race and did some tests at Thruxton and Snetterton. I went well in the car and I found it was very good to work with Dick Bennetts. We seemed to understand each other well so I was looking forward to the race. Obviously the TV race was very important for me and now that I have done well I hope it will help me to find the budget for next season.'

In fact Senna was stunning at Thruxton, the only man to get into the one minute 13 seconds in qualifying. He did it in both sessions. He took the lead from the flag (of course) and 'I was just making sure nothing could go wrong and that I didn't make any mistakes.' His only regret was that he didn't beat the lap record. The track was 'very slippery and the wind was a bit strong on the straight'. Henri Toivonen, incidentally, was fourth in a Ralt-Toyota, the same Toivonen who would become one of the best rally drivers in the world before he was killed in the 1986 Tour de Corse.

Dick Bennetts runs West Surrey Racing, an extremely professional team which had already had Formula Three champions: Stefan Johansson in 1980, Jonathan Palmer in 1981. This season of 1983 they would contest the twenty rounds of the Marlboro British Formula Three championship: a thorough testing ground for a young driver because it stretched from March to October (so he'd have to master many different kinds of weather again and, this being England, quite probably all kinds of weather). It would be fought out on six different circuits. But that was only the background. The foreground was inevitably drawn in sharper, harder shades. Formula Three represented the last step before Formula One; the rest, if you'll allow me to be so dismissive – karts, Formula Ford 1600, Formula Ford 2000 – had all been steps, too, but each leading only to the next. From Formula Three you could see the very summit, and it was inevitably bathed in beautiful sunlight.

'Ayrton brought some sponsorship over with him, so he'd got a bit of money,' Keith Sutton says. 'I think it was at that time that Ron Dennis contacted him and said he'd pay for the full season of Formula Three and Ayrton turned it down . . .'

He was more of a man than a teenager. The Face had filled out although it still seemed gaunt in structure. The torso had developed and this is important, extremely so. To be physically able to control a Formula One car demands strength and if you don't have it you can't play.

Already journalists writing their previews to the season were posing a single question: who can beat Senna and his Ralt-Toyota? Already Senna had tested the car twice and gone fast. Now, as the first race approached – Silverstone, 6 March – there seemed only one rival, Martin Brundle. He, too, was in a Ralt-Toyota, but with Eddie Jordan Racing . . . he, too, could see the summit . . .

The ingredients were present for a season which would become nearly poetic; it would move to pinnacles so extreme that in the end it captivated all motor sport in a way which had not happened before and has not happened since at the level of Formula Three.

'I knew nothing of him personally,' Brundle will say, his voice still carrying faint traces of a Norfolk accent, 'although I'd heard a lot about him. I'd seen him win a Formula Ford 1600 race in 1981. Now all I heard about was this guy who was going to dominate Formula Three and because he virtually hadn't driven in Formula Three it seemed a bit strange. The talk was of who's going to get near him and I found that strange, too.'

Nor could Senna expect a fond embrace from Jordan. 'He knows I gave him a free drive in 1982 at Silverstone and he hardly spoke to me in 1983 at all and I was fighting my balls off to beat him. It's only recently that he nods and says "Hello, Eddie." I don't like that so much. I gave him that first drive, I don't harm people, I help them. He is very much the professional, he is not a talkative person. I certainly wouldn't go out of my way to befriend someone who didn't want to be friendly with me. I'm not saying I'm perfect – far, far from it – but I paid and I know how difficult it was for me to survive in those days. As it's happened, he's turning out to be perhaps the greatest driver we've known . . .'

And so they came to Silverstone for that first race. In earlier testing Senna and Brundle had battered the club circuit record (53.94 seconds) set the season before; in qualifying for the race itself the wind blew down the straights full into the cars – Silverstone is largely treeless flatland like Snetterton – and a driver called David Leslie in a Magnum-Toyota took pole. This was as amazing then as it is now and would not be repeated. In twenty-one races, Senna would take pole sixteen times.

Senna was second quickest, Brundle fourth, Fish fifth and Johnny Dumfries, then twenty-three and in a Ralt-Volkswagen, sixth. Leslie held Senna to Copse corner – Leslie had the inside line, of course. Senna drove round the outside of him and after 5 laps his lead grew to 3.28 seconds. At the end, after 20 laps and 32.16 miles, he was 7 seconds ahead of Brundle.

The question came back immediately: who can beat Senna?

Nobody could at Thruxton. He took pole from Brundle and made an 'exquisite' start. In the wet — it had rained earlier — he was quicker through the corners, Brundle quicker along the straights. Senna described it like this: 'I could see that I was faster through the corners but I also knew that I had to conserve my tyres. I knew that whoever could make their tyres last longer would win. And my engine just would not pull more than 5,600 revs.' Brundle set fastest lap. Senna, rarely a conservationist at this stage of his career, won. It begs a different kind of question: why didn't he set fastest lap? He had influenza. 'I did not feel good but I was not making mistakes in the car so I felt it was OK. But I'm not sure I was going as well as I could have done.'

At Silverstone a week later — Senna on pole — it was wet again. Brundle would say from the heart: 'He is incredible. He always seems to find just a bit extra.' At Stowe Senna took him on the outside. 'Quite brilliant', Brundle said, again from the heart. The race was stopped after 6 laps by a downpour; a second 6-lap 'heat' was run later, Brundle led again and this time Senna took him on the outside at Becketts. Brundle: 'It was incredible. He had two wheels on the grass but he still kept going.' Bennetts: 'Ayrton got beaten off the line and then just drove round the outside. Martin was staggered, as he admitted afterwards.' Something else staggering happened. On the last lap Senna's fire extinguisher went off without warning, drenching him ('Cold' he said). It didn't disturb him at all.

At Thruxton (again) he took pole and won. At one point he was third, took Brundle, took the leader (Davy Jones) on a power play and finished a second ahead of Brundle. 'Why doesn't he ever make a mistake?' Brundle wondered wistfully. Senna was awarded the Avon Motor sports man of the month, £100 and a trophy.

Bennetts says crisply: 'We won the first nine races and I didn't know until someone looked in the records that Nelson Piquet had won eight (in 1978) so we had set a new world record. Of course, the bubble has to burst . . .'

Jordan says crisply: 'Senna had this tactic of doing the opening couple of laps in a blistering way and it broke the opposition. He was the one who started it. Other drivers actually couldn't cope with it. A lot of them were trying to find themselves at the beginning of a race. Senna demoralized them all during the first two laps. He made a fantastic effort – and you can see it now in Formula One – but in Formula Three he raised that to a new level. If you couldn't keep up with him you were finished, you'd never catch him back. Martin Brundle finally got around to accepting that if you couldn't stay with him you'd be beaten anyway.'

At Silverstone he took pole and won and – this is instructive – he went back to Brazil between Thruxton (4 April) and Silverstone (24 April). He needed to relax, did relax, said he felt better. Brundle took the lead, missed a gear, fell back into the pack and Senna won by five seconds from Jones. It was his sixth on the roll and seventh altogether, counting that one Formula Three at the end of '82 – and it equalled Piquet. At Thruxton two weeks later he beat it – you know, pole too, fastest lap from Brundle by 4 seconds but to general amazement failed to take the qualifying record, too. A strong wind made it 'impossible' to set the car up perfectly at both the complex and the chicane. Meanwhile Bennetts confirmed that Senna was in discussions with the Williams Formula One team. 'He's trying to speak to as many people as possible.' This would lead to a test session but was not intended to lead to more.

In qualifying at Brands Hatch on 8 May *Autosport* said: 'Yes, Ayrton had done it again – his seventh successive pole – but it was the manner in which he achieved his position that provided the talking point of the morning. Quite simply the Brazilian's car was sensationally fast through Paddock Hill Bend. "It's right on the limit at that corner," confided Ayrton, "and I can tell you that it feels quite dangerous!" A dab of the brakes, a flick down into fourth gear and throw the car to the right, hard on the throttle: that was Ayrton's recipe for success. And he was quite visibly the fastest through that particular corner. Once, during the second session, he missed his down-change, turning into the corner without any positive drive, but even that presented only a minor problem, the Brazilian sliding wide out on to the "old" circuit (which runs alongside) and quickly bringing the car back under his total control. His progress was very good to watch.' The margin Senna-to-Brundle in the race: just under 3 seconds. And that was number nine.

At Silverstone he took pole, set fastest lap. The margin Senna-to-Brundle in the race: nearly 10 seconds. And that was number ten.

Bennetts has already said that 'Of course, the bubble has to burst . . .'

It happened at Silverstone two weeks later. 'Senna was clearly very good in qualifying, so he was on pole more often than not,' Brundle says. 'Usually I was alongside him on the grid a tenth or less behind him but he seemed to catch me out for pole quite comfortably, really. But because you are side by side on a Formula Three grid – no stagger – it's not that important. It was all about the first corner. He was very aggressive into the first corner. He'd take all the risks a man could take on the initial two laps to put a gap between himself and his pursuer, which basically was me. In the first race he'd beaten me comfortably, in the second race I'd got on his tail at Thruxton, I'd followed him the whole way and given him a hard time. After the race he responded in a slightly surprising way by telling my mechanics that it had been too close for comfort and he'd have to do something about it. It really interested me when he said that. I realized for the first time that I had made him aware of me. We never chatted much during the whole year so I can't even remember the first time I spoke to him . . .'

And so we come to Silverstone, 12 June. It was a combined race, counting towards both the British and European Formula Three Championships. You could choose in which championship your result would be registered. Bennetts outlines the thinking in their camp. 'We had such a big points lead over Martin that we chose not to do the British part.' In other words, Senna went European.

Very few Formula Three races endure in the popular memory. By definition Formula One casts its long shadow over them; these young drivers are serving their apprenticeship and will only be properly measured when they ascend, when they find themselves wheel-to-wheel with Lauda and Prost rather than (to select two names at random who were at Silverstone that June day) Max Busslinger and Carlton Tingling.

This race endures.

In the first qualifying session, in the wet, Senna was second quickest. It forced Brundle to gamble. 'You could choose between European tyres or British tyres – they were for the British Championship, they were much harder and slower. I made a decision to go for the British points because it was my one chance to catch up some of the ground lost to Ayrton. Although I was the fastest British runner I was only twelfth on the grid. I thought: what's the point of that? I need to be at the front of this field. I made a spontaneous decision and to this day I don't really know why I did it. I decided to mount European tyres with a few minutes of the second qualifying session to go.' (Technical note: Brundle had run in the wet on Avons, was now changing to Yokohamas.) 'I said "Mark me up a set of Europeans, I'm going to go for it." I put it on pole.'

Brundle 1 minute 23.99

Senna 1 minute 24.08

Dumfries 1 minute 24.63

'All of a sudden I was in charge and it was one of the best decisions I have made in my racing career. I put some extra wing on, which was another flyer [motor-racing-speak: risk] to get more downforce on the basis that if I got away I wanted to be flat through Stowe and Club, which the European tyres would allow you to do. Once I got in front I was going to do a Senna. Nobody was ever going to catch me. And off I went . . .'

Brundle was in the lead at Copse, Senna second, Dumfries third. They crossed the line like that for the first lap . . . and the second. Dumfries felt that 'Senna seemed to be in a bit of trouble with his tyres and I caught up with him and we started to battle. I got a good run out of Becketts, I was alongside him going down Hangar Straight and he put me on the grass. I kept my foot on the accelerator and I got back on the circuit. Do I blame him? No. I would like to honestly, actually hear a driver say he has never put anyone on the grass. That's fair. But it was interesting because he was under pressure from me and he was also trying to catch Brundle.'

Senna did have tyre troubles. I quote a contemporary account: 'Senna had gambled on running three different types of tyre, including a harder "SH" on the front left against the advice of the Yokohama technicians in an effort to ensure that it would still be in good condition at the end of the race, but he was soon in trouble with excessive understeer.'

Senna would explain that 'after two laps the left rear wasn't working at all. There was just no grip.' Bennetts will explain that 'we opted for open tyres and we had an accident. Martin was on Yokohamas, Martin was leading, Ayrton put a wheel off at Club corner and must have had a puncture because when he got to the chicane he lost it,' to which Brundle says: 'So away I went. In an attempt to reach me he ended up in the catch-fencing at the chicane and that was the turning point, really.' Jordan comments: 'Senna made a mistake at the chicane, he went on to the top of the chicane and spun into the guardrail.' Jordan pauses, and Jordan pausing is an event worthy of note before he sets off at high speed again. You can hear his voice changing gear, first, second, third, fourth, fifth, sixth, seventh. 'We broke Senna that once at Silverstone – I'll never forget it – we broke him at Silverstone. It was a hard-fought season and we established ourselves (as a team) with the Brundle–Senna battle, mainly because Brundle kept at him. We were beaten nine times in a row [in this context, the '82 race didn't count] but we were all determined we were going to beat him, even though at the back of their minds everyone knows that he's a better driver than Martin. If I ever headed a Formula One team Martin Brundle would be one of my first choices because he has phenomenal talent, but you have to fill his head with the right kind of vibes. The thing about it is, we worked on him so hard that eventually he felt he was as good as Senna.

'It became personal, it was so competitive it was unbelievable, never have we seen a season like it. We got lots of TV and we got lots of credibility out of it. OK, maybe the financial climate wasn't as conducive then as it is now and as a result there weren't as many cars but it brought Formula Three alive because everybody was watching it.'

And a last reflection from Jordan: 'We were getting really top priority treatment from Novamotor and we always thought that we had a slight little advantage [Jordan is Irish, remember, and this is exactly how he speaks]. Whereas Dick went to John Judd. [Senna himself corrects this, saying it was Nicholson, McLaren.] On the Silverstone Grand Prix circuit Martin just, just, just had the legs of him.'

'So that began a little series of setbacks,' Bennetts says. 'Ayrton was just never happy to finish second. There was such determination that we often had pole position and fastest lap but he'd be beaten off the line and would run second – worth seven points (six for second place, one for fastest lap) – but might then crash trying to take the lead, losing the six points.'

Cadwell Park was one week after Silverstone and by now the duel was starting to draw big crowds. That gave it a feeling of importance, but Cadwell was to be something different altogether. 'You have to find your limit,' Bennetts says. 'If you are winning everything there is still a day when you must face the fact that you will be beaten and I think it doesn't hurt a driver to have one or two accidents.' (Clarification: the accidents are intended to show the driver that he has found his limit, not of course to hurt him.)

'The classic example was Cadwell Park. We already had pole position and he wrote the car off with about two minutes of qualifying left. He was on pole over Brundle and if memory serves Brundle was eight-tenths behind [it was Senna 1 minute 22.57, Brundle 1 minute 22.58]. Ayrton said: "I can go another four- or five-tenths quicker, just reduce a little bit of the understeer." We did that and apparently someone timing out on the course had him four- or five-tenths quicker but he didn't complete the full lap. He destroyed the car on the Mountain – it's a very tricky little area and it goes uphill quite steeply. He got it wrong through there and went off. He hopped out. A marshal was knocked over and Ayrton, I'm told, was more worried about the chassis than the marshal.' (In fact, as Senna makes clear for this book, 'I never realized the situation with the marshal!' and this is undoubtedly correct.) He'd strayed slightly wide coming out of the right-hander at the foot of the hill, kept the power on but ran out of road and struck the marshal's post virtually head-on. The car was wrecked and the marshal had to be treated for bruises and shock.

Senna was out of the race. As if to demonstrate just what Senna and Brundle were drawing out of each other, Brundle won it from Fish by more than twelve seconds. Jordan (cryptically) notes that 'he hit the bank going over the rise and we won that.'

Snetterton was two weeks away. Senna qualified only fourth and had no idea what was wrong with the car. Neither did Dick Bennetts. Brundle took the lead, Senna inevitably behind him, Brundle pulled away, Senna nibbled and nibbled and by lap 12 – half-distance – had caught him. Going along the straight to the S-shaped corners, Senna decided that the only way to overtake was seize the inside line. He crept up on the inside with two wheels off the main tarmac throwing dust and stones at the car behind (Jones). Into the left-hand kink Brundle moved across on to the normal line but Senna had his foot hard down, two wheels off the track, bouncing in the dirt. Spectators saw a 'tell-tale puff of smoke'. Senna's front wheel ran up and over Brundle's rear wheel. Senna spun across Jones and into the tyre-lined armco backwards.

'Let's put it this way, I was less than white, less than pure in the incident,' Brundle says. 'He asked for a tribunal and they got a load of spectators in who saw the incident and let's face it, there we are at Snetterton, Norfolk, my home track.

By now the war with Senna was pretty common knowledge and the tribunal was asking local people to make comments; so I didn't get fined and I didn't get my licence endorsed.' (Brundle is grinning while he says this.) 'The relationship at that point was at its lowest. We didn't speak very much. I got on with him very poorly because he very much felt that it was Brundle and Great Britain versus Senna.'

Well, it was certainly Brundle and Norfolk versus Senna.

'Gradually our points lead was being eroded and up to then I'd never really sat down and had a good talk with him because he's a very intelligent young guy,' Bennetts says. 'Some other young blokes you give them a bollocking every time they have an accident but with Ayrton being intelligent you know he really didn't mean to have it. But eventually, when I saw our points were eroding away, we sat down and had a chat. I said: "Do you realize this, it's better to finish second, you can't win every time." He found that extremely difficult to accept.

'There's only one place for him and that's first. He did realize his championship was slipping away.' Pause. 'Also we didn't find out until later that Eddie Jordan had a slightly different specification engine, so we were running fractionally less wing to keep up the straight line speed. There were no direct protests but Martin's car was found to be slightly illegal at one meeting – but that was the stewards at the meeting [i.e. not Bennetts]. I think between the drivers it may have got intense but Eddie and I have always got on reasonably well. We know each other, we do the best jobs we can.'

Between Snetterton and the next race, Silverstone, Senna tested the Williams at Donington. He did 70 laps, best time 60.90. What impressed Frank Williams most 'was that he got into the rhythm very speedily. He'd never driven anything as quick as a Formula One car but you'd never have thought so. I'm looking upon it as a kind of long-term investment in the future. There's no way we can handle him next year because of our current situation. And I think Bernie Ecclestone's going to offer him a deal. But he came to see me a while ago, asking for advice, saying that everyone was offering him 400-year deals and so on, the usual stuff. I told him that I couldn't really advise him but if it would help him to get the feel of the thing he could have a run in one of our cars whenever it suited him. I hope he'll remember we treated him fairly.'

Normal Formula Three service was resumed at Silverstone, Senna pole, fastest lap, victory, Brundle chasing all the way. But not at Donington, although Senna did take pole. For once Brundle got away first, held his nerve and the car steady to the first corner and then held both steady for the rest of the race. With Senna gnawing at him for the whole 30 laps it was an accomplished and mature performance – oh, and quite incidentally, the first time Senna had been beaten when he'd completed a race. The margin Brundle-to-Senna: 0.4 seconds.

Oulton, next, seemed only to confirm that Senna still could not accept second place, still could not accept driving percentage races to take the Championship. Brundle was in the lead and, as he says, 'we had a coming together which was really his fault. He took a slide up the inside of me, I mean never in a month of Sundays was that going to work, I would have had to have to turn off the circuit to avoid the accident.'

Jordan remembers that 'Senna made an absolutely suicidal dive up the inside (on lap 28) and the two of them went off – which was sad . . .' Another rare pause. 'Calvin Fish won that race.' And a last one. 'Possibly Ayrton didn't speak to us because it might have taken an edge away. He was mega-competitive, he knew I was up to all sorts of tricks to try and beat him. I mean, we had protested him,

A study in concentration: Senna in the early 1980s.

Senna crosses the line at Jyllandsring in tears, consumed by victory.

And that was 1981. Liliane seems pleased, too.

Testing at Oulton — with Keith Sutton
risking life and limb to get the shot!

It was dry
for
qualifying at
Estoril in
1985, Senna
now in John
Player
Special
overalls.

Perfect control at Adelaide, 1986.

Victory at
Monaco, 1987

The master of
Monaco: 1987

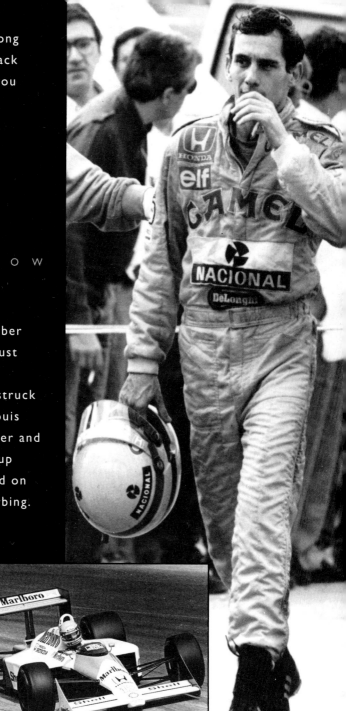

It's a long walk back when you don't finish.

BELOW

Monza, September 1988, just before Senna struck Jean-Louis Schlesser and ended up beached on the kerbing.

he had protested us ... after Oulton, he got fined and had his licence endorsed ...'

Senna's own view must be heard. 'I was right up his gearbox and I was going much quicker than him. I just braked late and went for the inside. I'm sure he didn't see me and he closed in on me when we were already going into the corner.'

(Meanwhile, rumours said that he had been offered a contract with Brabham, but it was now August and deep into the rumour season, anyway.)

Normal service at Silverstone on 29 August, though, Senna pole, and the margin Senna-to-Brundle a second and a half. The Championship: Senna 116, Brundle 94, Jones 60. (It was at this race, echoing Bennetts, that a 'discrepancy' was found at scrutineering on Brundle's car, one sidepod 1mm too low, but his points were not taken from him.) Bennetts, after some reflection, decided to appeal against the stewards 'for the way they handled the matter'. He stressed that he 'held nothing' against either Jordan or Brundle, and added that he had watched three attempts to get the car to clear the regulation 4cm. 'If it had finally passed I would have said "OK, it's close but it's fair enough." In the end, though, the scrutineers failed the car and made out a report to the stewards, who miraculously decided some two hours later that the car was OK.'

At Oulton on 11 September, fourth last race of the Championship, Senna took pole, Brundle took the lead, Senna after him, Jones after him. On lap 8 Senna tried to go outside Brundle at Druids and slithered off, buckling the front end of the car. Brundle, slightly incredulous (as was everybody else except Senna), mused that even if he won all the remaining three races and set fastest lap, Senna would still take the Championship by finishing second to him but he felt that 'it appears he can't accept finishing second'.

And now, for the only time in the year, genuine bad luck struck at Senna. Thruxton, 18 September. Senna pole, Brundle in the lead, Senna overtaking in the complex on the gravel when Brundle locked his brakes, Brundle overtaking just after the chicane because Senna took a ragged line through it. As they completed the second lap Senna peeled away into the pits, travelling slowly. The engine had failed. (It is a staggering thought that Bennetts's team had run in 65 Formula Three races since its formation and this was the only retirement through 'mechanical problems'.)

Brundle won comfortably from Jones and that made it Senna 116 points, Brundle 113, Jones 67. Now Brundle mused that if he won the last two races he'd be punished by his consistency. He'd have scored in eighteen of the twenty rounds and you could only count seventeen finishes. Nervously he scanned his season, and his eye fixed upon his worst finish, third and worth four points. (It is also a staggering thought that Brundle had only failed to gain points twice since 6 March, seven months ago, and his worst finish was third.)

Later the mystery of Senna's engine failure became clear – the team had been mistakenly supplied with two-star fuel, causing a detonation problem. 'Our supplier can't believe it,' Bennetts said, 'but that's what the results of the analysis were.'

Silverstone, 2 October, Jones on pole, then Brundle, then Allen Berg, a Canadian, then Senna who'd spun 'wildly' at Abbey Curve – backwards – touching the railway sleepers. And the race? Brundle from Senna all across Silverstone's broad acres and 20 laps of a total of 58.64 miles. On the last lap Senna toyed with taking Brundle on the inside at Beckett's but decided against. (It is another staggering thought that this was the first time he had compromised since 6 March, seven months ago.)

Brundle 28 minutes 55.23 seconds

Senna 28 minutes 55.87 seconds

Brundle 123 points

Senna 122 points

There was a round of the European Formula Three Championship at Donington on 9 October. 'I did the race and Ayrton decided not to because it wasn't a combined round of British and European,' Brundle says. 'I was on pole and won at a canter, which really showed the joint dominance of Senna and myself, if you like. He was a spectator that day, he came up to me afterwards and said: "Well, it just shows you where we're at, doesn't it?" I'd won against all Europe's best and I'd won so easily it was embarrassing.'

Brundle 37 minutes 47.09 seconds

Pier Luigi Martini (Ralt-Alfa Romeo) 38 minutes 02.03 seconds

James Weaver (Ralt-Volkswagen) 38 minutes 03.77 seconds

A few days later Senna caught a plane for the South of France and the Circuit Paul Ricard to see what a Formula One Brabham felt like. Then he was due at a place called Macau. Then he was due back to a place called Thruxton to decide the British Formula Three Championship.

CHAPTER SIX

For Whom the Bells Toll

Marlboro invest in the infrastructure of motor racing and, courtesy of McLaren, they gave three promising young drivers a taste at Silverstone that summer of '83: Brundle, Stefan Bellof and Senna. And because Marlboro and McLaren do things properly John Watson came along and drove a few laps to set a time – invaluable, this, because there was then a direct yardstick with which to measure the youngsters.

'I was so impressed by the whole thing,' Brundle says. 'I'd never driven a car with anything like that power. I mean, the fastest thing I'd ever driven was a Formula Three car with 150 horsepower and suddenly here I was with 550 horsepower and it was absolutely no problem.'

Memory's mechanisms are a mystery to me. I remember with some clarity Silverstone that day: how emptied it seemed, how intimate. You could wander and no official minded – only essential personnel were present. You could stand beside the car, chat to whomever you wanted. It was cold enough to need anoraks, cold enough to leave Brundle with one hand in a pocket, the other nursing a polystyrene cup of coffee. I remember – how can memory be this exact? – standing just inside the pit door with Brundle's father, a large patrician of a man. The instant Brundle moved away for the first time – that impossible growl-howl of the engine when you're close to it – I remember shouting (you have to): 'I hope he comes back.'

'Yes,' his father shouted as the red and white McLaren flowed down the pit lane. I don't remember Bellof being there at all that day. But he was, he was.

'We all did roughly the same lap times,' Brundle says, 'about a tenth apart. We had already blown dear old Wattle's set-up time completely out of the window although he didn't need to impress three young drivers. He'd done it all before and he's still won five more Grands Prix than I have. Every time I came in they cleaned the flies off the car, every time I got in the car on went a Brundle and a Union Jack sticker. They were so professional I just wanted to kiss Ron Dennis's feet for allowing me 30 laps in this wonderful piece of machinery. Senna managed to blow up on his first run.'

He did – it wasn't his fault, of course – but before that, to quote *Autosport,* 'he quickly got into the groove but incurred a finger-wagging from Ron Dennis for trying to go too quickly too soon and was hauled out of the car to cool off for a short while.'

Meanwhile out there, out at the back of the emptied circuit, a small, rather jolly man watched. He was Brabham's mole – if we may allow ourselves to stray into the terminology of espionage. He was called Herbie Blash. 'I went purely to watch Senna. We had Brabham and Senna in mind at that particular time. I was timing Senna, he did a lap – a 1 minute 11 – and then the engine blew up. It happened where I was timing him so I could see – and none of the McLaren people could – exactly how quick this lap would have been. When the engine blew he never made it past the point where they were timing the cars, so they never got the lap. Obviously I informed Senna. He said he knew it was quick but I was the only one who knew how quick it was. Obviously I didn't inform McLaren . . .'

'After my laps I got out and I was so excited about it,' Brundle says. 'Meanwhile Senna was negotiating a second run, much to my annoyance. I was a simple country boy from Norfolk. I'd got myself in a Grand Prix car and I hadn't got management around me, I hadn't got anybody around me [except Dad, still watching from the pit door], it was just me doing what I did naturally. Senna was there with managers and all that sort of thing. I was impressed by that, you have to take your hat off to the guy; and he was negotiating a second run . . .'

Ah, the tricks of Brundle's memory. 'I had absolutely no managers,' Senna says. 'It was myself and my father, that was all.' And negotiating a second run? 'I did it all myself and the simple reason was that during my first run something didn't work well! I can't remember what it was now . . .' After that second run, incidentally, Senna said: 'The McLaren is quite an easy car to drive and I know I could have gone much quicker. The steering is lighter than on my Formula Three car, although I wasn't really comfortable. My right leg was squashed [against the monocoque] and the blood wasn't circulating properly. I couldn't feel the throttle well because of that.'

Blash, Brabham's team manager, returned silently home a Senna disciple. 'I knew him from Formula Three, because I'm a friend of Dick Bennetts and after Silverstone, yes, we were really keen to sign him up. He tested for us at Ricard. He was very quiet – very, very quiet. He wasn't pushy in any way. He did a very professional job for somebody who you'd have thought was looking at the big world of Formula One. He took it very calmly, jumped in the car, came back, gave us very good feedback, very good information. From there you could see the guy was going to be a World Champion.' Herbie Blash is neither exaggerating nor joking (and just in case I might imagine he is, he locks his eyes on to mine to prevent any possible misunderstanding).

When the test was over Senna went hard for the airport. He had that appointment in a distant Portuguese enclave which, one must suppose, was linked to Brazil by the umbilical cord, just as Estoril in the karts had been. It was notable for casinos, slums, weird taxis which were very old and paddy fields. A travel brochure insisted: 'For those weary travellers who are looking for complete peace Macau is probably as near ideal as anywhere that can be found in Asia though the two annual bursts of noise – the Macau Grand Prix motor race and the Chinese New Year – might drive visitors to the beautiful green islands of Taipa and Coloane. It is still possible to relax, stroll or cycle round without playing life or death games with traffic.' That is just a touch ironic in the circumstances.

'There were several magical moments in 1983 and Macau was one of them,' Bennetts says. 'It was the first time there had been a Formula Three race there. Ayrton arrived very late and jet-lagged. He'd been testing the Brabham on the Tuesday, flew to England, then flew to Hong Kong. He arrived late Wednesday night. When he went out on Thursday morning for qualifying he hadn't seen the track before – others among the entry had been there in Formula Atlantic.

'It's a four-mile Monaco-type street circuit, it's got a long straight and two and a half miles on very twisty, narrow, bumpy road. [Cobbles, someone said.] He brushed a wall in qualifying, damaged a rim – he was that close – and then he put it on pole. No, it didn't surprise me because of his raw talent,' Bennetts says. 'The race? He just cleared off and won both heats.

'My personal belief is that a lot of it is the ability of concentration, the power of concentration. If you apply your mind to a lot of things you can do them. He had total dedication and concentration and talent as well. Some guys are very quick at learning circuits, others will drive round for two years and still not find the right line.'

Let us be clear: this was Senna's very first street race and he was not quickest in the first qualifying session. Guerrero (Ralt-Toyota) did 2 minutes 22.85 seconds, then Senna and Brundle both on 2 minutes 23.47. Senna had only three laps before he brushed that wall, damaging all four wheels but not the car itself. In the second session he bent a gear selector and, losing time for repairs, had only three laps again. It was enough. He did 2 minutes 22.02, Guerrero next on 2 minutes 22.18. The race was run in two heats. Guerrero took the lead in the first of them and quite naturally reached the hairpin – only 150 metres from the starting line – still in the lead. He reasoned that if he 'covered' the corner now rushing at them nobody would catch him afterwards. Guess who reached that corner in the lead? 'He came past me down the alley between the two corners,' Guerrero said. 'I couldn't believe what he was able to do on cold tyres.' Senna won, went to bed for an hour and a half – he still had jet lag, the weather was extremely hot and 'I wasn't feeling well.' The second heat? Flag to flag. He had quite naturally set fastest lap in both heats.

'Because it was all new to us we went out and had a very good night. Teddy Yip of Theodores, you know, put on a wonderful spread in the Lisboa Hotel after the race – a fantastic spread – and it went on until three in the morning. We got to bed about four-thirty, five, which you don't do in England when you're racing,' Bennetts says.

A week later the domestic Formula Three Championship would be settled. Thruxton, set in the gentility of English pastureland, has no slums, no casinos and you have to buy rice in packets from the corner shop; but for a motor race it's as good a place as any and better than most. Those who come to Thruxton – to drive, watch or parade as officials – care.

There was mist, hanging and lingering, insinuating itself around Church Corner – a very apt name, as we shall see – where the cars would have been going at top speed. They waited for the mist to clear, the faithful who had come to witness the culmination. They knew that Brundle had a one-point lead after nineteen rounds. They knew that, because of his consistency, Brundle was having to drop points and what he needed was simple now: to win. It was 23 October 1983.

What they didn't know and could not see was a proper, straight-up no-nonsense example of mechanical machinations which makes motor sport so devious, infuriating and interesting.

'We didn't know for a long time,' Dick Bennetts says in his quiet, reserved, almost nervous way, 'that Brundle had an engine done by Novamotor Italy. Our Novamotor engine had been rebuilt in England and we weren't given the latest developments. So for Thruxton we sent the engine to Italy, to where Brundle's had been done. Ayrton drove a car down with the engine in the boot. That's not unusual. We send a lot of our drivers to meet engine builders. We still didn't get the same modification as them but it was rebuilt.

'My honest view is that if we'd had the same spec engines midway through the year Ayrton possibly wouldn't have had so many accidents [i.e. wouldn't have had to push so hard]. But we didn't know about it until two or three races from the end of the Championship. I'd found out by looking at their car in scrutineering. They had a different pulley on the engine. It got me thinking. I rang Novamotor and they said: "It's just a one-off development." So we had our engine rebuilt but we couldn't get one with the special pulley. What we did have was 1984 sidepods and Eddie was upset then.'

Yes, Eddie was upset then. He says: 'This is a fact – we went into the last round of the Formula Three Championship one point ahead in a total long series. When you think back, when you see what Senna has achieved, I reckon as a little team – as we then were – running one car we were magic. I was furious with Ron Tauranac. It was one of the reasons I left Ron. He upset me because we fought so hard and he brought an unfair advantage. In the wind tunnel he had found a new underbelly. They weren't flat bottoms, there were wing sections underneath. OK, maybe Ayrton deserved to win because he was the best but we didn't deserve as a team and as a customer to be treated unfairly. I admire Ron but I have never ever forgotten that he brought it in. This was a completely new underwing. We used to get some stuff to try for him and Dick Bennetts used to get the same. Dick got his hands on this and he persuaded Ron that he should be given the opportunity – because he had tested it – to have it exclusively for the last race. Why Ron did that for him I don't ever know.'

Bennetts counters with this: 'Well, all I can say is that Novamotor gave him an advantage by giving him an engine which had a different cam pulley arrangement and we didn't have one.'

And Brundle himself: 'At a race before it was wet and what I was doing was short-changing, second, third, fourth coming out of the chicane. That's how I went so far off into the distance – but I was pulling too low revs. We went into the last round with an engine which was basically tired because I didn't have enough money to do anything about it. Senna went to Italy – I know because Stefano Modena is my current team mate [1989] and he's told me Senna stayed with him. He had an engine pulled apart, put on the dyno all under his supervision, decided he didn't like that, had another one put together, put on the dyno and decided he did like that.' ('Not correct,' Senna says. 'I simply took our engine to Italy, they rebuilt it in one go, straightforward, nothing else much, which proves that for half a season we were at a disadvantage to Brundle.') Now Brundle again: 'He brought it home personally (back in the boot) so he had a new engine for Thruxton. Also, Ron Tauranac had got two new parts ready for 1984, a push rod front suspension and new sidepods with five per cent more downforce. So I got the suspension and Senna got the aerodynamic package and the aerodynamic package was the thing to have.'

Now, this early morning of 23 October, the mist did begin to clear. The cars were able to go out at 9.28 for the first practice session. Wintry sun peered through the dispersing mist. Senna did a handful of laps, eased the car into the pits, Bennetts adjusted the wings, he went back out. The American Jones had done 1 minute 13.63. Senna responded with 1 minute 13.55 – and the record was 1 minute 13.55. Not that that mattered. Brundle did 1 minute 14.03.

And then the session finished. It had lasted exactly twelve minutes. Years before, local residents had obtained a High Court injunction to stop motor racing during the hours of worship and the circuit was always happy to comply, anyway. Now the bells from two churches with the same name – St Peter and St Paul, one near the circuit, the other in the nearby village of Kimpton – tolled across the flat land.

Senna said: 'I came across a couple of cars stopped at the complex on my lap (the fast one) and although the car felt good it wasn't perfect for the conditions. If the track stays the same I'm sure we can go much quicker.' He did, brushing aside the record in the second session with 1 minute 13.36, Jones 1 minute 13.90, Brundle 1 minute 13.88. 'To be honest, we're scratching,' he said. 'The engine is pinking like mad for some reason and there's also too much oversteer.'

The faithful had seen all this but now, quietly, discreetly, the man from 1982 – Dennis Rushen – moved unseen by them into the paddock. 'I have a lot of time for Dick Bennetts, he's a good guy. Dick's a brilliant engineer but if he has a weakness it's that he's not too good with drivers. Towards the end of the season he was having problems and he phoned me up and he said, "Harry keeps telling me to [expletive] off every time I say anything. Would you come down and have a word with him?" I went to Thruxton and I got him in the transporter. I said: "What the hell are you doing? There's one race to go for the Championship and you've got to get out there and do the job." He accepted it quietly. But that's how he can be. You've got to handle the guy. Harry wants to have his own way and you've got to let him have his own way or let him think he's having his own way. It's important to do that.'

With this piece of man management concluded, Senna took his place on pole position. He faced 15 laps, only 35.34 miles but long enough for an enormous amount to happen. Somewhere nearby his father, a man of obvious dignity and presence, watched intently.

Senna made a perfect start, Jones tucked in behind him, Brundle tucked in behind him but at the complex Senna was already a couple of lengths ahead. Brundle attacked Jones, urged his car alongside but Jones held him off. They came through the chicane feeding them on to the start-finish straight but Senna was gone. After two laps he was two seconds ahead.

What Brundle, hounding Jones, didn't know was that Senna had taken a risk. He'd taped up the oil radiator outlet to heat the engine more quickly. 'It worked perfectly. The oil was up to proper temperature within a lap or so rather than the usual six or seven.'

But now – it was lap 6 – with the water temperature rising he leant an arm out to tear the tape away. He couldn't reach. Surging towards the chicane he had to make a decision. Could he afford to wait, the temperature climbing and climbing? He unbuckled his safety belt – and he'd taken care to practise this many times the week before. He angled his body forward, opened the air flap but the chicane was on him. He thrust himself back into the seat but there was no time, no time at all to clip the belt up again. He had reached the chicane. 'By the time I looked back up, I was almost up to the chicane. I thought I had lost it for a minute. All of a sudden I was not part of the car. I was sliding around inside.'

A memory returns of that day: Senna, buckled up again, moving away, moving away, Brundle flicking and darting behind Jones, trapped, Senna moving away, moving away. The lead became seven seconds and still memory holds Brundle at the chicane, the snout of his car probing at Jones. In the end, it became the most simple of all motor racing stories: he had the will but lacked the speed.

Senna eased back for the last couple of laps and on the final one his hand was held high out of the cockpit in salute. He'd won it. He stood on the podium with both arms raised, both fists clenched. 'I struggled, I really struggled,' Brundle says. 'Davy Jones beat me and it was one of the few times in the year when I didn't finish first or second. I hadn't got the power, I hadn't got anything. I saw Senna have a big wobbly moment while he was taking the tape off, but then he won and he won fair and square. On the podium, and in front of his father and mother, he was very magnanimous and after that there was an interview with both of us and he was busy telling the whole world that I was the best British driver who had emerged since Jim Clark. I think we ended up realizing we had done each other an awful lot of good. If he'd won the Championship at a canter – sure, he was Senna, he was going upwards anyway, no problem – that wouldn't have been the same thing. Me being near gave it an awful lot of credibility. We had national and international coverage, we had done a lot for each other, and of course if he hadn't been there I would have won the Championship at a canter [Senna had 132 points, Brundle 123, Jones 77] but it wouldn't have had much credibility. I needed him there and he needed me, we elevated each other straight into Formula One.'

'If he won the Championship, there was no point in doing it again in 1984,' Bennetts says. 'He sought my advice a little bit, not too much. He pretty much had his own thoughts on things, he was a very intelligent man for his age. I didn't know the Formula One people that well in those days. I can speak with Ron Dennis and Peter Warr and those guys now, but I'd only been doing it since '81 then.'

Senna would go his own way.

That night he, his father and mother, Bennetts, some members of the team and Keith Sutton went to a restaurant at Shepperton, near where West Surrey Racing were based, to celebrate with a meal. He was very happy and it was, Sutton says, 'a really nice evening'.

This meal was not, as it happened, the end of 1983. He had an appointment with Toleman.

Chris Witty remembers that: 'He tested for Toleman and it was the same day Brundle drove the Tyrrell. Ayrton had the TG 183, the thing that Warwick had been driving. It was at Silverstone, a nice, bright, cold day but the engines love it when it's crisp in autumn time. He got in this thing and instantly he was on the pace and he ended up about a second quicker than Warwick had done in the Grand Prix. Mind you, Brundle went quicker that day than Rosberg had done in the Williams at the Grand Prix. Rory Byrne, the designer, said: "This is the guy." He had the ability even at that stage and at that age to know what a car was doing, know what he wanted a car to do and converse with an engineer. Rory said: "He's brilliant, we've just got to have him."'

CHAPTER SEVEN

The Transporter

The room is rather large for an office. You can hold small conferences in it. It has a view of suburban England, a solid, timeless, becalmed grey stone church, semi-detached houses fringed by trees. During the day you can hear the hum of an ordinary English shopping street not far away, just up there by the traffic lights. Brentwood, on the very outer reaches of London, is functional; just as Alex Hawkridge's office is. The office is also deep within the heart of the headquarters of a company called Toleman, who are well-known for an extremely anonymous activity. They deliver cars from ports to salerooms. On any British motorway at any given moment you might see their transporters lumbering along laden with brand new cars. (An employee once said: 'We can't even advertise. Who cares who delivers their cars?') Ted Toleman was no anonymous man. He was (and is) an incorrigible adventurer who can't resist offshore power-boats or the Paris-Dakar rally. And one day – it must have been the late 1970s – while he was buying me an extravagant lunch at his extravagant country club he began talking of his Formula Two team. The conversation drifted easily into the realms of conjecture. Namely Formula One. They made it in 1981, won their first points in 1983 and that year Derek Warwick made what appeared to be a prudent decision. He joined Renault, which seemed to offer him the chance of becoming World Champion.

It was to fill Warwick's vacancy that Senna journeyed to Hawkridge's office. Hawkridge: 'He got engaged in this contest with Martin Brundle in Formula Three and both of them knew that one of them would drive for Toleman the next season. They were the two drivers. If Ayrton hadn't signed and Martin had been prepared to, Martin would have been our driver for 1984. Ayrton knew that. So it went to the guy who got the Championship, in essence that was it. We did the deal here in these offices. It was well into '84, it was real last-minute stuff. There was Bernie Ecclestone, Ron Dennis, Lotus ... I think he'd had a pretty liberal sprinkling of promises. Along the way he'd had contact with just about everybody. As the pre-season progressed to a crescendo he was acknowledged to be somebody that they ought to be interested in. Formula One is such a closed world [implication, goddamned hard to get into] that I don't think anybody apart from us was actually serious.'

Peter Warr of Lotus was. He had had Senna in his office, but what happened next illustrates the conflict of interests which operate within Formula One. The main backers of Lotus were John Player Special and at Brands Hatch for the Grand Prix of Europe in late '83 JPS were the sponsors of the race, too. 'One of our drivers, Elio de Angelis, put his car on the front row,' Warr says. 'Nigel Mansell was on the second row. The next morning I opened up the British papers and the headlines were screaming: Mansell on the second row! JPS [a British company selling their cigarettes primarily in Britain] said we'd better keep the Brit and we did.'

'We had to be serious for different reasons from the others,' Hawkridge says. 'We couldn't hire a superstar (money) or even a current experienced driver on a minimum retainer – our cars wouldn't get a fair showing in the hands of an average Formula One driver. We had to go for young talent. That was the only way forward for Toleman. We had to have somebody good enough to progress the car and we knew Ayrton was capable of doing that. Martin would have been, too. Either of those guys would have done justice to our product so, to be honest, I wasn't really bothered. The pluses and minuses were about equal. I don't think there was any difference in speed between them. I don't think there was a great deal of racing difference between them. Martin is very accomplished, just as Ayrton is. However I have to say that on balance results speak for themselves. I believe in the performance system: Ayrton won the Formula Three Championship and Martin came second. Even Martin can live comfortably with that.'

He can. 'It all came down to the Toleman drive, really. I was in Alex Hawkridge's office and they made it quite clear that they wanted me to drive for them but that Senna was top of the list. I think Senna was going to Brabham at the time but Piquet wouldn't have him, so he came back and got the Toleman drive.'

Herbie Blash of Brabham confirms that and expands on it. 'I was sad in one way but in another way we were more than happy to keep Piquet because he was our World Champion. Piquet said no [to having Senna] and Piquet was involved with our Italian sponsors [Parmalat]. So it was very difficult to say "Oh, I felt really sorry for Senna." Bernie was the one who told him.'

Witty, then of course sponsorship director of Toleman, 'saw a lot of Ayrton in 1983. I was the one who used to go to the Formula Three races and keep tabs, talk to him and generally try to woo him – because certainly when he started going well in Formula Three Ron Dennis came on pretty strong. Then it got to the situation where Bernie wanted him. That was quite good fun. I mean, that was Bernie in some ways wanting to prevent him going to Ron. Bernie is very persuasive. But at the end of the day it suited Bernie not to have him – because of what Bernie's package was at the time. [Piquet, Parmalat.] You can understand why.'

'I don't think Ayrton had any choice,' Hawkridge says. 'We were his last stop but the issue for him was: Before I sign for this team rather than retire from motor racing altogether I have to be absolutely sure. He said in conversation before we'd signed the contract: "If the car isn't good enough and if you stop me changing to another team I will leave racing. You cannot force me to drive a racing car. Either you make a term in the contract to allow me to take another chance if it comes along or you give me no option but to leave racing if I don't think your car is competitive. I'll stay with you if possible and I'll give you a hundred per cent every time I sit in the car." What can you say to a guy who says that to you? You can't say "That's unfair, Ayrton," you can't say "That's not the way we do things in Formula One," you can't make a guy give you a hundred per cent – but he did every time, he gave us everything he had.

'Would he have retired? I never know with Ayrton. He's a self-assured, confident negotiator and I'm sure it's the same dilemma for anybody that he deals with. You just don't know how far he'll go, how far he believes what he says. I don't doubt him.

'The negotiating was completely one-sided. He got what he wanted. It wasn't money, money wasn't a problem at all, it was the conditions of the contract and in particular the buy-out terms of the contract – the one area where I disagreed with him. I'm talking about the terms of the contract as we understood it. But I can appreciate the over-all problem because you're dealing with a Brazilian who is working in a foreign language with a legal document which is resting on lawyers on the end of a telephone. That's what we had. We were sitting in this office with an open telephone line to his lawyers in Brazil. I didn't have our lawyers. I reckoned it was unfair enough as it was, so I was anxious that it was fair to him, anxious that

110

it was something he could live with and that we would never have to use.

'In other words, if it became a usable document then the relationship between us and our driver was finished. We approached it on that basis but nonetheless he was very particular about every single sentence, wanting to know exactly what it meant and adding words throughout the agreement. With his lack of command of the English language he did a hell of a job to meet his requirements. It was an insight into him. Whatever he does he goes into it and does it to the maximum of his ability.'

This outpouring is centred, as you must have gathered, on the buy-out clause, intended (by Toleman) never to be used. It said: if Senna wants to leave the Toleman team he has to tell us before he signs for another team and pay us a certain amount of money. In due course, when Senna did use it, his action gave Formula One one of its regular convulsions.

'The meeting went on well into the early hours of the morning, thrashing out the interpretation of the words. He would accept some explanations, he would insist on others being changed. Don't think he is just a good racing driver, he's good at whatever he does. He is a man who will excel at anything he puts his hand to.'

Senna judges that 'it was the best offer, the best situation that I could have at that time. Toleman was coming up, it was a new team. They really believed that I could learn with them and do a good job. They were prepared to commit themselves a lot with me so I felt it was the right thing. Taking everything together, I'm sure it was at that time, given the conditions.'

Just before we move into the season of '84, just before we journey to Brazil in late March, we must consider tyres. Because a Formula One car is what it is, a small difference magnifies itself. You – if you are a casual tele-spectator –

might imagine that all tyres are virtually the same. They aren't. It is an accepted axiom within Formula One that you virtually cannot win on uncompetitive tyres. This would become central to Senna's first season and would give Formula One another of its regular convulsions. Three companies were supplying the fifteen teams.

Michelin: Brabham, Ligier, McLaren, Renault.

Goodyear: Alfa Romeo, Arrows, ATS, Ferrari, Lotus, Tyrrell, Williams.

Pirelli: Osella, RAM, Spirit, Toleman.

The big boys, then, were grouped around either the French or American company; the small boys around the Italian company.

And they all went to the Jacarepagua circuit. Witty remembers that Senna had 'asked for something like thirty-five passes, some ridiculous number, and Bernie said to tell him the facts of life. He thought he could have as many as he wanted.' Now please listen to Senna. 'To my mind the number of passes was as usual very restricted and what we decided was on the basis of what we had in our hands – so people were going in and out under a system where everybody had an opportunity to see a little bit of Formula One. Don't forget this was my first Grand Prix and it was in Brazil.' By everybody, he includes members of his family who, as Witty says, 'idolized him. Ayrton was a demi-god, even to his family. It's almost like a little cage in Brazil and they didn't actually come into the area where we had the car. His mother sat there nearly all day in the shade and I thought this was idolization of the eldest son ... but, I mean, he's a pretty good kid to idolize.'

To those who imagine the Prodigal Son is selfish and

self-centred please listen to Keith Sutton: 'I'd kept in touch with him over the winter and he said he wanted me there at his first Grand Prix – Brazil, of course. He said he'd look after me. He did, my flight to and from Rio, my hotel.'

He qualified on the eighth row of the grid but lost turbo boost pressure on lap 8.

Witty had noticed something in Brazil, apart from his family, and it presaged, he believes, the beginning of the end already. 'I think it actually started as early as that Grand Prix. He appeared with a Marlboro patch on his overalls and a Munroe shock-absorber patch. His contract said he could have anything he wanted but he had to clear it with the team and he hadn't. Alex brought Ayrton up to Brentwood and there was Peter Gethin, myself and Alex, and Alex tore into him and I actually saw a tear in the kid's eye and I thought: "Oh, Christ, he's being belittled." Alex was really laying into him a bit, and I think Ayrton thought: "Should I really have to go through with this?" Technically Ayrton was wrong but the problem with him was that if you gave him an inch he'd take six. I mean, he was fairly good at making sure he got what he wanted but I felt we were a bit hard with him.'

Gethin remembers that meeting at Brentwood. 'Ayrton was crying, in fact he was crying quite a lot. I saw him suddenly realize what was going on and it was like a drawbridge going down in front of his face. In that moment he went from Senna the child to Senna the man.'

In South Africa he qualified on the seventh row, finished sixth. He'd had to drive part of the race with no nose cone – he'd hit something, probably a stone – which made steering exhausting, and at the end had to be helped from the car. He had not, of course, driven anything like seventy-two consecutive laps in a Formula One car before; and as a point of interest Martin Brundle, after an extended pre-season test in Brazil in the Tyrrell, had to be helped out, too.

Only time in the cockpit prepares the body for the special strains.

'Ayrton was very difficult to cope with,' Witty says. 'He knew what he wanted and always got what he wanted. Alex, as I've said, was pretty strong with him in the early days, maybe a little bit too strong, and Ayrton thought: "Right, I know where I'm going, sod you guys." He did have a sense of humour although he was unbelievably intense. He just knew that if you are going to be successful you've got to detach yourself from the distraction. That would no doubt be the same for a tennis player or whatever but it seems to me particularly so in Formula One. If you are going to deliver you've got to give it one hundred per cent.

'I remember Zolder vividly. We had the old dog which was, well, the double-wing thing from the year before. He'd driven it in Brazil and retired, he'd driven it in South Africa and got his first point, he came to Zolder and he knew that we had the new car sitting back in the factory and he was a bit upset.' Toleman were negotiating with Michelin, having decided that they were going nowhere with Pirellis. 'We felt politically that we should transfer all the allegiance of the new car on to Michelin. He said the old car [the TG 183] was an absolute dog to drive. I thought he'd do five laps. The guy did the whole race. He finished seventh, subsequently promoted to sixth when Stefan Bellof was disqualified [allegedly Tyrrell added lead ballast to the fuel]. To me it said so much for the guy that he knew the car was a dog, didn't want to drive it but did the job.

'People have found him difficult to get on with and one thing in the early Toleman days, he was very sceptical of journalists – particularly those in Formula One that would suddenly want to become your best mate.

'We had Stefan Johansson later that year, Stefan is a

114

big mate of mine but he's too nice. That's why Stefan has had about four second places and twenty-three third places. There were great social scenes and, when he got to McLaren, Stefan was quite happy to be in the shadow of Alain Prost – but he wasn't a winner. Ayrton is a winner.'

Now, as we move towards the next race, Imola on 6 May, the tyre situation was becoming acute. As Hawkridge says: 'We'd been with Pirelli, we'd always been with Pirelli, we'd never had an opportunity to run on anything else. We believed that our engine wasn't the problem and we had a reasonably competitive package – well, a hell of a competitive package. We were convinced that tyres were our problem. Pirelli had stopped listening to us long before, we could make no progress. We said: "There's no future in this relationship, we've lost all confidence" – and this was the team talking because my relationship with Pirelli was an arm's-length one; but the morale in the team was so bad over the tyre issue that the team would have gone downhill. It was a make-or-break position. We either had to find an alternative or stop Grand Prix racing. It was our Waterloo. We had to obtain a different tyre manufacturer and prove once and for all whether our team had any competence or not. If, having changed, the car was not competitive, that was a reason to stop. If the car *was* competitive it was no guarantee of success but at least it was a way forward.'

Hawkridge approached Michelin.

'The first time we ran on Michelins I went to the test. That was when Ayrton impressed me more than on any other occasion. By agreement with Michelin we would run their previous year's tyres which, by their own acknowledgement, were uncompetitive. We were made no promises that we would ever have the same tyres as McLaren. McLaren had some sort of golden vote that would exclude us from getting comparable equipment. We ran on their old tyres, cross-matching different compounds. Ayrton was able to keep improving the car. It amazed even the Michelin technicians.

'This was Dijon, after the race at Imola. We decided to change to Michelins the race after Imola. The reason was we didn't want to embarrass Pirelli on their home ground. So we had an agreement with Michelin that no announcement would be made. That was a Michelin request. The drivers [the other was Johnny Cecotto] were frustrated as hell, Senna in particular, having run on the Michelins. He was transformed. "This is a different ball game, now we're with the front runners." I tell you within five laps of running on Michelin tyres he said: "We're on the pace." '

But not at Imola. Toleman took a drastic step, there were suggestions of a financial dispute between them and Pirelli, and Toleman did not take part in the Friday qualifying session at all to 'pre-empt any hostile reaction from Pirelli' (*Autocourse*). This left Chris Witty with the impossible task of trying to maintain good public relations.

The Tolemans did go out on the Saturday but a fuel pressure problem prevented Senna from doing a lap any faster than 1 minute 41.585 seconds. It was not enough to get him into the race.

'The decision had nothing to do with me, that was a team decision and was between the team and Pirelli, so there was nothing I could do about it,' Senna says. 'I was not upset that we changed, I was upset that we didn't have the opportunity to race in Imola because we did not run during the first day of qualifying and ended up not qualifying. I was upset for that but during the season it was a good decision because the Michelin tyre was a better tyre.'

'We were never off the pace from that point on,' Hawkridge says. 'Look at the results, look at the qualifying, look at the race performance on year-old tyres and

116

you'll see that the only people who could beat us were McLaren. Ayrton? I mean that guy has an absolute knowledge of where he's at, what he's capable of and he also knew the car was good. He was right to be pushing for a change, he was the guy who motivated and made that change happen. He made full use of it when it did.'

Witty 'spent a lot of time with him when he failed to qualify for the San Marino Grand Prix – which is the only time in his life he did fail to qualify. Ayrton and I went off on the Sunday. We had to be at Dijon on the Monday morning to test a new car [the TG 184, with the Michelins] and we went off to Linate Airport in Milan, missed the plane and decided we'd take the car all the way. We drove together, we talked a lot about marriage and about my marriage and I asked him about his brief marriage and we got on pretty well. He said to me: "How do you find you get on with your wife when you are travelling all the time?" I said: "I find it very difficult." (Remember Alison and I are divorced.) I said: "It is difficult because when they're not working they want to be with you," and he said for him it was difficult, he'd married very young and he knew that what he needed to do needed no distractions. I think it was just a question of incompatibility at a very early age.'

Friends would find themselves drifting away, too, among them Keith Sutton. 'With all the Formula One pressures, all the Formula One people and contacts coming up to him, I kind of lost touch with him; and he started earning lots of money whereas I was only going up steadily. He still sends me a Christmas card every year "to my good friend Keith" but that's about it. I say hello to him and everything, but it's not the same as in the old days. In those days we'd go out for a drink, music, girls, and we'd talk about what young men of the same age talk about. But after that, I don't know, I lost him.'

Between Imola and Dijon, Senna contested a celebrity race to open the new Nürburgring. John Watson was among the other drivers. 'It was just before Mercedes launched their 190Es and everyone in the race had an identical one. Obviously the race was a good chance for publicity for Mercedes and the track. The field was a celebrity one with a host of Formula One drivers past, present and future. Ayrton took it very, very seriously. He thought that if he could beat Lauda, Prost and Rosberg it would bring a lot of attention to him. He'd be noticed by a wider public. You have to remember that at this point he was only an up-and-coming driver. My own view of celebrity races is that you do your best to win, of course, but it's not exactly the end of your career if you don't. Senna's attitude was that he had to win it. That day was cold and wet and he did a bloody good job.'

He did. He covered 12 laps in 26 minutes 57.58 seconds. Lauda was behind him, 26 minutes 59.16, and this is the rest of the field Senna beat (in finishing order): Carlos Reutemann, Keke Rosberg, Watson, Denny Hulme, Jody Scheckter, Jack Brabham, Klaus Ludwig, James Hunt, John Surtees, Phil Hill, Manfred Schute, Stirling Moss, Alain Prost, Udo Schutz, Jacques Laffite, Hans Herman, Elio de Angelis. Alan Jones retired. 'It showed us,' Watson concludes, 'what this guy was all about.' Immediately after the race Senna said to Russell Bulgin, a journalist and friend: 'Now I know I can do it.'

At Dijon Senna qualified on the seventh row on Michelins. He was openly enthusiastic but had only one set of qualifiers and, at the very moment he chose to use them, Lauda left oil on the track. He was up as high as ninth, fell back a place before the turbo went on lap thirty-five. They went to Monaco, an enclave where the traffic is so choked that millionaires favour mopeds. The Monégasques are particular about whom they welcome as tenants of the apartments, which is a polite way of saying: if you're not rich, please don't apply. Monaco is a symbol rather than a place.

Monaco is also a motor race, and a deeply infuriating one. Because it is around the streets you can't overtake without express permission of the person in front – which is why, once the racing drivers have gone, the millionaires are back on their mopeds. They can't overtake either. I am not being entirely flippant about all this. I am trying to sketch a background – an authentic background – for the Monaco Grand Prix of 3 June 1984. Senna was again on the seventh row after qualifying. (Forgive Alex Hawkridge for telescoping and generalizing memory. Neither Senna nor Toleman were invariably 'on the pace' when they got their clutches on Michelins.)

It rained. This is worse at Monaco because the churning walls of water are coming at you along narrow, armco-clad corridors and the corridors are so damn narrow: exactly, in fact, the width of an ordinary street, but you're not limited to 45 kph, you're expected to average (if it's dry) 144.242 kph, which is what got Alain Prost in the McLaren pole position. To appreciate it, multiply that 45 kph speed limit in a built-up area, add corners, add a tunnel, add a couple of outrageously tight hairpins, then cover it all with rain, real, heavy rain, and if you are anything but consummate in your touch you'll be a sandwich against the armco before you even see the armco.

Prost led, Mansell overtook him on the tenth lap and Mansell led a Grand Prix for the first time in his life. It lasted five laps. He hit the armco and hit it hard. He subsequently claimed that the car had slithered on the white line in the middle of the road – the normal broken white line painted to keep normal traffic apart. Whatever happened doesn't really matter now. Just that any miscalculation would be punished.

In these circumstances – and memory holds it even today, each car emerging from the tunnel, descending the sharp incline to the chicane and then Tabac corner spitting its own ball of water – Senna attacked the circuit.

Lap 1: ninth. Lap 2: ninth. Lap 3: eighth (overtaking Laffite). Lap 4: eighth. Lap 5: eighth. Lap 6: eighth. Lap 7: seventh (overtaking Manfred Winkelhock). Lap 8: seventh. Lap 9: sixth (Albereto spun). Lap 10: sixth. Lap 11: sixth. Lap 12: fifth (overtaking Rosberg). Lap 13: fifth. Lap 14: fourth (overtaking Arnoux). Lap 15: fourth. Lap 16: third (Mansell crash). Lap 17: third. Lap 18: third. Lap 19: second (overtaking Lauda). They crossed the line and Senna was 34.355 seconds behind Prost. The hunt began in the walls of water. The figures tell it as well as any words:

Lap	Prost	Senna	Difference	Gap
20	1:56.684	1:56.170	−0.514	33.841
21	1:56.264	1:57.551	+1.287	35.128
22	1:56.144	1:55.226	−0.918	34.210
23	1:57.618	1:54.674	−2.944	31.266
24	1:56.873	1:54.334	−2.539	28.727
25	1:56.641	1:55.650	−0.991	27.736
26	1:56.848	1:55.253	−1.595	26.141
27	1:59.669	1:55.232	−4.437	21.704
28	2:00.193	1:56.628	−3.565	18.139
29	1:59.436	1:56.666	−2.770	15.369
30	2:02.598	1:59.008	−3.590	11.779
31	2:03.766	1:59.433	−4.333	7.446

At this point Jacky Ickx, the official starter, decided to stop the race. The decision remains controversial. Why did he do it now and not a long time before? Certainly for several laps Prost had been gesticulating from the cockpit to have it stopped. At the end of lap 32 – and with 46 laps left –

the red flag was shown and Prost slowed. Senna, moving like a thunderstorm within a thunderstorm, caught and passed him on the finishing line and thought he'd won. Unfortunately the positions were calculated from the end of the previous lap – 31 . . .

'Monaco was a quirk,' Hawkridge says. 'We were supposed to be running on the year-old Michelins but they didn't have year-old rain tyres. Come the race, surprise, surprise, Michelin said to McLaren: "Sorry, we have to give Toleman tyres and we only have one sort of tyre. We can't send them out on dries." Suddenly McLaren had this youngster called Ayrton Senna in a ridiculous car called a Toleman on the same tyres as they had and they were going to lose the race.

'If some diligent official [Ickx] hadn't jumped out and stopped it just before Prost was overtaken . . . well, the race had been horrendous for the preceding fifteen laps and when it was stopped the track was by no means in its worst state. Everyone who was there shared the sentiment, I think, that Ayrton was robbed of his first Grand Prix victory. He took it completely calmly, he wasn't [visibly] upset. I'm sure he was disappointed but he showed no emotions that were uncontrolled at all. It was not a racing-driver reaction of thumping his helmet and banging the car or anything, he just said: "Well, what do you expect? This is the Establishment we're taking on." That was his attitude to it. "They're not going to let me and Toleman blow their doors off at Monaco." He had Prost completely sussed. He wasn't driving over the limit, within the laps to go he would have easily overtaken him.

'Monaco was the highlight of our racing career. It was a hell of a race. We could believe it was happening. We knew it would happen, we absolutely knew. He runs his own race, incidentally, he doesn't do anything else. He doesn't compete with other people. The word competition actually means seeking together and he doesn't do that. He rises above other people. He has to prove that he's in his own race and he's in a different class.'

That sodden night in Monaco, when darkness mercifully drowned the whole dripping mess, Hawkridge knew something else. 'It was pretty clear that we had the makings of a bloody competitive Formula One team.'

However he contained his feelings Senna was 'very, very angry because we were almost leading after a hard race and suddenly it was stopped halfway through. Maybe I would have taken the lead and crashed myself after another five laps and have nothing, but I believe we could have won. After some time just reflecting, I thought it was a fantastic result because of the way the thing developed. I probably got more publicity than if I had won.'

From this moment on the perception of Senna was altered. He had thrust himself on to the big stage and almost taken the leading part, too. One day he clearly would, perhaps even tomorrow.

CHAPTER EIGHT

The Losing Game

Montreal was anti-climactic. He qualified on the fifth row, finished seventh two laps behind the leader (Piquet) – the car was never on the pace. Detroit was anti-climactic. He qualified on the fourth row, crashed on lap 21 (a broken rear wishbone). And they all went to Dallas. In retrospect it was a mistake to have a Grand Prix there – a new circuit, of course, which the drivers didn't like much at all, and when Can-Am cars had used it on the Saturday (after Formula One qualifying) they tore the track surface to pieces. Quick-set concrete laid overnight didn't set and the warm-up was delayed then postponed altogether.

'It was red hot and the track was breaking up at every corner in practice,' Hawkridge says. 'They were actually laying cement between sessions and quick-drying concrete and all kinds of things in a disastrous situation. I walked with the FISA delegation and I could kick the tarmac out with my foot – ridiculous.

'The track was strewn with marbles and it was quite clear nobody would go out and improve their time on it. Peter Gethin was our team manager then and Ayrton came walking out of the garage, overalls on and his helmet on, and Peter said: "You ain't going out in this." Ayrton went absolutely berserk, just absolutely blew his cool completely, just total emotion, he went absolutely crazy with Peter Gethin. He wanted to go out. Peter came to me and said: "Alex, what do you think?" I said: "Peter, you're team manager, I don't interfere in those things but I'll talk to Ayrton and I'll certainly reinforce the decision you've made." So I went to Ayrton and I said: "Look, Peter's the team manager, he has to decide, he's got that job to do and that is his job." Ayrton said: "Well, if you don't change it I'll act accordingly." I think we actually lost Ayrton at Dallas that day because we didn't agree with him.'

Gethin did not hear Senna say the words; what Gethin did hear was the Toleman going round the track when 'I'd turned my back'. Despite everything Senna had gone out. When he came back 'it was the only time he had a mouthful from me. He walked off up the pit road like a spoilt child.'

'My understanding is very clear,' Senna says. 'I had been on the circuit the previous day and also that morning – so to me nobody at that time was in a better position to judge the situation with the circuit. I am happy to agree with somebody else's point of view as long as it is shown to me and explained to me in a dialogue, but not as an order imposed, as at Dallas.'

Gethin remains, however, a staunch admirer. 'Ayrton is the best driver I have ever encountered and the most single-minded. I think he knows how good he is. I think he's a terribly ambitious bloke, I think he's terribly mercenary in terms of he'll put everything aside to do what he wants to do. His one thought in life is motor racing and winning motor races. I think he realized early on how good he was. I'd have put a lot of money on him becoming World Champion even in the Toleman days. He is shy outside motor racing and basically I think he's a nicer bloke than he appears to be. He's just terribly hard on himself and anyone else around him who is going to give him something which is going to be winnable in – whether it's a Ferrari, a Toleman or a Lambretta. I thought he was the best driver I'd seen since Jim Clark. He's got everything.

'I liked the bloke, overall I liked him. I thought he was

124

a very tough little man, a very hard little man, who knew what he wanted, where he was going and where he was going to end up. If he said to me he was running for president of Brazil I'd say yes and wouldn't be surprised if he became so. We had times when it was very difficult [the tyres] but, you know, that's life. Sometimes you have to make decisions, whether they are good or bad. In that tyre business, in all the things I saw and heard going on, I thought a stand had to be made. I had a great admiration for Alex.'

That day at Dallas – and from the third row of the grid – Senna was fourth at the end of the first lap but kissed a wall, needed four new tyres, kissed a wall again and retired on lap 47 (out of 67) when the driveshaft went. Of the twenty-six starters, twelve retired 'hit wall'. Senna was not alone.

Between Dallas and the next Grand Prix, Brands Hatch, Senna was asked to drive for the Newman Joest team in the World Sportscar Championships, 1000 kilometres of the Nürburgring. He would partner Henri Pescarolo and Stefan Johansson in a Porsche 956.

'At that time I didn't know him at all,' Pescarolo says. 'Reinhold Joest had been told there was a very good young Brazilian driver, you should try him. Joest said: "Why not?" We were allowed to have three drivers in the team. I met him in the pits while we were waiting to start practice. He was very shy. He wasn't speaking to anybody because he didn't know anybody.' (Sportscars are an off-shoot of single-seaters in one sense – Grand Prix drivers past, present and future do take part in them – but a separate world altogether in another sense.) 'He didn't know the car and it was the first time he'd driven a big car like that.'

Johansson and Pescarolo took the morning session. Senna went out in the afternoon – inevitably it was wet – and did but a single lap. He brought the Porsche smoothly into the pits and earnestly enquired what all the cockpit dials and switches did. (Truly. And he'd done a lap without knowing.) They told him and, as Pescarolo says, 'he was competitive straight away, you know. After a few laps he was doing a good time. I wasn't really surprised because I'd been told he was promising but he coped with the big car, the big engine and it looked very easy for him.'

He was seventh fastest in the wet. A contemporary report said he had an 'uncanny smoothness'. Eventually the Porsche qualified eighth. The race was unhappy, and wet, too. Pescarolo began, had a puncture, they lost eight laps with clutch problems and towards the end water was getting into the electronics. They finished eighth. Pescarolo: 'Because he didn't know anybody, he stayed in his part of the pit, speaking very little. After the race he disappeared, that's all.'

At Brands for the British Grand Prix he was on the fourth row, worked his way carefully up to third place and stayed there. He tracked Elio de Angelis (Lotus) and every time de Angelis squeezed out a little lead he came back at him. With five laps left Senna took him on the inside going towards Paddock on a power play which had the crowd on their feet. And that was third place. On the rostrum Brian Jones, microphone in hand, waited to interview him. Was it only four years ago that, in exactly this same place, he had said to Jones: 'No, I finish with racing, I go back to Brazil'? Lauda, who'd won, was grinning his toothy grin and Senna waved his right arm, his whole face consumed by a vast smile.

In Germany his rear wing failed after 4 laps (when he was fifth), in Austria the oil pressure went on lap 35 when he was fourth. Brian Hart, who produced Toleman's engines, of course, recounted one of those interesting little stories which float briefly round Formula One and then die but give you instant insight. During the Austrian Grand Prix, out there in all the loops down the slopes, Senna saw a car ahead, recognized it and its driver, noticed the car was travelling slowly and reasoned (1) it's probably dropping oil and (2) the driver is too lazy to park it and walk back. There *was* oil. Senna went round it. Prost, charging along, didn't and spun off in a mad carousel into the armco. I mention this not to criticize Prost (who probably had no chance to see) but to try and show you how Senna's mind works at 250 kph.

Brian Hart was very impressed indeed.

'Then,' says Hawkridge, 'the unbelievable happened. Michelin announced their withdrawal. We had put all our eggs into their basket – bearing in mind that we'd blown Goodyear off in Formula Two, so we'd already shut one door and we'd shut another by changing from Pirelli to Michelin. Then the Michelin door shut. Michelin's withdrawal was nothing, I'm sure, to do with our performance, it was for purely commercial reasons. That company is so professional that I don't doubt it was anything else. Ayrton knew of it beforehand, he knew there was a likelihood that it could happen. We just believed that it couldn't happen to us. We'd been through enough! They just couldn't! I suppose it was wishful thinking. We didn't have anywhere else to go and I'm sure at that point that was it as far as Ayrton was concerned – but I think if you are realistic it goes back earlier, to that incident at Dallas.'

They went to Zandvoort. It was to be in no sense an ordinary weekend. 'There are tremendous up sides to Ayrton, but the fact is he's not a team player and the warnings are there for anyone to see,' Hawkridge says. 'The first we heard was when two journalists arrived in our motorhome with a press release on Lotus paperwork telling us Ayrton Senna had signed for them. I mean, it was so embarrassing. We had umpteen guests and sponsors, we were negotiating a multi-million-pound sponsorship which could have taken us into the big time at that meeting.

So it destroyed our credibility – that we didn't know what the hell was going on within our own team.'

Lotus had a proper sit-down luncheon under the awning against their motorhome to make the announcement, while immediately outside it Witty whispered through to me: 'Remember every word that's said. I want to know afterwards.' Hawkridge, a little further off, was pacing about incandescent with rage. Ted Toleman wandered a bit further off again. His habitually benevolent face seemed bemused. Nor was it so easy when Nigel Mansell came in under the awning. A glance told him we all knew he was being replaced by Senna.

'It was embarrassing for me when Ayrton came into the motorhome,' Hawkridge says. 'I tackled him on it and he said: "I'm sorry, I have not agreed to this." Then he changed his position. He wasn't saying he didn't have an agreement with them but he hadn't signed an agreement with them. Then from that, he hadn't signed an agreement with them so they weren't authorized to put out a press release – but that was over a period of several weeks, not that weekend.

'I don't blame Ayrton or Ayrton's management for keeping their ears permanently to the ground because everyone's doing that, it's part of the lifestyle. I don't even blame Ayrton for deciding his future wasn't within Toleman. He had the right to do that, the clear and expressed right. What he didn't have the right to do was enter into an agreement with anybody else before he'd advised us and released himself from his contract through an agreed payment. The payment wasn't that large, for Senna it wasn't even an issue and in fact he paid the money that was due. He's an honest man, he's not dishonest, he's genuinely not dishonest – but he's liable to interpret events liberally.'

In Holland he was ninth on lap 19 when the engine went.

And they went to Monza . . .

Hawkridge remains unrepentant. 'We took the car off him. The reason was a simple one: we had to settle the issue of whether we were going to end up in court because he had clearly breached the agreement, no doubt about that. Journalists at the time saw and read his agreement. There is no doubt about whether it was right or wrong, it was patently wrong. We weren't on about money, we were on about the humiliation that he'd caused us, and the embarrassment, and the fact that he'd probably put us out of motor racing forever, breached the credibility to such an extent that Toleman could no longer continue in motor racing and get support from sponsors and suppliers. He'd accomplished that in one hit – all the credibility I'd been working flat out for years to achieve. He didn't just cost us the possibility of Formula One, he cost us the possibility of being super-competitive with a major engine manufacturer. It was a catastrophe. I felt he shouldn't be allowed to get away with that. He wasn't worried about courts or legal fees or whatever: the one thing that hurt Ayrton, the one thing he couldn't tolerate, was to be stopped from doing what he loved, which was driving a Grand Prix car round a Grand Prix circuit. We just stopped him driving. He went out there and I'd told him before he went that he wouldn't be driving. He laughed. He didn't think we were serious at all. I wasn't there on the first day of practice, and I wasn't in England either so I wasn't contactable. I got home on the Friday evening and the phone lines were melting. Bernie wanting me, Marco Piccinini wanting me, Balestre wanting me. There were so many names I'd have been twenty-four hours on the phone ringing them all back. I spoke to Peter Gethin and I asked what had happened. He replied: "Just what you said would." Then he went on to say Bernie had totally supported our position – but you'd expect that from Bernie, wouldn't you?'

129

Yes, I would, although I must be careful not to impute motives to Mr Ecclestone, who does not always see Formula One drivers as God's Given Creatures (like light bulbs, unscrew one, screw another one in) and who does see a contract as a contract; and he – having worked flat out for years to give the whole thing credibility – cannot have welcomed anything hinting of anarchy.

'It was the only way you could get through to Ayrton,' Gethin says. 'I think that's right. I do think he needed taking down a peg or two and that was the only thing that he did understand. It wasn't a matter of fining him, although he doesn't like to be fined. I think driving is his one kick in life – it was and I'm sure it still is above everything else. Most drivers I knew liked the odd girl or two, but I think Bo Derek for Ayrton was a Ferrari. That's the way he is.'

'Piccinini tried the conciliation role. He said: "Are you really sure?" He couldn't see what all the fuss was about. Here was a guy who had just regally screwed us and all we were doing was saying we don't really require this driver's services which, under our contract terms, we were allowed to do at any point in time. The first time we wanted to exercise it – massive outcry, all this lobbying, all this pressure for us to do something we didn't want to do. We put Stefan [Johansson] in the car and he came a glorious fourth, which frankly proved an enormous point. I'd have been very unhappy had we not proved it: that the car was on the pace ... and on year-old tyres again,' Hawkridge says.

It is time, high time, to listen carefully to Ayrton Senna. 'Basically, to me, I was giving indications to the team, and particularly to Alex, that I had in mind the desire to leave since the Grand Prix at Montreal. The reason was simply to give the team a better opportunity to find the best choice for the next season, even if in doing that I was putting myself in an uncomfortable position. But to my mind it was the right thing to do. The whole thing at Zandvoort was disgusting. I was very annoyed with Peter Warr – no release, no news was supposed to go out at all. Before anything could be said it was my desire and duty as a professional to inform Toleman that I was 100 per cent leaving plus where I was going – so it was a bad start in my relationship with Warr, but this is Formula One and I have learnt from it.'

It is also time, high time, to listen to Peter Warr's side of this. We have heard how, at the European Grand Prix in late 1983, 'I had already had Ayrton in my office discussing driving for us in 1984 and we were not far off having an agreement in principle. As it was Elio put the car on pole at Brands Hatch, Nigel was on the second row confirming the resurrection of Lotus to its role as one of the leading teams after the depths of despair following the death of Colin Chapman. Our astonishment at the newspaper coverage the next day was only exceeded by the pleasure of John Player because the headlines were not "Team Lotus back on pole" but "Nigel Mansell second row!" This convinced the sponsor that, against the team's wishes, we had to retain Nigel for 1984 and we suspended negotiations with Ayrton.

'Convinced as I was that Ayrton was "the man of the future" we stayed in touch and built up a dialogue to the point where serious negotiations were in train' – following a 'furtive' meeting between Warr and one of Senna's advisors at Dallas – 'during the summer months of 1984, with meetings taking place between us and Ayrton and his new manager Armando Boteilho. These culminated in a very protracted series of meetings going on late into the night with Ayrton's lawyer Tony Clare, one of the most careful and meticulous of men. His very fastidious approach to matters, whereby every "i" had to be dotted and every "t" crossed, alone guaranteed that what happened at Zandvoort could not have happened had there been no prior agreement in place.

'We were aware throughout that Ayrton was only able to sign for us as a result of having a buy-out clause in his Toleman contract, which had been shown to us with only the amount of the buy-out deleted. Incidentally the eventual fee in our new contract with Ayrton was almost exactly ten times the figure on the table the previous autumn!

'Now the scene shifts to Zandvoort. Team Lotus's contract with John Player had a renewal date in August and the option to continue lay with them. Prior to this, however, a new sales and marketing director, Brian Wray, had been appointed and replaced the rather gentlemanly way of doing business with that company with a Harvard Business School approach of "stack 'em high, sell 'em cheap" which negated a great deal of the classy, upmarket black and gold image we had been cultivating with their leading brand. Wray had to be convinced of the value of the motor racing sponsorship and came to Zandvoort having been promised' – although not by anyone at Team Lotus – 'one of the by-then traditional motorhome lunches with the British press so they could get to know him and he would have an opportunity to impress them with a release of team news which would have them all running for the telephones to file the story. From that point on Team Lotus and I had very little control over the situation.

'It is true to say that Ayrton knew of our intentions to make the announcement that weekend but it is also true to say that he had requested the opportunity to inform Toleman first, as a matter of courtesy and to let them know that he would be exercising his buy-out option. But then another factor came into play.

'At that time it was a not altogether agreeable practice for some journalists to align themselves with certain drivers, acting as their unofficial or official spokesmen – or even managers. Others doubled up their duties as pressmen with being PR representatives of teams. All this meant that any prior knowledge of news stories had little chance of remaining confidential.' Zandvoort was 'a case in point. As a result *the embargo of the Team Lotus press release was ignored by a few* and by the time their colleagues had seen them moving about the paddock with a "hot" piece of paper the damage was done, the story out and the Team lunch became the forum for some animated discussions. I had little or no control of the accelerating events but it was a matter of some regret that our relationship with our new driver had got off on a wrong and seemingly unprofessional footing. Nonetheless Ayrton seemed to understand and accept the explanation offered. So the pressures on Hawkridge and Co were no greater than those on us and his somewhat hysterical reaction plus his supposedly "blow by blow" accounts of my words, statements and conversations were bewildering to say the least. Until I went up to him on the grid that Sunday at Zandvoort I had never met or even spoken to the man before!'

Witty, who felt he had a relationship strong enough to talk frankly to Senna, did so. 'When it came to the bust-up, I was sitting with him once in the Toleman offices at Witney [where the racing team was] and I said: "I'm asking you a question personally. Why are you doing this, why are you going to Lotus? Without you, we become a hell of a lesser team." He said: "The problem is, when I joined the team I had a lot of belief in the management and I questioned the technical ability of the team. Six months later I have total faith in the technical ability of the team but I question the management."'

Senna was back for the Grand Prix of Europe at the Nürburgring but crashed on the first lap. And they went to Portugal . . .

He was walking briskly down the alley between the canvas walls of hospitality units that day in Estoril. He wore white flameproof overalls and he wore the withdrawn, almost haunted look that he usually did, The Face somehow serene, the facial muscles somehow never taut. Thirty, forty minutes to go before the race. He was just another driver, really, just one of many moving around the maze of the paddock or sheltering in the arbour of their motorhomes, and this would not be his day or theirs. It would belong – forever – to either a certain Niki Lauda or a certain Alain Prost. Lauda, back from the dead these many years, was poised to win the World Championship. In the simplest terms, even if Prost, his team mate at Marlboro McLaren, took the Portuguese Grand Prix and Lauda finished second, Lauda had the title by half a point.

But that was only the most obvious of the dimensions: there was, too, a swell of emotion for Lauda. You only had to glance at him to see why: the still-seared ear, the areas of molten skin fossilized now, the damn near macabre moment whenever he took off his cap (rarely) and only a strange plateau of tufts of hair remained from the fire at the Nürburgring in 1976. Nor was it purely emotion. Lauda had become the drivers' spokesman over safety. Lauda had become a most respected man and if he wasn't loved, which drivers are, anyway? But this October day in 1984, as the clocks moved towards 2.30 and the race, he was already an historical figure, to some a mythological and superhuman figure, twice champion already but in another era, the 70s, and now surely about to do it again. The fact that he'd retired between 1979 and 1982 and scarcely even watched a race on television was one dimension; the fact that he'd come back and mastered turbo engines to this extent was another.

He'd qualified eleventh and that was yet another, particularly with Prost on the front row. Lauda was going to have to do some overtaking and it was making the other drivers tremulous. What if, even inadvertently, they baulked him, brushed against his McLaren, sent it spinning off? Could they, as racing drivers, move tamely out of his way? Or dare they, if they could hold Lauda, stay in front of him, be the one to rob him?

I'd already broached this delicate matter with a driver and he had said: 'Well, what would you do? I'll tell you what I'll do – get the hell out of his way. History isn't going to remember me as the clown who cocked up the Championship.'

Exactly. Probably it was a commonly-shared sentiment. Some, of course, would calculate it in a more refined manner, put on a bit of a show, lay on a bit of the old cut-and-thrust and then get the hell out of his way. As Lauda himself realized, it looked better for them on television like that; and the cameras would certainly be tracking him. And from nowhere, as it seemed, a breathless whisper travelled through the paddock. Marlene's here! Marlene Lauda never went to the races, Marlene Lauda thought all the drivers were crazy, races were crazy, the whole ethic of the thing, the whole desire for the thing was crazy, and there she suddenly was, regal as Habsburg – that stately progress with friends in attendance as she moved along the back of the pits, that defensive Royal Family perma-smile. Marlene was at Estoril to witness the consummation. In its rarity it was a news event all by itself; and another dimension.

Ayrton Senna da Silva is walking briskly down the alley between the canvas walls towards his Toleman car deep in the pits up there, up the slight incline from the paddock. He was twenty-four, he was in his first season in Formula One, a rookie and with a small team. He stopped to answer the question: Well, what are you going to do? For an instant he seemed not to understand. He shook his head but that was bemusement, not an answer. I explained the question more pointedly: Will you get out of Lauda's way? His eyes invariably look straight into yours and they were doing that here, posing their own question: How can you ask me something as silly as that? To the original question he didn't have to stretch his English vocabulary at all. He covered it in one word.

'No.'

He finished third. 'The climax was that we were running two cars in the top four at Estoril [a trick of memory. Johansson got no higher than sixth, but never mind] so we went out with our best, most competitive position,' Hawkridge says. 'In fact – and this shows the character of Ayrton and that our relationship really wasn't as bad as everyone would imagine and how realistic he is – we said we really wanted to do some comprehensive tyre testing. "We haven't had a chance to do any all year and we want to test some other drivers. Ayrton, will you stay over after Estoril and run the car each day and set a pace? Then we can measure the other drivers." He went out and on his fifth lap he took the lap record apart. He was like a second and a half inside the lap record on the same tyres he'd used in the Grand Prix the day before. He came in and he said: "This is what I've dreamed about, it's the first time I've driven a Formula One car on the limit" and he was the happiest I'd seen him all year.'

So he'd been nursing the Toleman all that time . . .

'He went out and he had no worries, no responsibilities. If he'd written the car off – it would never happen – but if he had it wouldn't have affected Toleman and it wouldn't have affected him. He blitzed around and made the McLarens look like lemons. (Prost had been on the front row of the grid, remember.) He showed what he was capable of. Stefan had stepped in and done the job and Ferrari hired him on the strength of that, but what Ferrari didn't see

136

was what we'd seen Senna do after the last race. We knew what he could do and he knew. Nobody else knew.'

They were soon to find out and as a matter of record, that Monday Senna did 1 minute 21.70 seconds. It equalled Piquet's time which had taken pole in the Portuguese Grand Prix and it was set on race tyres, albeit of a soft compound. Piquet of course had been on qualifiers . . .

'I remember doing a deal with Sergio Taccini, the Italian sportswear company – in fact a bonus deal because we'd had them as a sponsor but Warwick had moved to Renault and they wanted to stay with Warwick,' Witty says. 'They said to me: "We'll do a deal with Senna" but they didn't think he'd be on the podium many times so it was a high bonus. At the end of the season, I think he'd earned more than Warwick had done!

'We knew that the guy was good. He destroyed Cecotto mentally, right, he didn't really get a chance to destroy Johansson because Johansson was only in for three races. In a funny sort of way Stefan accepted the role that he played later with the Alboretos and the Prosts. At the Portuguese Grand Prix we had three cars, right, and Stefan went out in his race car intending that maybe he would use the spare, but Senna is very clever. I don't know whether he did it on purpose but I think it's in the back of his mind. He went out and did about three laps in his race car, there was a problem with it, he gets into the spare, monopolizes the spare for the rest of the warming-up session.

'It was very clever tactically the way he got guys like Rory Byrne [the designer] and the team to work around him, very difficult if you were a number two driver to do anything about it. Ayrton wasn't really a whinger but everything had to be right. But you don't mind if he turns it into lap times like he used to do. I've always been an admirer of Ayrton because I think I've been able to touch him a bit. I spent a year working with him and I can see

137

Victory in Europe in the 2000, at Zandvoort, 1982.

Senna's first taste of Formula One power, courtesy of
Frank Williams, at Donington.

Senna at
home with his
mother,
Neide.

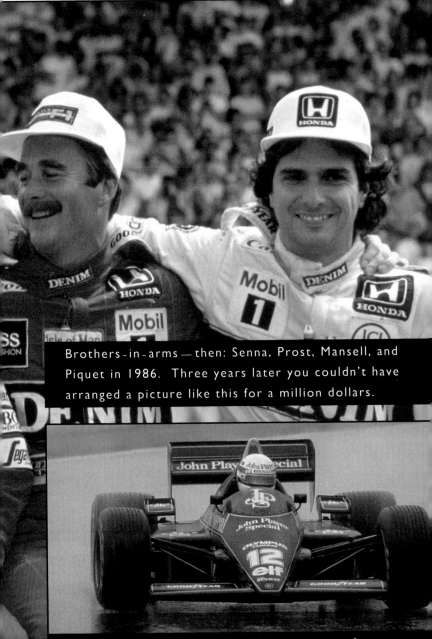

Brothers-in-arms — then: Senna, Prost, Mansell, and Piquet in 1986. Three years later you couldn't have arranged a picture like this for a million dollars.

The rain master at Estoril, 1985 — winning of course.

A pastoral backdrop and that sinking feeling in Austria, 1986. The engine died.

The street master strikes again at Monaco in 1987.

The intensity of the man, here contemplating Marlboro McLaren Honda power in 1988.

There was *entente cordiale* – then

Suzuka, 1989. Senna and Prost, locked together, have flowed helplessly towards the escape road at the chicane. Prost prepares to climb out of his car. Senna takes a different view of the situation.

Suzuka, the Championship is decided by a crash and now Senna and Prost begin the lonely walk back.

Senna's annual glass of champagne – if he wins a championship. This is Suzuka, October 1990.

CHAPTER NINE

The Warr Zone

'If you're inclined to the view that, well, perhaps Elio de Angelis wasn't as good as we thought he was, why Johnny Dumfries didn't make it, they had no chance. The guy was driving at a super-elevated level.' These are the words of Peter Warr and they represent a homage to Senna. We have heard many homages already but this one is more important. Lotus could give Senna the World Championship. Lotus had given it to others before him, Clark, Graham Hill, Emerson Fittipaldi, Jochen Rindt, Mario Andretti. Lotus were still, in 1985, a big team.

What really happened when Senna left Toleman for them is absurdly simple, no mystery at all. He knew Lotus could give him the World Championship, he knew Toleman couldn't. Lotus, Senna concluded, was 'definitely a better opportunity'.

'The first time I met him was at the factory,' Nigel Stepney will say. 'I didn't really have a lot to do with him because I was working on Elio's car and he was in the other one, but you could see that when he was in his car he was totally oblivious to everybody else. He could wind himself up into a very great intensity. You could watch him standing there or sitting in the car concentrating and somehow he was completely different to anybody else you could meet.'

Stepney was, of course, a Lotus mechanic then. He has gone now, gone to Benetton. Warr was in charge of the whole thing then. He has gone now. Elio de Angelis was an experienced driver then – he'd been racing since 1979.

139

He has gone now, gone in a shocking, churning moment in testing a Brabham at the Paul Ricard circuit. He is still lamented as a good man and true. I've never met anybody who didn't like Elio de Angelis.

Warr's evaluation of him is not insensitive and must not be seen as that; Warr is evaluating only the driver, not the man, and he is entitled to do that, just as anyone can evaluate any driver killed. You could barely speak of motor racing at all in an historical sense if you didn't. Many, many are gone now, Clark, Hill, Rindt . . .

And Colin Chapman, too. He died in 1982, not that long after de Angelis won in Austria, and this had been Lotus's first victory since 1978. Chapman was a turbulent, self-made strong man and quite possibly in the originality of his thought a genius. He saw what others did not see and founded an empire on that. He made kit cars (they virtually came through the post) called Lotus Sevens which were low, light and a sensation on the roads. They had competition clutches – it was either in or out – and absolutely direct steering, no play at all. They went precisely where you pointed them. The price of the kit was so modest that people to whom a Jaguar, Ferrari or Porsche were but a misty dream made an interesting discovery. Once the postman had delivered the kit, they had something which would accelerate faster . . .

Chapman made other, more exotic, more expensive cars but he remained a racing man. From 1958 Lotus would win seventy-two Grand Prix races until a heart attack ended it. To Peter Warr came a difficult, uneasy inheritance and he set about it as Chapman himself might have done: decisively. He hired a designer, Gerard Ducarouge, who built an entirely new and competitive car in five weeks.

In 1985 Warr was three years into his inheritance and now he'd got Senna. It was a coup. Senna, meanwhile, wintered in Brazil and contracted a viral infection of the inner ear so that he could not blink his right eye. It inflamed part of his face. 'It helps you to realize how weak you are,' he said. 'How inadequate you can be. You control yourself more, be careful, give more attention to yourself, your mental and physical condition, everything.'

'When he first came to us Elio had been there a while [since 1980], he'd only been in Formula One a year and Elio was a bit worried, I think,' Stepney says. 'Everybody used to like Elio but Senna came along and – I don't judge he did it on purpose – after a while had the whole nucleus of the team working for him. It just happened.'

He qualified on the second row at Brazil and was third on lap 48 when the electrics failed. Then – Portugal, a lap of 1 minute 21.007 and his first pole position in Formula One. That was done in the second qualifying session. The first session had been wet. Steve Hallam was a senior team member and he says, 'Ayrton set an unbelievable time when the track was in that condition, unbelievable.'

Senna 1 minute 21.708

de Angelis 1 minute 22.306

Lauda 1 minute 23.670

'So he had provisional pole and the next day he simply consolidated it,' Hallam says. On the Sunday it rained hard. Of the twenty-six who started, only ten would be running at the end. Senna was completely and typically candid. 'They all said I made no mistakes, but that's not true. On one occasion I had all four wheels on the grass, totally out of control . . . but the car came back on to the circuit.' It did. The sodden mechanics raised their hands in salute, Peter Warr danced like a man who had vindicated his professional life, and Senna had won his first Grand Prix.

He took it placidly, you know, what's all the fuss about, didn't you expect me to win? His car control – despite going off – was from another dimension altogether, precise, sure, easy. It can be best expressed by this judgement: all the others were slithering in a thunderstorm, he seemed to be driving a dry race.

He was just goddamned fast: pole at Imola, pole at Monaco, front row in Canada, pole in Detroit. 'Ayrton was almost two seconds quicker than anybody else,' Hallam recalls, 'and Joe Ramirez of McLaren said: "OK, which short cut did he take?!"' Stepney, too, recalls: 'The street races stand out most vividly in my memory. He was simply so much quicker than anybody else. They all take risks but I don't believe he took bigger risks than the others. He had not just speed but a purity, he cut every corner finer, he went closer to the barriers; and he didn't do this for just one lap but lap after lap after lap, he could do it for a whole race, he drove like that all the time. That's the difference.'

He put the Lotus on the front row in France, only the second row at Silverstone, only the third row at the Nürburgring ... only the seventh row in Austria (the car didn't like the bumps on the track), only the second row in Holland, pole at Monza despite an amazing lapse. He had not, of course, driven Monza before and 'on the first morning I arrived at the chicane flat in fifth because I'd forgotten it was there!' He was on the front row at Spa, pole at Brands Hatch, only the second row in South Africa. Oh, and he won Spa by 28 seconds from Mansell, was second at Brands.

John Watson emerged from retirement to drive the Marlboro McLaren (Lauda was ill). 'In qualifying I was coming down from Westfield Bend and I was on an in lap – going to come into the pits. Round Dingle Dell dip into Dingle Dell I saw this car coming very quickly behind me. Just at the bottom of the dip Ayrton came through on the inside – I'd left him room. I witnessed visibly and audibly something I had not seen anyone do before in a racing car. It was as if he had four hands and four legs. He was braking, changing down, steering, pumping the throttle and the car appeared to be on that knife edge of being in control and being out of control. It lasted maybe two seconds. Once he had checked the speed of the car and he'd got the right gear, what he was trying to do was maintain boost pressure. On a turbo you lift off and the power goes away very fast. He got to the point of the track where he wanted to make his commitment to the corner. The car was pitched in with an arrogance that made my eyes open wider. Then – hard on the throttle and the thing was driving through the corner. I mean it was a master controlling a machine. I had never seen a turbo car driven like that. The ability of the brain to separate each component and put them back together with that rhythm and co-ordination – for me it was a remarkable experience, it was a privilege to see.

'I was so moved that I went down to the Lotus pit and I said to Peter Warr and Gerard Ducarouge "I've just seen something" and they said "Yes, yes, we know."'

We might dwell, in contrast to this, on the final race, Adelaide, where Senna gave a chaotic performance, crashing and banging, and his maturity was called directly into question. He defended himself stoutly enough, analysing each incident and then, broadening it, added: 'The drivers have different lives outside racing so we never see each other. At the race track we have the opportunity to talk but when I am there I find I have so much to do with my team that I hardly find time to eat. My attitude is to make my car as quick and as safe as I can and then try to drive it as well as I can. That's the way I see it, and I suppose that's not good when it comes to forming relationships with other drivers.' He had 38 points and fourth place in the Championship. De Angelis, on 33, was fifth. He left for Brabham and now Senna convulsed Formula One.

Lotus needed him more than he needed Lotus, and he proceeded to exercise a veto over who would be his number two driver. Senna's defence: 'The principle was that in '86 they would concentrate behind one driver. Otherwise we would have compromise situations.' In this, Senna was uncompromising. Derek Warwick, available because Renault had dropped out of Formula One altogether, was an obvious candidate. Senna said no. Senna: 'It was bad, bad. Until then I had had a good relationship with Derek.'

This did not endear Senna to the British motoring press, who – by sheer weight of numbers as well as diversity – represent collectively something of a force. Who the hell was this upstart Senna, with only a couple of seasons behind him, making decrees? How the hell is it that he doesn't have to pay his lip service to tradition, serve his apprenticeship, keep his mouth shut in deference to people who know better than him? Worse, Warwick was (and is) immensely popular, truly one of the lads.

Senna's words come back. 'I could never be just another Formula One driver.'

He intended to be *the* Formula One driver.

(While the indignation was gathering strength someone – I won't name him – said calmly and clinically: 'Senna is doing the right thing. Lotus are no longer big enough to field two front runners, they'd dissipate their strength.' This is not only interesting, it is accurate. Senna was not frightened of competition, never had been, never would be, but he was frightened of the dissipation.)

The choice fell upon the Earl of Dumfries, known as Johnny. 'It was far from ideal circumstances,' he will say, 'but it was a chance to get into Formula One. For sure it had negative sides to it but I would have been stupid to turn it

144

down. If I could turn the clock back I still would have taken the drive. But I'd have behaved in a different way if I'd had more experience then. I think I was too naive at the time, I didn't capitalize on opportunities. Most people are pretty naive when they get into Formula One. I didn't have time to capitalize on the experience of my first year.'

You see it clearly: Dumfries was happy to be there at all, which is what we discussed when Senna was having discussions with Toleman. The whole lot of them are going to be happy to be there at all at the beginning – except Senna. (Don't forget Hawkridge: 'He intended to dominate Formula One.') Dumfries: 'I wasn't particularly sociable with the other drivers when I'd been in Formula Three [in Senna's year, 1983], I just didn't want to be. I was there to beat them, not socialize with them. So I didn't really get to know him until I came to Lotus. There are lots of guys who are touted as being brilliantly promising drivers. I don't pay too much attention to what I read in the press and I think Senna has always suffered from being written about too much. People tend to write about him in extremes. That's a bit unfortunate for him but, by the same token, I don't think it really bothers him either. The impression I received was that he's the sort of person who doesn't need a lot of friends. He probably has quite a small group of friends whom he trusts, because he's not the sort to go out and make lots of them. He doesn't need to and he doesn't want to.

'It was strictly a working relationship between us and conducted on that level. I don't think I was compared to him. He knew that I was the number two driver. I was in my first year in Formula One and he was in his third, he had established himself in the team. He's always been clever in picking the team he thinks is going to be best for him. That is an asset because as driver you tend to become too emotionally involved and sometimes it's

145

difficult to make rational decisions. His decisions have been good.

'What tended to happen was that the team would polarize around him. I'd sort of split off with my own race engineer and we'd do our own thing. I didn't want to feel I was hanging on the edge of their circle. I can't be bothered with that. So I'd go off and we'd discuss what we thought was the way to go. If you do that there's always pressure, there's pressure generated from inside yourself. I wanted always to be as quick as possible in the car.'

Stepney became Senna's mechanic in 1986. 'For me it was good because you knew you were in with a chance and as far as I'm concerned there's not much point in going to the races unless you are in with a chance. He expected everything to be right and in those days at Lotus it was hard in any specific car to get it absolutely right to the point he wanted. In some respects he expects a lot more than you can actually do for him. I don't know, but I expect he's calmed down a bit now he's won the World Championship. You could see he was going to win the World Championship. He was that kind of person.

'He knew the weak points of the car and he could read the car mechanically going round a circuit. He knew what the limit of the car was – not just in driving it but the actual car itself. He had to have the brakes a hundred per cent, the gearbox a hundred per cent and if he had one doubt about the gearbox he'd make you take it out – if he'd missed one gear he'd make you take it out. He was into everything on the car.

'He would stand for hours looking round the car, just generally looking. He knew a lot about the car. You could never hide anything from him. If anybody ever did and he found out he didn't like it.

'I remember at Detroit he'd done his warm-up lap and came to the grid and we were checking over his car and the rear skids – the plates under the gearbox – had disappeared because he'd gone over a manhole cover [they were all over the place at Detroit, a street circuit, of course]. We were told not to tell him. It could possibly have damaged the car because it could have damaged the gearbox, but we couldn't put new skids on.

'It wouldn't affect the car but because he didn't know about it he kept on driving over the same manhole cover on the same line. If somebody had told him he would have changed his line and missed it. He'd have said: "Yes, I know where that happened and I'll miss going over that point again." After the race he heard about it and he said: "Next time tell me, I want to know everything."

'His precision was unbelievable. When we had the fuel metres – fuel in the turbos was always on the limit – you'd listen to his debrief and he'd be going round the circuit and he could tell you at what place he was point one of a litre plus or minus on the lap. He could tell you when that figure changed – before or after the bridge, on certain corners, at different parts of the circuit. He was that intense.

'You'd got this gauge in front of you and it was changing the whole time. If it changed earlier than he anticipated – at, say, the bridge – he knew he was using too much fuel. He remembered it and this was through the whole race. His mind? On a debrief he could spend five or ten minutes telling you about one lap, every bump, every entry, every exit, every line he'd taken through the corner. I think he wore Ducarouge down with his memory power and his explanations of what he'd done. He'd stay until eight or nine o'clock at night and he wouldn't simply go even then, he'd always come and say goodbye. He wouldn't just clear off, he'd speak to everybody and not only the people working on his car but the people working on the other one. Whether it was a general interest or an

147

interest to see what was happening on the other car I don't know.

'He was a very good guy to work with. He was the kind who could pull out a second and that second would come from him, not the car. Say he'd be half a second off pole. Next minute he'd be sitting there on his last set of qualifying tyres, out he'd go and find a second, just like that. He did that so many times in '85 and '86 in the final five minutes of qualifying: he'd sit there, wait, do it. I can't explain that. I think only he can explain it.

'In a team he feeds off other people's information and he can do that because of his memory. He listens to everything that is said and he listens to the other driver's debriefing and he feeds off it. I can't see anything wrong in that.'

Let us put this directly into racing performance: across 1985 he had taken pole position seven times, now he would take it eight times. Only two men – Lauda in 1974 and 1975, Piquet in 1984 – had more, nine; the eight equalled James Hunt in 1976, Mario Andretti in 1978. It beat Clark, seven, in 1963.

The first pole of '86 was in Brazil. 'He worked hard to get that one,' Hallam says. 'He was absolutely exhausted after the lap. We were dealing with Piquet in the Williams, Ayrton went out on his second set of tyres and he gave everything from himself for that lap. I remember seeing him on the back straight slumped in the cockpit when he'd done it – not slumped so much as hunched. He'd given absolutely everything.' In the race Senna finished second to Piquet, Dumfries ninth and three laps behind. 'I had the fourth quickest race lap,' Dumfries says, 'but it was very difficult to repeat that speed in a race again. I don't know why. But it was very, very frustrating.'

After Brazil the journalist Bulgin was made redundant by the magazine he was working for. He rang Senna and said he wouldn't be going to the next race, explained why. 'How will you manage?' Senna asked.

'I'll be all right, I've enough to pay the mortgage.'

'If you ever need money, anything, contact me.'

(Looking back on this, Bulgin says: 'Senna was the only person who offered me help rather than commiserations.')

That next race, Spain, was a classic. Senna beat Mansell by 0.014 seconds. 'Physically I was at the end,' Senna says, 'but because I had won I recovered quickly. Winning is the best medicine to regain strength. In the evening I had fully recovered and I drove the race again in my mind. I wanted to enjoy my victory once more that way.'

He explained also how he managed to get such good starts. 'I may look slow but people don't know what a Grand Prix is. There are so many things you have to do, think about and even learn in those few hours before the start. For me the only way to be stronger is to concentrate deeply. I try to remember everything, every small detail of my preparation. You must think of everything in this enormous turmoil at the start. It is wrong to recognize people, except your mechanics perhaps. I run the whole picture in my head. I inspect the surface of the track. That is important to determine your tactics in the race and your choice of tyres. I believe I am the only one who does that. I go through a sort of check list like a pilot except we have nothing on paper. After the warm-up lap I check everything once more. People always think the start of the race is something terrible, that your heart beats like mad, that your brain is about to explode but it's a totally unreal moment, it is like a dream, like entering another world. Your spirit goes and the body sets itself free. When you accelerate there is only one thing that matters, not to fall behind, to take the lead. Really the most beautiful moment is the moment when the light turns red. Everything in me is programmed then, everything is discharged, bang, bang,

bang, the tension, the waiting for hours, minutes, it all disappears.'

So now you know.

A wheel bearing went on lap 11 at Imola when he was fourth; he was third at Monaco, second at Spa, fifth in Canada, won Detroit. Stepney puts that into context. 'When he won he didn't celebrate much, no, as far as he was concerned that was the job that was meant to be done. Where his limit is I don't think anybody knows. When he's just sitting there in front of Prost [my interview with Stepney was in 1989] for sure he's got a lot left in him, because he won't push the car for the sake of pushing it. He'll be conserving his tyres. You learn so much about that from him just because of the way he explains how he looks after them. He will only use a car as much as he has to in order to do the job. OK, Detroit, places like that, he blasts off into the distance but he still won't be pushing it any more than he has to. I believe that even at Detroit he still had plenty left in hand. We won't find his limit until somebody actually starts pushing him.'

In France he spun off and marched back and apologized to the mechanics. At Brands Hatch the gearbox went on lap 27; he was second behind Piquet at Hockenheim, took pole in Budapest. 'He was quick all the way through there,' Hallam says, 'and he was always saying "No grip, no grip, we've got to improve the car!"' He was second behind Piquet in the race, the engine went on lap 13 in Austria, the transmission went right at the start at Monza, he was fourth in Portugal, third in Mexico, the engine went on lap 43 in Adelaide. He had 55 points and was fourth in the table.

John Player were very serious sponsors who did more than write large cheques and post them to Team Lotus, Ketteringham Hall, Norfolk. Their promotions executive, Peter Dyke, was an almost Rabelaisian figure, knew the journalists well, enjoyed life and drove a Rolls-Royce (which Ducarouge once took for a flying lap at Brands Hatch, much to Dyke's anguish and apprehension). Dyke was conscious of the overall Player responsibility as well as the good name of the company – when he heard that market stalls just outside the paddock at the Österreichring were selling black and gold anoraks with JPS on them he rose from his glass of wine at the motorhome like a wrathful schoolmaster to go and make sure the anoraks were approved (or removed).

It was Dyke who acted as master of ceremonies at a dinner for journalists at Cascais, not far from the track at Estoril on the eve of the Portuguese Grand Prix.

The place might have been a minor château. Through high arched windows you could see manicured lawns. Waitresses flitted here and there dispensing drinks from trays. Dyke loomed, slightly larger than life, joking to make people giggle and guffaw while his knowing eye roved the room, making sure all was well.

The conversation ebbed into silence when Senna came in. Instinctively people found themselves looking at him – as if he was a presence, not a mere person. It was awkward for him: so many faces turned to his. Dyke covered it by making an announcement – 'Gentlemen, I think you already know Ayrton' – which broke the silence.

By good fortune I sat next to him at dinner. He drank one glass of mineral water in careful, rationed sips and towards the end asked timidly for another. When the white wine was brought and the waitress worked her way along the table he covered his glass with the palm of his hand and smiled politely at her.

I wondered about the perfect lap? He pondered the proposition. 'It is like tying both ends of your tie so that they are exactly the same length. Experience tells you that you can do it, practice tells you that you can do it – but you can't.' For someone who was supposed to have a limited command of English, it wasn't bad, was it? (Later, I have to report, I wondered about how he could live in Brazil with money amongst widespread poverty and his defence of his own country was so perceptive, so rational and so vehement that the man from *The Times* thought it prudent to change the topic of conversation. As you might expect, he achieved this effortlessly by saying something like: 'Tell us please, Ayrton, about last year, when you won in the rain here.')

You and I don't know what it feels like to be gazed at, to be a moving exhibit, to have artificial silence and a couple – or a dozen, a hundred, 100,000 faces – always peering into yours every minute of every place you go until you close the hotel bedroom door; it must be damn near intolerable, must drive a strong man towards screaming and if Senna seems withdrawn that is one way of coping; you see the faces in a haze, or as you might see trees, not as separate trunks but just as woodland.

Senna confesses as much. 'It is very pleasant to be able to go to a restaurant without having to book a table even when the place is very busy. On the other hand when I want to be alone and people won't let me I am annoyed.'

He may have been rude to people but I've never heard him. (And, breaking the chronological sequence of the narrative for a moment but pursuing the theme, when he'd won at Spa in 1988 he was asked a question, moved into a lengthy reply and was interrupted by another question. Slowly, in his strangely modulated English, he said: 'Please, let me finish my reply.' It was said with a daunting mixture of firmness and politeness – to such a degree that it brought nervous smiles from the assembled journalists.)

I suppose that everybody knew 1987 would be a decisive season in Senna's relationship with Lotus. It would be his third, and if he didn't win the World Championship, or get extremely close, his hunger for that Championship would inevitably take him to another team where he felt he could win it. Interestingly, Juan Manuel Fangio was extremely mercenary in this matter, always went for the team with the best chance and this is his sequence: 1950, Alfa Romeo; 1951, Alfa Romeo; 1953, Maserati; 1954, Maserati, Mercedes; 1955, Mercedes; 1956, Ferrari; 1957, Maserati; 1958, Maserati. Presumably everybody else would have done this, too, and kept on doing it through to the modern era – to today – if they'd been good enough to have the choice. Certainly drivers have never been coy about leaving losing teams to join winning teams, which was why Senna left Toleman for Lotus and would leave Lotus for exactly the same reason. Lotus were a winning team, as he had proved. The question was much, much larger: were they a World Championship winning team?

He was twenty-seven, nearing that point in his career which is a balance of youth, experience and the need still to do it. He could exploit the Lotus fully, but if the Lotus was inherently incapable of taking the Championship he could do no more. Even for Senna it is the art of the possible. Nor would the season be in any sense easy: Piquet and Mansell at Williams, Prost at McLaren, Alboreto and Berger at Ferrari, and he had to beat all of them.

The man himself? He'd learnt early on that Lotus were serious but had a human face. They'd pulled the cream cake trick on him – sniff it, Ayrton, to make sure the cream hasn't gone sour – and when he did they'd pressed his nose into it. Lotus had learnt early on that he was serious but had a human face. He pulled the dyed sweets trick on them. He offered them sweets from a bag, they accepted and found their mouths dyed blue.

'At the end of a race you'd have a bit of a laugh and a joke,' Stepney says. 'He was a practical joker but he picked and chose his moments when he'd do that. We'd have water fights, stuff like that. People look at him and say he's cold, you know, but he has a sense of humour, a very good sense of humour. It takes a long time to get to know him and I don't know him fully.'

Before we examine 1988, listen to Senna himself on how he drove a Lotus. 'I used to cover the palms of my hands because if I didn't I'd get these terrible blisters and that made steering difficult. I don't do that any more now. My new car is lighter, easier to handle. I clean the visor. It is strange but something like that can cost you your victory. I perspire a lot during a race but I have a tube through which I can drink. A tube like that must be fitted carefully so it doesn't come loose. That happened to me once and I almost lost the race. In my head I consider every detail. It's never finished. The smallest error in checking, the smallest error in setting the wing mirror could cause a catastrophe. On the circuit it's too late to think of that. I check if all the buttons are in the right place, if they work or not. There is so much to think about, there is never enough time – or room in your mind – to process all the information adequately . . . and then it gets tiring.

'Whenever I think it's one of those days when nobody can touch me I call out through the radio link "I'm fine." I think they like to hear that. When I cross the line first it is an overwhelming feeling . . .'

Moreover, Lotus now had Honda engines instead of Renault. Peter Warr discusses this in retrospect. 'I'm not sure that even now [1989] we have got all the facts and figures and data together, but . . . maybe it served us a little bit badly because [paradoxically] the Renault engine was a better engine than Senna made it appear. Maybe it was only because he was driving it so fast that its fuel consumption was bad. Maybe it was because he had this throttle control technique – blip-blip-blipping in the corners. The reason we have suspicions like this is because he

154

keeps on coming up as the worst of the four Honda drivers on fuel consumption. That's partly because he's going the quickest and partly the blipping of the throttle.

'People were saying "Well, the Lotus is a good car, Senna is a bright up-and-coming driver but they are handicapped by the Renault engine which hasn't got the fuel consumption." But who knows if the truth wasn't this: the engine was absolutely fantastic and very powerful, the chassis wasn't that good and Senna was having to drive it above the level of which it was capable of being driven to be competitive – which was why the fuel consumption was bad.'

With Honda engines came a pleasant, experienced man called Satoru Nakajima to partner Senna. He would be immediately useful. Lotus tested at Donington, Senna brought the car into the pits after a couple of laps and said: 'There's something wrong with it because it's vibrating, it feels like it's going to shake itself to pieces.' Nakajima got in, did a couple of laps, came back and said: 'No problem. That's the way the engines always are.'

'I greatly valued my collaboration with Renault,' Senna says. 'The motor racing people are very competent at Renault Sport and we obtained excellent results on pure performance. But at that time Renault's involvement was on the decline. Honda were investing totally, with maximum means and a Japanese mentality of taking-it-to-a-conclusion.'

Brazil: Lotus had an 'active' suspension system which brought problems and Senna spun during the Friday qualifying session. He was quicker on the Saturday and started from the second row of the grid. He had a strange sort of race: in the lead by lap 8, in the pits with handling problems on lap 14 pitching him back to eighth, charged, was second on lap 39, stopped altogether on lap 50 – separator in the oil tank broke.

Imola: pole. In the end he simply couldn't catch Mansell in the Williams and finished 27.545 seconds behind.

Belgium: row two of the grid. Mansell took the lead, Senna following. Far back down the field Philippe Streiff, breasting the rise after Eau Rouge, lost his Tyrrell and it hit the armco hard enough to bisect itself. Jonathan Palmer in the other Tyrrell couldn't avoid the wreckage. When he got back to the pits he was in that 'hyper' state of delayed shock, face white, talking too fast. And when Streiff's Tyrrell was brought back to the parc fermé it drew gasps from people wandering by. It looked as if it had been savaged by a pack of wild animals; that Streiff had survived unhurt seemed unbelievable (in the proper sense of that word). The race was re-started and now Senna took the lead, Mansell following. They reached the corner called Pouhon – a left – and as they came out Mansell was very close. Along the short rush to Les Fagnes – a right – Mansell moved out and, as he drew alongside, was on the racing line. The two cars went into the right-hander together and their wheels touched. Mansell said he thought Senna had missed a gear or the engine had 'hesitated' and he moved left to overtake. 'The next thing I knew, I was being pushed off the circuit.'

Senna judged it a different way. 'I can tell you that nothing happened to my car at the previous corner. I took it flat. Maybe you find the car in front of you appears to slow if you hit the boost button on your steering wheel and have an extra 100bhp. But I couldn't believe what he was trying to do – overtake on the outside at a place like that. I tried to get out of the way, brake as much as possible, but you can only do so much in a situation like that. I was committed to the corner – there was no way I could stop.'

They spun off as if they were locked together, Senna came to rest in the sand trap, Mansell limping back out and on. Mansell went as far as lap 17, came into the pits and his eyes were ablaze with anger. He strode to the Lotus pits and seized Senna.

'When a man holds you round the throat, I do not think he has come to apologize,' Senna commented afterwards. Three Lotus mechanics were needed to get Mansell off Senna, who regained his composure and wandered to the pit lane wall to watch Nakajima finishing fifth.

Monaco: Mansell on pole, Senna beside him on the front row and what would happen when they reached the right-hander at St Devote? Nothing. Mansell got there clearly and cleanly first, held the lead until lap 29 when the waste-gate pipe went and Senna ran comfortably to the end, finishing 33.212 seconds ahead of Piquet. Prost now led the table with 18 points, Senna three points further back.

Detroit: Mansell on pole, Senna beside him on the front row and what would happen when they reached the left-hander at Turn One? Nothing. Mansell got there clearly and cleanly first, held the lead until lap 34 (cramp) and Senna ran comfortably to the end, finishing 33.819 seconds ahead of Piquet. Senna 24 points, Prost 22.

France: second row of the grid. Senna didn't like the balance of the car and ran a percentage race to finish fourth. Senna 27, Prost 26, Piquet 24, Mansell 21.

Britain: second row of the grid. This time he was hampered by fuel consumption and drove a percentage race to finish third. Senna 31, Mansell 30, Piquet 30, Prost 26.

Germany: Lotus tested there ten days before the race and at high speed Senna had a tyre deflate. Warr was so concerned that he rang Goodyear in Ohio to warn them that they might have a 'tyre wear' problem similar to the one which had – with shocking speed – caused one of Mansell's tyres to explode at Adelaide, the last race of 1986. It turned out to be an ordinary puncture. Mind you, it was a hell of a moment. Senna had been moving out of the stadium complex towards the first chicane and the

157

Ferrari speed trap clocked him at 206 miles an hour. The left rear deflated, tearing the rear suspension off the car; and the car kept on in a straight line for 600 metres. The 'active suspension' had been battling to compensate for the deflation.

Senna was now pondering his future. He had already spoken to Ron Dennis before the season began and now, in the German Grand Prix, finished third but a lap behind Piquet and Stefan Johansson. He made a judgement: the Lotus could not compete with the McLarens and Williams. A few days after the race Warr received a letter from Senna's English solicitors saying that he wouldn't be with them for 1988. (Senna: 'Before the letter was sent I told Peter Warr myself during the weekend at the German Grand Prix as a matter of education' – i.e. common decency and information.) He was talking to Dennis. On the Saturday after the German Grand Prix, Warr flew to Nice and had a long talk with Piquet. On the Wednesday – just before the Hungarian Grand Prix – Piquet flew to London and signed. 'I hadn't spoken to Nelson before that Saturday but I felt we had to act,' Warr says. (Senna: 'Nothing was signed but all the negotiations had taken place and I believed in Ron's word on the deal.') Now Warr again: 'It was quite obvious that Senna thought he was going to be the first to sit down in the game of musical chairs and that everything else would then follow. I wasn't prepared to wait for him – and run the risk of having to choose from the left-overs at the end of the season.'

Senna did not know the team had hired Piquet. (Enigmatically, Senna says that 'there is a lot more about this Lotus-Piquet-Senna-McLaren-Honda deal but I am keeping it to myself.') He only heard about it when he reached Hungary. 'It amazes me that a company as big and famous as Lotus should behave so unprofessionally. They could have called me on Wednesday – the day he signed –

to let me know. Instead I found out here on Friday morning.'

Hungary: third row of the grid. He finished 37.727 seconds behind Piquet.

Austria: fourth row of the grid. He finished fifth, two laps behind the leaders. Piquet 54 points, Senna 43, Mansell 39, Prost 31.

Monza: Dennis confirmed that Senna had joined McLaren. Senna saw it as a 'great opportunity for me. From a personal point of view I am very happy to work with Alain: two top drivers working together can only make a team stronger.' And significantly McLaren were getting Honda engines. Honda liked what Senna did – a lot. He was on the second row for the race, took the lead on lap 24 and lost it on lap 43 when he slewed slightly off – tyre wear – and couldn't catch Piquet, although the difference was only 1.806 seconds at the end.

He got no points in Portugal, was fifth in Spain and the Championship had virtually gone. Piquet 70, Mansell 52, Senna 51, Prost 46. When he spun off in Mexico (clutch) it had gone. He was second at Suzuka, second at Adelaide – then disqualified because the brake ducts on the Lotus were irregular. It constituted a sad end to three years. Of Lotus, he says: 'I knew the team from the inside, it was a team which counted for me. I made friends there.'

I never did discuss the question with Peter Warr because it seemed hardly necessary. Everyone knew why they couldn't hold Senna, none more than Warr himself. His face was wistful, full of quiet resignation, as we moved around the topic, not through it. There was nothing to say.

Prost had won the Championship twice with McLaren, and now, as we've said, Honda engines would be added for 1988. Since 1984 the team had won twenty-five races – and taken Lauda to the Championship, too. For Senna, it was the main chance; perhaps it was always where he had been

159

going and all the rest merely an apprenticeship, although that's a hard judgement on Toleman and Lotus and the good men at both places. He was still twenty-seven, it was still an age to retain big ambitions. Before we leave Lotus let's reflect that in an uncompetitive car he had taken 57 points and was third in the Championship. The final words must go to Peter Warr: 'Ayrton Senna's time with Team Lotus was undoubtedly a very, very exciting period in modern motor racing. The thing that really marks him out is that he was the first driver since Jimmy Clark to arouse the sort of emotions that Clark did within the team. He was certainly the first driver since Ronnie Peterson to have people as excited about some of the things he could do with a race car – you know, things you just couldn't believe.'

CHAPTER TEN

Diary of a Championship

Bologna, Tuesday 22 March 1988, evening. McLaren International's Falcon 20 landed from Heathrow; a freighter bearing the McLaren MP4/4 racing car had landed earlier. Steve Nichols, who headed up the design team, looked for the transporter to take it to Imola. There had been a misunderstanding. The transporter was not there, it was at the track thirty kilometres away. They phoned, waited until it came and they reached the track at nine, fussed around, went to their hotel. Nichols had what he remembers as a 'fitful night's sleep'. A question gnawed at him: what if the car is a 'turkey'? It hadn't run yet, McLaren had not run a Honda engine yet, building the car had been a rush and the new season was two and a half weeks away.

Imola, Wednesday 23 March. Nichols: 'We arrived, warmed up the car, Prost went out and did the first few laps and I mean it was just incredible. Within three laps and before we'd changed anything, he was only a few seconds off his previous best time at the track. He came in, the engine was checked all over, out he went again and he was doing competitive times.'

Prost's best: 1 minute 28.5.

'We changed to Senna and by lunchtime he was quicker than any of the other teams had been in the whole test. By the end of the day our drivers had done times two seconds quicker than the Ferraris, and they'd been the quickest in the previous two days.' Senna did 1 minute 27.6. Berger – in one of those Ferraris, of course – had done 1 minute 29.90. At least, Nichols concluded, the car is not a turkey.

Senna made no public comment. There was no need. The car had made the comment.

Rio, Friday 1 April. Senna and Prost were quickest in the untimed session for the Brazilian Grand Prix and both said the handling wasn't quite right. The temperature crept up towards 40 degrees and in the afternoon Senna did 1 minute 30.218, Prost behind Mansell (Williams), and Alessandro Nannini (Benetton) on 1 minute 31.975. Senna: 'We have not had any serious problems. Our car is virtually brand new and we are still finding out about it, so it is only to be expected that we will be adjusting both the chassis and the engine. The circuit is still developing grip, so tomorrow I think we can improve quite a lot.'

Rio, Saturday 2 April. Senna was right. He thrust in 1 minute 28.096, then Mansell (1:28.632), then Prost (1:28.782). Senna: 'I was quite lucky with the traffic but the most important thing is that we seem to be more competitive in spite of the inevitable minor problems that are to be expected with a brand new car.' Osamu Goto, Honda Formula One Project leader: 'We are delighted with Ayrton's performance in a new car with his new team. We have been able to work out the best engine settings for the race but of course we may have to adjust them if the climatic conditions change.'

We were back, somehow, to 1983 and to the start of the Formula Three season in England. The question posed then was the one being posed now: who can beat Senna?

Rio, Sunday 3 April. It rained, the rain stopped. Senna brought them round slowly on the parade lap to the green light – was he trying to make the others overheat? – and the moment they formed up Senna's arms were out of the cockpit being waved like flippers. Behind him smoke belched from Ivan Capelli's March as if it was a bonfire. Senna had a gear selection problem. The start had to be abandoned. Worse, a 'fan' rushed towards Senna's stationary car and had to be manhandled away by a posse of men in yellow shirts. They were not gentle with him. Senna would start from the pit lane in the spare car. He watched as the cavalcade went by and came from that pit lane fast. By lap 2 he was up to nineteenth, and now he moved in a hurry: lap 3, seventeenth, lap 4 fifteenth, lap 6 thirteenth, lap 7 eleventh, lap 8 tenth, lap 9 ninth, lap 10 eighth, lap 12 seventh, lap 13 sixth, lap 16 fifth, lap 17 fourth, lap 19 third, lap 20 second. Prost lay ahead. Senna slipped back to sixth when his pit stop went wrong. The engine stalled, frantic hands were waved and he was stationary for 32.01 seconds.

On lap 31 an official in a lime green uniform and wearing headphones wandered rather sheepishly out on to the rim of the track. In his right hand: a small black flag. In his left – and held in front of him like a matador's cape – a wide black board with the number 12 on it. As Senna passed him the official wandered back on to the grass. It was over.

Senna came in, talked for a while with the mechanics from the cockpit, clambered out, went into the pit-lane mêlée taking his driving gloves off. He had been disqualified for changing cars after the green light for that first aborted start – technically it was not a new race so he wasn't allowed to. 'Why wait until now?' Senna wondered. A good question. Actually Ron Dennis had been arguing his case with the officials; hence the delay. Prost won from Berger, Piquet, Warwick, Alboreto and Nakajima.

Monza, Tuesday 19 April. He tested, did a 1 minute 28.94, did that again across an extended test of 42 laps and also did a complete spin at 160 kilometres an hour, thumping the barrier.

Imola, Friday 29 April. He was second behind Prost in the first session for the grid; and faster than Prost on the Saturday. Senna: 'The pop-off valve fitted to my engine was giving trouble so the Honda engineers had to fit a new one. Although I knew the valve was not operating correctly I did not come into the pits immediately because I was worried that it might rain.'

Imola, Sunday 1 May. Nichols: 'Although we had gone well in testing, Imola is thirsty, it was supposed to be the sort of place where a normally-aspirated car would win. Everybody was thinking: will we be good here?' Senna took the lead and was not to lose it. Senna: 'We set a quick pace – so far as the fuel allowed, we were racing. This was a question-mark race for us. I never really felt confident I would finish. I thought: there's another race gone for me. The balance of the car was beautiful, the engine fine, the consumption good but quite early I had smoke and a burning smell coming into the cockpit. Later the gearbox started to feel loose.' Senna stopped just beyond the line, 2.334 seconds ahead of Prost. Nichols: 'It wasn't absolutely bone dry.' (And Geoff Lees, Honda test driver in Japan: 'Fuel consumption can be calculated to within 200 metres over the full distance of a Grand Prix. It is that precise.')

Monaco, Thursday 12 May. Senna took provisional pole with a staggering 1 minute 26.464 and there was only one direct comparison, Prost on 1 minute 28.375. Now Senna said something staggering: 'We had a problem with poor engine braking in the morning untimed session which the Honda engineers were able to cure for the afternoon but we still have a slight delay in the power pick-up from slow corners.' Slight delay? Hmmm. On the Saturday Senna challenged credulity with 1 minute 23.998 and again the only direct comparison was Prost, 1 minute 25.425. Prost: 'Fantastic. There's no other word, is there?' Senna: 'To be honest I can't tell you if I got an absolutely clear lap or not. It's all so frantic here that you can't separate individual laps in your mind. But to be really quick you have to use all the road and you have to take big risks, yes.'

Monaco, Sunday 15 May. He led to lap 67, lost concentration just before the tunnel and hit the armco. He was out. Senna: 'Monte Carlo was the turning point in the Championship. It was nothing to do with the car or the equipment. The mistake I made changed me psychologically and mentally. I changed a lot inside. It gave me the strength and the power to fight in critical moments. It was the biggest step in my career as a professional, a racing driver and a man. It brought me closer to God than I have ever been. I was feeling easy in front. It was a hundred per cent perfect weekend. Suddenly I lost concentration, made a stupid mistake and threw everything away. It made me reflect about a lot of things. I had good help from my family and other people who gave me power and strength. It has changed my life. I am the same person but my mental strength has changed.'

Prost won, and the Championship was: Prost 24, Berger 14, Senna 9, Piquet 8 . . .

Mexico, Friday 27 May. Senna took provisional pole, took pole itself on the Saturday. Prost won the race, Senna second. 'The pop-off valve opened unexpectedly when I took second gear at the start. After that I did not want to risk using too much fuel so I decided not to chase Alain.' Prost 33, Berger 18, Senna 15, Alboreto 9. 'By the time I got myself into a rhythm Alain was already some way clear. He drove very fast today, never backed off and he deserved the race, sure.'

Montreal, Friday 10 June. Senna quickest from Prost and again on the Saturday. Prost took the lead and held it to lap 19, Senna always behind him – directly behind him. They came to the left-right kink, Senna darted out, ran briefly alongside Prost and reached the right turn on the inside . . . on the racing line. It settled the race. Senna: 'For all 69 laps we were on the limit of the fuel so Alain and I were pacing each other. In some places he was quicker and at others I'd gain on him. I knew that I had to be patient. Passing him is never very easy but when I saw the chance I made my move and everything came good.' Prost – courteously and prudently – moved out of the way. Prost 39, Senna 24, Berger 18, Piquet 11.

Detroit, Friday 17 June. Senna quickest, then Prost. Senna: 'The tyres were most effective only in the first two or three laps but apart from that everything is going fine.' Everything did not go fine on the Saturday; the track started to break up and Berger and Alboreto were quicker than Senna, although his Friday time was enough to give him pole, his sixth on the roll. 'It was very slippery,' he said. That six poles, incidentally, equalled the record of Stirling Moss (1959–60) and Lauda (1974).

Detroit, Sunday 19 June. Senna gave a consummate performance, led from flag to flag in what Goto called 'a survival race'. Goto added: 'As we had anticipated, the temperature was exceptionally high at 34 degrees, which is hotter than it was in Brazil in April. Our priority therefore was reliability and in fact the McLarens started the race with 140 litres of fuel instead of the permitted 150 litres. This gave the brakes a slightly easier time in the first few laps, which gave them an advantage.' Twenty-six cars set off into the contorting 'tunnels' between the armco and after the 63 laps only eight were running. Senna was exhausted. 'This race is very hard, both mentally and physically. You're racing against the heat and the walls. When the crew told me to come in for a tyre stop (on lap 42) I did not want to do so. But when I saw that Alain had stopped (lap 39) I was happy to do the same.' Prost 45, Senna 33, Berger 18, Piquet and Boutsen 11.

Silverstone, Monday 27 June. Senna tested and said: 'I have to be as close to perfection as possible because Alain is always like that, too – close to perfection. I have to be exact in setting the car up, exact in every decision I make. We are in the same factory team. If I want to compete with him I have to give the same as he does. For me it is important to have a competitive car like I have now. It is the first time in my career I have been in such a situation and I feel quite happy. With Alain, I expected it to be as it has turned out and I can't see any reason why it should change. In other words, harmony not friction.'

That was the mood of the moment and as I've recounted elsewhere (*Conquest of Formula One*) Senna spoke the words to me while this was going on: I set my tape recorder on top of my briefcase rather than hold it, and place the briefcase, side up, directly in front of his feet. As he speaks he begins to tease the briefcase with his toe, gently but rhythmically, so that the tape recorder wobbles and then rocks to and fro – but does not fall. You wonder how someone speaking a foreign language (English) could simultaneously do that with such precision ... Senna is grinning hugely as if he's doing something very, very naughty and getting away with it ...

And:

I go off to Stowe, where there is a wooden platform inside the corner – a superb vantage point because you can see a panorama of cars coming out of Becketts Corner into Chapel Curve, all the way to the *Daily Express* bridge on the other side of the track. After a few minutes Senna arrives in a hire car, hops nimbly out – he's wearing a Marlboro anorak which makes him look broader – skips up the platform and watches. You sense that he does not wish to be disturbed. He wants to see what the others are doing and how they are doing it: he's not spectating at all. His eyes track each car, locking on to them, his head moving in time with them. It is as if he is using the eyes as binoculars, using his mind to dis-assemble the cars as they pass.

And:

He skips down the steps and I assume he's going off to his hotel. It's late afternoon, anyway, and only three or four cars are going round. He's already seen them. The hire car moves off along the wide, undulating runway which is inside the circuit and leads towards the distant paddock but Senna swivels off on to the wide grass verge flanking Hangar Straight. Halfway along a man sits hunched over a speed trap. Senna stops, gets out, goes directly to him, stoops, looks at the speeds, starts to ask questions . . .

Silverstone, Tuesday 28 June. Prost arrives, says firmly that he has to be perfect because of Senna and insists that they are functioning as a team, not factions within a team. That really was the mood of the moment. Senna meanwhile was out at the back of the circuit flying his model aeroplane, the one he'd kept firmly in the boot of the hire car yesterday. An echo of the man comes back, and in his own words: 'I can't do anything without thinking of technical things. If I'm surfboarding I'm curious to know what the board is made of and why.' (The McLarens, incidentally, were testing rather than trying to blitz lap times; Prost did 1 minute 12.500, which was slower than Berger – 1:12.120 – Senna did 1:18.596, slower than Piquet, Boutsen, Nakajima, Alboreto, Warwick and Mansell. Not that it mattered.)

Paul Ricard, Friday 1 July. This time Prost was quicker than Senna (although, Prost said, the handling seemed 'a little bit nervous'). Astonishingly it happened again on the Saturday, so that for the first time in 1988 Senna did not have pole. He would have to share the record with Moss and Lauda.

Paul Ricard, Sunday 3 July. Prost took the lead, Senna hounding him, Prost had a troubled tyre stop and when he emerged Senna was in the lead by 2.9 seconds. Prost hunted Senna and overtook him in a great, incisive swoop at the right-hand loop of Beausset – Senna momentarily baulked by two back-markers, Prost seeing this, screwing everything out of the engine and taking the inside line. Prost: 'I think Ayrton lost downforce when he was following another car through the fast corner because he ran wide on to the dirt. I caught him there and then I braked very late at the next corner.' Senna: 'I cannot remember exactly when but the gear lever began to feel spongy. I started to miss the odd gear, I had a problem with my gearchange when I was leading and it just got worse and worse. Alain behaved very correctly.'

Silverstone, Friday 8 July. And the miracle did happen, Alboreto and Berger quicker than Senna and Prost, who said: 'The balance of our revised chassis was good in testing here but we couldn't find the same performance today.' Senna: 'We have a lot of understeer at Copse and Becketts which is losing us time.' The miracle endured on the Saturday, Alboreto and Berger again quicker. Senna spun twice – complete rotations at high speed – and continued as if nothing had happened at all. Both spins were at Stowe. 'The car was not handling very well there and I was more on the limit than I had been yesterday.' Actually, it was a glimpse of Senna's mastery, the spins so controlled that he might have been doing them as party tricks to entertain the crowd. When a car breaks loose your first reaction is: my God, let's hope it's not a big one. By the time you'd thought that, Senna had the McLaren pointing directly forwards and was on his way, you know, as if nothing really had happened at all . . .

Before we leave Saturday, a couple of interesting thoughts. In the morning untimed session, Senna's engine needed changing. This was achieved in one hour fifty minutes and Senna thanked the mechanics very sincerely indeed, the way he'd always done. Goto: 'While we regret we were not able to get pole position, the problem with Senna's engine gave us some new data which we think

169

will be useful. We still think we can have a good result in the race.'

Silverstone, Sunday 10 July. It rained, grey rain tumbling from a slate-grey sky and this sky had the look of permanent, unmoving cover. It would rain all day. The race would be dangerous, as all wet races are, but more dangerous here because Silverstone is fast, fast, fast. Berger took the lead, held that to lap 14 when Senna dipped left and moved past Berger – he was travelling fast, fast, fast towards the *Daily Express* bridge, Prost, hobbled by engine problems, on the edge of the track about to be lapped. Picture it: a back-marker and Prost poised to turn into the sharp left-hand corner just past the bridge and Senna inside them. They would turn across him . . .

Senna's car twitched under braking and he slithered towards Prost who had to turn sharply away. 'Alain and I almost touched. It was a bad moment because the visibility was so bad. Then we had some unexpected problems with the fuel consumption which was worrying until I got the situation under control.' And: 'At the speed Berger had been running I couldn't make the finish on fuel. I was pretty sure he couldn't, either.' Prost had clutch problems. 'Because of that I stalled at the start and I was very lucky to get it re-started. The handling was bad and I did not think it was worth taking big risks to fight for fifteenth place.' Prost retired. Prost 54, Senna 48, Berger 21.

Goto said that 'today's conditions were severe because of the extra drag which is induced by the wet-weather tyres so we were only able to make a rough estimate of how much fuel would be required. Ayrton had to drive under our control, a situation which he accepted as a good team member. He quietly judged the situation and made it possible for us to continue in the search for more records.'

But the harmony of the season was being broken. The

French press savaged Prost – you know the sort of thing, he's a beaten man, hasn't even the stomach for a wet race any more – and Prost was very indignant indeed. He said that the clutch problem had made no difference to his basic resolve, which was to cease the moment he felt it was too dangerous to continue. Why, he mused, do we have to race at all in the wet? Other sports don't, even golf (the British Open had been stopped a few days before and golf isn't exactly dangerous, anyway). What do you think it feels like, he mused further, trying to listen to the engine noise from the car in front to estimate when he's braking because you can't see him, all you can see is the equivalent of waves breaking over rocks? Ron Dennis was angered by the criticism of Prost and came forth to say he had the two most professional drivers in the sport and if they ever decided to stop he would give them his full support.

All unnoticed, McLaren and Honda had won their eighth successive race, an absolute record for a single season.

Hockenheim, Friday 22 July. Senna quickest, Prost next; but a radical change on the Saturday, Prost then Berger then Alboreto, Senna tenth. Tenth? Senna: 'We took the decision to concentrate on a race set-up, running with a full fuel load before the start of the season. From my point of view the worst that was going to happen was that Alain might knock me off pole position, but I wasn't too worried about that at this circuit, so we figured it would be more worthwhile running through some chassis settings.' Senna did keep pole – Prost couldn't get within a second of Senna's Friday time. Dennis: 'With the track conditions offering less grip we concentrated simply on setting the cars up for the race. That's all there is to it.'

The traditional after-session press conference was ugly. The press room was crowded by a couple of hundred journalists and photographers who milled and mewled waiting for Senna and Prost. One journalist, enraged by the delay, set off to find Dennis to protest. When Senna and Prost did come they protested that they had had a debriefing and they had been harassed by journalists who wouldn't wait for the press conference, had been made to say all the things they would have to repeat at the conference. Senna let Prost speak – it was a face of Prost we rarely see, moving towards bitterness – and then asked for the microphone. His voice was almost trembling and made so by the profundity of what he wanted to say. 'Since my childhood I have been taught that it is not honourable to ignore people and therefore when journalists come up to me I try to answer their questions.' In other words, you're crowding me all the time and I'm not impolite enough to tell you to clear off. Why can't you wait until the press conference?

Thus the pressure was gathering around the two men who were, anyway, the only people journalists wanted to talk to. Eight races (including the German Grand Prix) remained. The pressure could only increase, and very likely day by day.

Hockenheim, Sunday 24 July. It rained, but not like Silverstone. The sky was not so leaden, not so intimidating. A wet race, yes, but it might become a dry race. Piquet risked dry tyres and any doubts he must have had about that were resolved at the first chicane when his Lotus found itself in closest acquaintance with the tyre barrier and out of the race.

Senna made a flying start, Prost did not. 'In these wet conditions I was not very confident – which was why I did make a bad start,' Prost said. He was fourth as they crossed the line to complete lap 1, second by lap 12. 'Alain was pushing hard to get back at me so I just concentrated on maintaining the gap,' Senna said. 'With wet tyres over a full race distance and no pit stop it was a bit difficult.'

He added: 'The conditions were changing constantly, particularly out in the forest where it was much wetter than in the stadium.' Deep into the race Prost spun, recovered and finished 13.609 seconds behind. Prost: 'I kept up the pressure until I spun. I think my wet tyres were a bit more worn than Ayrton's and the brakes were not perfect either – but that was because we had expected the track to dry out much more as the race went on.' Prost 60, Senna 57, Berger 25.

Hungaroring, Thursday 5 August. It was damp and overcast and Prost went quickest, Senna only fifth. 'At the end of the session, when the track was almost completely dry, it was just a matter of getting a clear lap and I didn't get one. Tomorrow . . .'

Hungaroring, Friday 6 August. The sun came out and Senna came out with 1 minute 27.635 – pole, of course – Prost only 1 minute 28.778 and a place on the fourth row of the grid. He'd had a vibration in the engine of his race car and used the spare. Senna: 'It was hard work and it is going to be a long, hot race. It's good to be starting from the front row because overtaking is so difficult.'

Hungaroring, Sunday 7 August. Senna led from start to finish, Prost squeezing up to second by lap 47. The gap: under two seconds. Now Prost harried and hounded Senna. They turned on to the straight. Two back markers were hugging the left. Halfway down the straight Senna dived out into the middle of the track and Prost – screwing the engine just like Ricard – went to the extreme right, surging, surging. The corner at the end of the straight: a right-hander. Prost, almost level with Senna, would have the racing line . . .

As they reached the corner Prost did have it and he was fractionally ahead. He took the corner but his impetus flung him wide as he tried to angle the car to the next corner rushing at them, another right-hander; not very wide, but wide enough – the width of a car. Senna was through on the inside like a thief. It was the decisive moment of the race. Senna: 'Alain was pushing hard and he was quicker than me. He managed to go through and we avoided each other – I held my breath, for a moment I thought we would both go off the road.' Prost: 'The moment with Ayrton was the most worrying thing. I was surprised because Ayrton did not try to close the door. It could have worked – then almost immediately something happened at the front of my car and I got a huge vibration.' It was tight enough at the end, Senna winning by 0.529 of a second. Hardest I've worked all season, Senna said. Senna and Prost 66, Berger 28.

It was Senna's sixth win of the season. All manner of records were moving rapidly into focus, but most immediately that of greatest number of wins in a season. This stood at seven, by Prost in 1984 and Jim Clark in 1963. (Interesting how the name Clark keeps coming into the narrative, isn't it?) Senna had six races left to equal and beat it, six . . .

Somewhere in Britain, Tuesday 16 August. Prost tested Honda's new V10 normally aspirated engine at a circuit sealed against prying eyes. Senna was at Monza testing the Honda turbo engine. On Thursday Prost tested the V10 at Silverstone, then flew to Italy to test the Honda turbo. Senna flew to Silverstone to test the V10. He crashed 'heavily' at Copse and did considerable damage to the car. This made Peter Warr wonder out loud how Senna was coping with a normally aspirated Formula One engine. He had not of course driven one since he'd had a brief go in the Williams and McLaren, 1983.

Spa, Friday 26 August. Senna quickest, Prost next. 'The engine was working well. The last lap with the second set of tyres was really good and I think I might have been able to go quicker on a later lap if I had not been forced to back off because of Tarquini's incident.' (Gabriele Tarquini,

Coloni, shredded a tyre and was limping towards the pits on three wheels.) Saturday was wet, Prost didn't go out at all and Senna was fourth quickest. 'I used the spare car in the untimed morning session so I wanted to check my race car. In fact I drove both in qualifying and everything was fine.'

Spa, Sunday 28 August. Senna led from start to finish, Prost half a minute behind. Senna: 'Today was not as hard as Hungary, for example, but the car's handling deteriorated because of the oil on the circuit and I had to keep it consistent. Although I have to carry on the way I have been doing, I must agree that Alain is in a difficult position now for the World Championship.' Senna 75, Prost 72, Berger 28.

Prost said that 'Ayrton is better than me at the moment. I changed the settings of my car before the start for less downforce and better fuel consumption but although I saved a lot of fuel the car was a lot slower on the oily track. I am not upset. Now we are going to try and win all the races [McLaren as a team, of course] and Ayrton is going to be World Champion.'

It was an enigmatic selection of words and everyone wondered, everyone wondered. Five races left and in the next Prost was to conjure a master stroke which argued very forcibly that he did not accept Ayrton Senna was going to be World Champion. And before we leave Spa . . . McLaren had taken the Constructor's Championship, Senna had equalled the record for pole position in a season – nine – and, of course, equalled Prost and Clark's total of wins in a season. He had five races left to beat it, five . . .

Monza, Friday 9 September. Goto: 'The experience from testing here has been useful but we have not yet done full tank testing which will be necessary for Sunday.' Senna was quickest, Prost next. One-tenth of a second lay between them, and that over 5.80 kilometres. Senna: 'I only used one set of tyres on the race car because I wanted to check that everything was OK with the spare car that I am using this weekend. The traffic was not too bad but I made a mistake in the spare car and went straight on at the second chicane.'

Monza, Saturday 10 September. Senna took pole from Prost and that broke the nine-in-a-season total of Ronnie Peterson (1973), Lauda (1974 and 1975) and Piquet (1984). Senna dedicated the record to 'his team and all those who had helped him get it'.

Monza, Sunday 11 September. Senna went off into the distance, Prost grappling with a misfire. Prost sensed he wasn't going to finish the race and wondered . . . and wondered . . . and wondered what might happen if he turned the boost up and pushed Senna hard. Fuel was marginal, as they say. If Prost pushed Senna hard, would Senna – not knowing the magnitude of the misfire – respond, guzzle fuel in an attempt to hold Prost off and run out himself before the end? A provocative prognostication. Prost acted on it, dropped out on lap 35 and because Nakajima (in the Lotus Honda) had also had a misfire Goto 'instructed Ayrton to slow down for the sake of safety'. But both Ferraris were chasing him hard now, towards the end of the race, and 'Ayrton once again had to increase his speed'. With just under two laps to go Senna could see both the Ferraris in his wing mirrors, drawing closer and closer. He was not, he would insist, 'worried'.

Going into the chicane Jean-Louis Schlesser (Williams) lost control and Senna thought he could nip through. Instead Schlesser came back and punted Senna hard. The McLaren was pitched across the track and came to rest straddling the kerb. Senna was out of the race. How much fuel did he have left? No-one has ever answered that question. All Honda would say was that 'Ayrton did not wish to apportion blame for the accident.' But why had he been there at all? Why didn't he wait, overtake Schlesser at his leisure a few moments afterwards? Because Senna lived by risk in such circumstances, and sometimes that took him to the wrong place at the wrong time.

Estoril, Friday 23 September. Senna was quickest, Prost next but Prost took pole on the Saturday – only the third time Senna hadn't. And on the Saturday Prost began to apply psychological pressure in the most obvious way. With fifteen minutes of the session left he changed into his civilian clothing, slung a purple pullover across his shoulders and made his way to the pit-lane wall to watch. He was saying to Senna: I've done 1 minute 17.411 and I know you can't beat it. Senna didn't beat it. Now Prost compounded the pressure by saying: 'I was not terribly interested in getting pole. There was no point in taking any more risks just for the sake of a tenth of a second. It's the first time in a long while that I have been completely satisfied with the set-up of my engine in qualifying specification.' Senna: 'With my first set of tyres I had already done 1 minute 17.8 seconds when they were worn. Normally on my second try I would have expected to go even faster. Unfortunately it was impossible to get a clear run.'

Estoril, Sunday 25 September. Senna took the lead at the first corner but as they rounded the right-hander into the long pit-lane straight Prost was directly behind him. As they reached the start-finish line Prost jinked right and drew abreast. They were doing 190 miles an hour. Senna now moved over, forcing Prost toward the pit-lane wall. A cluster of pit boards were dragged backwards, people ducked – if the cars had touched they could have cannoned anywhere. Prost: 'It was very dangerous. I could do nothing – if I'd backed off I might have hit his rear wheel. If we have to take risks like that to settle the World Championship . . . well, I don't care about it,

OK? If he wants the Championship that badly he can have it.'

Senna said only that he was angry because Prost had almost forced him on to the grass at the start.

The pressure had reached Senna. His anger had taken him to a moment where his judgement went completely and he did something bordering on the crazy. I repeat: if he had hit Prost the cars could have cannoned anywhere. Prost won the race, Senna – worried by high fuel consumption and oversteer – was sixth. Prost 81, Senna 76, Berger 37, Boutsen 25, Alboreto 24.

Afterwards in the quiet of the motorhome Prost sat and beckoned Senna over. 'Ayrton,' he said very softly, 'I didn't know you wanted the World Championship that badly . . .'

And that was the harmony broken.

Jerez, Friday 30 September. Senna was quickest, Prost fifth. Senna: 'It is quite difficult to get the car to work here. We changed the chassis set-up quite a lot after the morning session, which made an improvement, and I was lucky to get my one clear lap when I did because the car and the engine were working well.' Prost: 'There is no traction at all and the car feels very uncomfortable.'

Jerez, Saturday 1 October. Senna pole, Prost next to him on the front row. Senna: 'We have to concentrate on getting the chassis set-up to be right through the full distance. Let's hope the computer works accurately and we can use the engine to its best performance.' Prost: 'In qualifying, with my driving style, it is difficult to use the boost but I think I can be much better under race conditions.'

Jerez, Sunday 2 October. Prost led from start to finish and Senna, who was getting 'minus' reading from his fuel gauge, nursed his car home fourth. Prost 84, Senna 79, Berger 38, Boutsen 25, Alboreto 24.

Now we must look at mathematics. In the Formula One

World Championship you can count only your eleven best finishes and Prost was already being punished by that. Spain was his twelfth, and all he could discard were second places (worth, of course, six points). Senna was in a much stronger position. Spain had been his eleventh but he could discard the single point from Portugal, then the three from Spain. It meant this: if Senna won in Japan he became World Champion. Senna, incidentally, was not idle in the month between Spain and Japan. He tested the V10 at Imola and recorded a time which, as someone pointed out, would have put him third fastest in qualifying for the San Marino Grand Prix in May – slower only than the times he and Prost had done with the turbo engines, but before we leave Spain we must listen to the words of Osamu Goto. They were to create a furore. After the Grand Prix he said: 'There is no difference between the turbos and the aspirated engines here. However, we controlled the drivability, response and consumption of our engine – consequently Alain was able to get a good result by his effort. Now, with two races to go, Honda will be ready to give our drivers an equal chance to win, and we hope for more good competition at Suzuka and Adelaide.' It was an unfortunate choice of words because it implied that Honda had not been doing that already. What it meant was: Honda will keep on giving their drivers an equal chance to win.

Paris, Monday 17 October. From Jean-Marie Balestre, President of FISA to Tadashi Kume, President of Honda: 'As you know the Fédération Internationale de l'Automobile (FIA) comprises 92 member countries representing 72 million motorists. The greatest marketing experts consider the FIA Formula One World Championship to be one of the world's major competitions, along with the Olympic Games and the World Cup. Each Grand Prix is watched by several hundred million spectators.

'This year the manufacturers' World Champion is Honda

179

Motors Co [sic] and I should like to congratulate you on this great success. However, there are still a few World Championship events to be run in 1988 and all the world over eyes will be riveted on the Japanese and Australian Grands Prix, the results of which will be decisive for drivers.

'We should make every effort to ensure that utmost technical objectivity reigns over these two competitions and that equipment (car or engine) of equal quality be made available to the two drivers of the MacLaren [sic] Team, for otherwise the image of the World Championship, present and future, would be tarnished.

'I thank you in advance for helping the FIA to achieve this end of giving the necessary instructions to all the Honda technical executives who may play a part in these two forthcoming events.'

Balestre expanded on this to Brazilian journalists. 'I will do everything to obtain guarantees from both Honda and McLaren that Prost and Senna are treated equally during the final two Formula One Grands Prix. It isn't that I've had any cause for doubt; just that, this year, we have found ourselves faced with particular circumstances with the domination of one team.' If Balestre found that equal treatment was not being given, 'serious sanctions would be taken'.

Press room, Suzuka, Thursday 27 October (on notice boards). Tadashi Kume to Jean-Marie Balestre:

'I thank you for your letter of 17 October.

'I would like to congratulate the FIA, the FISA and yourself, as president of the FIA, for the successful efforts put forth in establishing the Formula One World Championships, and the prosperous condition of motorsports today.

'I believe that motorsports should be conducted in the spirit of fair play and safety, in order to obtain the interest and emotional involvement of spectators and people concerned.

'Honda Motor Co. Ltd sees fairness as the highest requirement of its philosophy for conducting business, and sets this quality as an ideology in its corporate dealings. From the outset, Honda, as a Formula One engine supplier with such a background, has been careful to supply engines having identical levels of performance and technology to racing teams and individual drivers who contribute their highest levels of skills, incorporating the firm attitude of our policy.

'As you mention in your letter, the Formula One Championship for this year is drawing to a close, leaving just two events to be run: the Japan Grand Prix and the Australia Grand Prix. We also appreciate that this year's series of races has been a most exciting and significant championship.

'For the last two races, Honda will continue to supply identical engines which will allow the drivers to give supreme demonstrations of their skills, as we have always done in line with our basic philosophy.

'Finally I would like to express my sincere gratitude to you for consistently performing your important role as president of the FIA.'

While this was reverberating (and it did reverberate), somewhere over the polar route two men were asleep in their seats in a Jumbo. One was Robin Green, the other Dennis Rushen. They had both sensed that Ayrton Senna was going to become World Champion at Suzuka. They would both be there to see it.

That Thursday night Prost didn't sleep more than an hour. 'I should have taken a pill, I suppose, but the later it got the more I was afraid to, in case I was drowsy through the morning.'

Suzuka, Friday 28 October. The untimed session: Prost quickest (1 minute 44.620), Senna next (1 minute 44.484). The timed session: Senna 1:42.157, Berger 1:43.548, Prost

181

1:43.806. Senna's time was achieved – and it was an achievement – on his first set of tyres early on. 'Unfortunately on the second set I could not get a clear lap before the tyres were too far worn.' Prost: 'It is a combination of chassis and engine problems. I think the track has changed since this morning, but I am finding that the power is coming in very suddenly and then fading along the straights. I am sure that it is something that can easily be cured and I expect to be faster tomorrow.'

Suzuka, Saturday 29 October. The untimed session. Prost had a fuel leak, his overalls were soaked. He moved quickly into the pits, climbed quickly out of the car and began dousing himself with water. Petrol burns. That had been the spare car. Now Prost took his race car and ran on full tanks. The engine was fine, just fine. At lunchtime Prost felt optimistic. In the timed session Prost was on the track within five minutes of the start and put himself alongside Senna on the front row. Then it rained – more of a drizzle, really – after ten minutes. The rain stopped at 1.30 and Mauricio Gugelmin lost control of his Leyton House March and it hammered into the armco. 'My fault,' Gugelmin would say. 'It just kept coming round until it hit the rail and although the impact didn't feel hard it's torn the engine mounts.' Taking the car away needed sixteen minutes. A few minutes of the session remained. Inevitably it would be a cavalry charge.

Prost went for it but was baulked by Stefano Modena (Euro Brun); Senna went for it and somehow found a clear lap. 1 minute 41.853. With two minutes left Prost made a final assault; he got a clear lap, too, but exiting the chicane took second gear instead of fourth: 1 minute 42.177. Senna had his twelfth pole position of the season. Senna: 'If there had been no rain we would have been able to do a little bit more work on the car but I was lucky to get a clear road on my last lap – because it was my second run on my last set of tyres and they were not optimum.' Prost: 'I missed a gear at the last corner on my quick lap and I have to say that it was my own fault. We also had a problem with the pop-off valve which gave me less boost than normal.'

Suzuka, Sunday 30 October. Morning. The warm-up. Senna 1:46.372, Mansell 1:46.745, Boutsen 1:46.885, Prost 1:47.063. It had been sunny then but now grey cloud was moving across. Afternoon. Light rain stabbed down and with fifteen minutes to go teams were readying wet weather tyres. The rain passed. It was still a dry race although the track might be greasy at the beginning. On the parade lap Senna and Prost set off as if it was the race itself – but that was only to see what the track surface was really like, how the cars would behave on it. They slowed. They came to rest on the grid, the twin columns stretching away behind them. Ayrton Senna faced the great moment of his life, the moment he had fashioned his whole life around. He needed to cover 51 laps – cover 298.809 kilometres – all the way back to where the car now rested, and be faster than all the others. He needed to wait, as he scanned the track ahead and he needed to obey his dictum: 'You must think of everything in the enormous turmoil at the start of a race. It is a totally unreal moment, it is like a dream, like entering another world . . .'

He had waited many times in many places with his eyes on the red light since that very first time at Brands Hatch, March 1981. Now the red light came on, quick as the blink of an eye. Three seconds later it blinked to green. Senna knew the clutch was 'sensitive', let it out and the car hiccoughed about four metres forward. Both his arms were out of the cockpit, flailing the air, warning – and pleading with – every one of the twelve cars in the column behind travelling in a wild rush towards him: miss me, miss me . . .

Prost had gone. Berger, directly behind Senna, pitched the Ferrari left, taking the middle of the track to go past

183

Senna; Piquet, behind Berger, pitched the Lotus right, the car slithering towards the pit-lane wall under the stark power of acceleration, Piquet caught that and was gone.

Inside the cockpit of the McLaren Senna thought crisply and clinically that 'it was all over for me. I dropped the clutch and got the car moving again and then the engine stalled again.' The car was drifting forward so slowly a pedestrian might have overtaken it; but it was drifting forward, because the track sloped . . .

The middle of the grid – Alboreto, Patrese, Gugelmin – were surging by. Senna's engine caught. 'I staggered away. I was really lucky.' He was. He was also lost in the pack, fourteenth, as they wheeled and turned into the first corner. Prost was in the lead . . . far, far away with Berger harrying him. Prost drew Berger away from the pack. Only Capelli could stay with them. The rest were back there over the hill. On lap 1 Senna had moved up to eighth. In other words he had overtaken five cars. (Mansell had nudged Warwick and gone into the pits.)

On lap 2 he took Patrese and Nannini. That lifted him to sixth but it didn't seem important. Senna was cutting through the field like a man prepared to risk everything to vindicate his life. No man was as incisive in dealing with traffic, the car wielded as a surgeon might wield a knife . . . but it had to take time, even Senna couldn't overtake everywhere. As he crossed the line to complete that second lap many hands in the crowd flicked their stopwatches. The gap Prost-to-Senna: nine seconds. And Prost had a clear road, no obstacles at all. The feeling he had was 'perfect'. There was, as he drew further and further away, an 'occasional gear selection problem' but nothing too serious. 'I was controlling the pace, taking care of the fuel.'

On lap 3 Senna took Boutsen and that was fifth. The stopwatches flicked again. The gap Prost-to-Senna had gone out to around ten seconds. On lap 4 he took Alboreto just before the chicane – he flung the car on to the inside line, the McLaren's wheels almost caressing the grass at the side of the track, and that was fourth. The stopwatches flicked again. The gap had gone out to 12.936 seconds. In the dispassionate language of statistics this is how it had unfolded:

Prost	1:55.293	Senna	2:04.246
	1:51.028		1:51.579
	1:49.431		1:52.210
	1:49.837		1:50.490

On lap 5 the gap went out to thirteen seconds. Senna held fourth place across laps 4 to 10. 'I started to find my rhythm and I was going quicker and quicker.'

Prost	1:49.190	Senna	1:49.474
	1:48.425		1:48.104
	1:48.306		1:48.625
	1:48.341		1:48.186
	1:49.888		1:49.160
	1:49.234		1:48.527

On lap 10 the gap had steadied to 11.628 seconds and Senna moved on Berger. He took him on that and was third. Meanwhile something interesting was happening up front. Young Capelli was challenging Prost and what Prost couldn't afford was second place, especially since Senna would then be directly behind him – and charging. Worse – for Prost – the sky was darkening. No man on earth could make a racing car go faster than Ayrton Senna in the wet. On lap 14 Capelli was right with Prost and those spitting drops of rain had begun to fall from folds of white-grey cloud. As they crossed the line to complete lap 15 Capelli angled the March out and drew level with Prost, just got ahead before Prost responded. Capelli would say that 'I was so happy it happened there where all my team could see it and see their efforts rewarded. I didn't have long to enjoy the moment . . .'

Still Senna was coming, coming, coming and as Prost held off Capelli at the end of the straight there he was, within sight at last, rounding the corner at the other end of the straight. From lap 16:

Prost	1:51.379	Senna	1:49.115
	1:55.865		1:53.254
	1:57.550		1:58.101
	1:56.330		1:51.507

They were together now, Prost, Capelli, Senna and suddenly Capelli pulled over to the right of the track, his engine gone. Senna stole through. It was raining harder. And there was Prost, filling the road in front of him, and there were three back-markers filling the road in front of Prost. At the end of lap 27 Senna nipped out and took Prost – on power – along the finishing straight. As it happened, Prost had missed a gear . . .

Could Prost stay with Senna, then get back at him? He clung from lap 28 . . .

Prost	1:51.008	Senna	1:49.295
	1:47.824		1:46.965

1:47.402	1:47.006
1:46.491	1:46.801
1:46.522	1:47.615

Prost: 'The gearbox problem got worse which was frustrating because I'd make up time on Ayrton then lose it again with a single missed change. But the worst problem was definitely the traffic.'

With five laps to go Senna's hand was repeatedly out of the cockpit, the index finger stabbing towards the heavens. Stop the thing now, he was saying, it's raining and the track is extremely slippery. The irony of that. He'd have won his first Grand Prix at Monaco in '84 if they hadn't stopped it and given it to Prost . . .

Senna's tyres glistened. Prost was shed now, lost somewhere back there.

Even James Hunt, commentating on British television, caught the mood – perhaps unconsciously – as Senna moved calmly and clinically round the final, triumphant lap. 'Unless there is an act of God, we are looking at the new World Champion.' That was one aspect which was never going to worry Ayrton Senna. God was with him in the cockpit. As he rounded the last corner he raised a fist – only shoulder high – and shook it in a tight, taut gesture of exultation. As he crossed the line both hands were out, and that was another, more expansive gesture of exultation. In the crowd Brazilian flags waved and fluttered. And still he kept shaking his fists, bang, bang, bang all the way to the first corner. Then – it was almost a private moment, almost unseen – he let his neck muscles go slack, let his head fall gently back against the hump of the cockpit. He'd done it.

He faced the television cameras and his eyes were veined red. He must have been crying. 'It was,' he said, measuring each word, 'a lot of pressure. I still can't believe it.' At the press conference he added: 'Even after I got through into the lead it was very difficult with the back-markers. They did not behave very professionally with Alain and me.' It was true. It was just a curious time to say it, as if the mechanics of the race wouldn't release him.

He came from that press conference, Ron Dennis at his side, and he saw Rushen. 'Ayrton was overcome with emotion, well overcome. In the early days we'd taught him swear words because that's a natural thing you do with foreign drivers. One particular expression he thought was great but he'd say it at all the wrong times. He'd send me Christmas cards with the words on. So as he walked by at Suzuka I said "You're still an [expletive expletive]" and he didn't know whether to laugh or cry.'

Later, he sat on the pit-lane wall. Keith Sutton: 'There was only a French photographer and myself still there. He was doing an interview with Brazilian television and actually watching a re-run of the race on a big screen at the same time. The light was fantastic, a beautiful sky. We were taking pictures with the flash. It was very emotional. And he did the interview with Brazilian television and the television chap had been very close to him when he started, a bit like me. He said: "Now you're World Champion the pressure will be off. You have been very, very dedicated and you have pushed a lot of people aside during your years, a lot of close friends. Will this change?" Tears rolled from his eyes.'

CHAPTER ELEVEN

The Bitter Year

Alain Prost craned his craggy face towards the microphone and said: 'Ayrton has a small problem. He thinks he can't kill himself because he believes in God and I think that's very dangerous for the other drivers.'

In a direct response for this book, Senna says: 'That's his own thoughts, his own conclusions and words. They don't reflect my thoughts and my beliefs at all.'

Adelaide, November 1989 and it had come to the first of the two cold autumns; and bitter cold it was, conducted in great outpourings and great silences, compounded by crashes, judged by tribunals, fed by accusations and counter-accusations. Carefully constructed friendships were broken apart, fines levied, appeals heard, the behaviour of some of the leading players publicly questioned, the integrity of Formula One hacked and hammered around day by day, FISA itself seen as inconsistent. There were even motor races, too – and strange creatures they were, each chilling it more and more until in the end a permafrost covered the whole thing.

The season began hot, of course, in Rio a few seconds after the start of the Brazilian Grand Prix. Senna, on pole, put the power down and the McLaren slewed slightly into the middle of the track towards Riccardo Patrese in the Williams. Gerhard Berger thrust the snout of his Ferrari up into them trying to get in between, couldn't, flung the Ferrari right to take Senna on the inside as they all coursed down to the first corner, a right-hander. As Berger drew alongside, Senna twitched right – making Berger twitch

189

even further right, two wheels almost off the track. Patrese now turned into the corner and that sandwiched Senna, who still had Berger on his right – and Berger did have two wheels on the grass. Senna and Berger touched; Senna had to go into the pits, losing a whole lap, and would finish eleventh. 'Really, the car ran perfectly – apart from that first corner where the only way out of the problem would have been to go straight up in the air. Patrese and Berger trapped me and I lost the nose section. That's all there is to it.'

Berger quite naturally saw it the other way. 'Senna chopped across twice to try to make me back off but he shouldn't try that with me. Never in my life will I back off in that situation.' Senna says now, reflecting on it: 'Today my honest view is that three cars tried to do the same corner at the same time and there was only room for one.'

At Imola Senna won. 'The car wasn't going too well under heavy braking at first and with Alain pushing me hard it took a while to settle into a rhythm, but once the gap reached six seconds I was able to maintain that pace and after Alain spun the pressure was really off.'

Behind these most innocent words the whole season began to break up. What happened looked innocent, too, a simple, safe overtaking move at a corner called Tosa. Berger had crashed, survived a dreadful fire and the race was re-started. Prost took the lead, held it round the graceful curve of Tamburello and positioned the car in the centre of the track on the short surge to Tosa. Senna jinked left, went round Prost on the outside – Tosa is right then left – and had the racing line. He was in the lead. He did not lose it.

Prost was visibly angry after the race and said he didn't want to say much at all, which itself was instructive because invariably Prost is eloquent whether he's won or lost. What he did suggest darkly was that an 'accord' had been breached. Accord? What accord could that be?

Only later did details emerge – whichever McLaren got to the first corner first would not come under attack from the other McLaren, and demonstrably Senna had overtaken there. Prost was so angry he did not attend the post-race press conference (and was fined 5,000 dollars) but vanished in a helicopter.

McLaren tested at a track called Pembrey near Llanelli, Wales. Ron Dennis would say: 'They had agreed that whoever made the better start would exit the first corner ahead. Alain made the better start, but Ayrton took the corner, which was not consistent with the agreement they had made. A subsequent discussion between them at Pembrey resulted in an apology from Ayrton. The problem is now resolved . . .'

It wasn't.

Senna would look deep into himself before he explained, patiently and laboriously, the case for his defence in this curious matter. 'Yes, there was an accord, and not only at Imola but elsewhere. It was also present several times last season and it was he who proposed not to attack in braking for the first corner, not me. At Imola we had spoken about it.' Senna now explained that Prost had made the same proposal at Imola the year before. 'It was his idea. I had never found myself in this kind of situation before and I said OK. We respected this agreement for several races. Then, as our relationship deteriorated, we stopped doing so. This year after the winter breaks we were on more friendly terms again. Then came Imola. I remembered the agreement of the previous year and I put the question: what shall we do about the first bend? He replied: the same as '88. So that was the situation. Only, I think there is a divergence of interpretation of the concept of this accord and then, above all, a disproportion between the consequences of the overtaking move and his reaction after it. At the re-start he got away a little better than me

191

but I was immediately on his tail to profit from the suction. I thus gathered speed and I made my move well before the braking area. My overtaking move was begun, in my opinion, well before the first corner and as a result outside the terms of our accord. What should I have done? Lift off in a straight line because I was going faster than him? We're in races, yes or no? And I braked later than him, I was better placed, that's all. Never have I wished to betray our accord, not for one second did I think it was dishonest [and, subsequently and poignantly], the agreement has always been that no overtaking manoeuvre would happen *under braking* [author's italics] at a first corner. My overtaking was initiated by slipstreaming Prost during the straight and by the first corner we were side by side!

'After Imola Ron Dennis spoke to me about it for a long time and I explained my point of view. He told me Prost had taken it very badly, that he was disgusted, that he wanted to retire, etc ... Ron was very disquieted at the idea of our reunion at Pembrey. Ron exercised an enormous pressure on me to smooth things over. At first I didn't want to because I didn't find that correct. But he insisted and he said to me: if you say sorry it's forgotten, everything is back in order. And I did it. It was stupid because it meant I had changed my opinion on the concept of our accord and on the overtaking move. Now, I have never changed my opinion. I said sorry for the good of the team, to calm it down, because I was almost compelled to. I wiped a tear away because at that moment it was harming me. Ron did a good job convincing me to accommodate things but it wasn't easy. Perhaps I have the air of a very cold, frosty person but that's wrong, you know. I have a heart and I received a very gentle education. Perhaps I am strong as far as my job is concerned but I am no less a human being because of it. The three of us were there and Ron said: "That will stay between us, we won't speak about it any more, OK?"'

Two days later Prost told the French sports paper *L'Equipe*: 'I do not wish to drag McLaren into difficulties caused by the behaviour of Senna. McLaren has always been loyal to me. At a level of technical discussion I shall not close the door completely but for the rest I no longer wish to have any business with him. I appreciate honesty and he is not honest.' As words go, they don't come any stronger.

When Senna arrived at Monaco 'people were speaking only about it [the interview in *L'Equipe*]. I am persuaded that in acting like that Alain wanted to implicate me, make me carry the can, make me culpable, in a phrase: put the pressure on me. I decided not to react.'

Only later, in a sudden, heartfelt sentence would Senna say, conjuring finality: 'Since that day at Monaco it's finished, I don't want to hear any more talk about that guy.'

He could isolate himself from it, of course, retreat to his private places, and that is what he did. On the Saturday at Monaco Senna produced one of the great laps in qualifying – 1 minute 22.308 seconds, while Prost could do no better than 1:23.456. Typically, Senna conceded that it 'was obviously a very satisfying lap. I had a little too much understeer on my first set of tyres but everything was fine when we put on the second set. On my second lap with them I got a clear run and recorded my best time, despite making a slight mistake at Casino Square [!]. The engine was fantastic.'

So was the boy himself.

Flag to flag, as they say, in the race. 'At the start I didn't want to push too hard but when we came to lapping traffic I began to pull away, perhaps rather more than I expected but it was just as well because I suffered gearbox problems in the second half of the race, losing second gear then first. It made the car extremely difficult to drive in traffic but I kept pressing on as hard as I could because

I didn't want to give Alain any indication that I was in trouble . . .'

Prost's summary was also pitched on to the pragmatic rather than passionate level. 'I had a really difficult time when we started lapping slower cars, then I lost about twenty seconds when the gearbox stuck in neutral at the hairpin, so I settled for second place after I re-started because Ayrton was so far ahead . . .' Prost just hadn't realized.

In Mexico, Prost 'tried to speak to me. I refused. I didn't want to fall into a trap. I didn't want to speak to him any more, it didn't interest me.' Senna won Mexico and took his total of pole positions to thirty-three, equalling Jim Clark. He beat it in Phoenix. 'I feel rather light-headed, with no weight on my shoulders now that I have established this new record. I take the record from Jim Clark, a man I never saw racing but who by his results was obviously a very special driver. It is a big moment for me.'

In Canada Senna drove one of the great races in a storm which recalled sodden memories of Monaco '84 except that here it dried. After four laps, Senna – leading – came in for slicks, was fifth when he emerged. He was up to third when the rain began again, up to second when Boutsen pitted and actually started to attack Patrese for the lead. The rain was heavy, Patrese was on wet weather tyres and Senna was still on the slicks. Even Senna could not maintain this almost fantastic assault – no other man on earth could have mounted it at all – and drifted back. Even Senna would need wets and on lap 21 pitted again, sixth when he emerged and almost sixty seconds behind the current leader, Patrese. He bided his time and then he charged, a proper, classical motor racing charge. It was almost hypnotic to watch, this certainty of control. Patrese pitted for more wets and Derek Warwick (Arrows) found himself in the lead, Senna coming at him like a storm himself. Senna took him and seemed to be cruising it. The track began to dry and Senna went on and on in lonely isolation up front until with only three laps left the engine let go. 'For the last twenty laps I had a blistered left rear tyre. The engine gave no indication there was a problem. I just felt it tighten up and that was it.' Never once in the bitter season would Ayrton Senna voice complaints about mechanical unreliability to the waiting ears; he would accept it with The Face downcast for a moment and then with considerable dignity.

At least France was dry. Senna did not take pole – inevitably if it didn't go to him it went to Prost – and didn't even complete the first lap of the race. 'I was just changing from first to second when the drive simply vanished. There was nothing more I could do about it.' Senna parked the car and walked away, displaying that dignity again. Later on he would receive some astonishing and undignified criticism for what he did while the car was actually moving.

He took pole at Silverstone, took the lead but 'I had difficulty selecting third gear on the downchange almost from the start. Four or five laps before I finally spun off I almost went off at the same place. Eventually I couldn't get the gear and that was that. I could not take the corner in neutral!' That start, incidentally, had had dramas all of its own as Senna moved past Prost, who suggested that if they'd been 10cm closer 'we'd have crashed'.

As Prost and Mansell passed Senna's marooned car Mansell waved congratulations to Prost, whom he could clearly see grinning in the cockpit. How did Prost feel? 'Happy . . .' Nor can we ignore the reaction of the crowd who waved their arms in pleasure that Senna had gone off, a most un-British reaction and one which, if truth be told, demonstrated how far Senna was from a place in their affections. Over the years they had seen only what he had permitted them to see, the cold, frosty person.

In Germany in the Friday morning session Senna crashed. 'I made a mistake and spun off. I damaged the car and the mechanics had to work very hard to repair it, a task they managed with twenty minutes of the qualifying session left. The spin was my fault. I put a wheel on to the kerb under braking and the car snapped round on me. It was a stupid mistake. It was quite a big impact and I had a slight headache.' In those twenty minutes he took pole a fraction more than a second faster than Prost. He was lucky in the race. With three laps to go Prost, leading, lost top gear and Senna was by in an instant, swift as a knife thrust. 'I did not have any particular strategy to pass Alain. I was concentrating first on getting as close to him as possible. I was easing towards him . . . I felt I was close enough to profit by any mistake he might make . . . then he had a problem . . .'

Hungary belonged to Mansell, Senna second, Prost fourth; and they came to Spa, where, in the wet, Senna was superb, leading the whole way. 'I had tremendous difficulty keeping the car safe on the ground. There was so much water the car was aquaplaning so you don't feel safe at all to go fast. It's difficult to motivate and to push, but as far as the car was concerned the beginning was very good for five laps or so, very stable. Then I think the front tyre pressures got too low and it started to be even harder for me. The back-markers? As usual it's always difficult in the water when you see nothing and if you wait you lose five, ten seconds. It was a very big risk and very dangerous but that was the same for everybody.' And those tyre pressures? 'We put the blankets on the tyres and the front blankets didn't work – well, they only started to work a few minutes before the start so I think we got the wrong pressures. It meant that when the race did start the rear tyres were at a different pressure to the front because the rear tyres were hot.' Towards the end Senna slowed dramatically – and I

196

am not using the word carelessly – especially on the last lap. 'There was no reason to carry on going fast. I only needed to cross the line first – by how much was not a problem.'

The miraculous – yes, miraculous – aspect was that, like Canada, none of this was evident to the spectator, who saw only smoothness, ease of style. At Spa neither Lotus qualified for the race and Senna was moved to a great melancholy. His voice sounded heavy, almost cumbersome and he spoke the words slowly. 'If you make the wrong decisions in this business, sooner or later you have to pay but I know most of the people there and they are very nice, very good. I feel extremely sad.'

It is time to look at the points. Prost had 62, Senna 51, Mansell 38, Patrese 25, Boutsen 20. Five races remained. Clearly Prost would have to start dropping points soon – you can only count your eleven best finishes, remember, and departing Spa he already had ten, Senna six.

Between Spa and Monza, a period of two weeks, Prost talked and Senna talked, although not to each other. Prost revealed that he had spoken to Dennis at Monaco, saying to him: 'It's with McLaren that I would still like to drive but I will drive better in another team.' Prost continued: 'I had already spoken to him about it on the telephone. I even thought of stopping then. It was close. I decided to join Ferrari in Belgium. Regrets at leaving McLaren? No. Everything I did over six years with them was positive. I leave with my conscience clear thanks to the certainty that I have given the best of myself. I was living in a fantastic atmosphere. I had the possibility to say no to Senna joining the team but I thought the team would have need of a driver of his worth when I stopped.' (Senna: 'Correction. One year earlier than McLaren having Honda, both Ron and Prost even went to Japan especially to convince Honda to come to McLaren and yet Honda came to Lotus [1987]. As for 1988 I initiated the work towards Honda and Prost wouldn't have had Honda in 1988 if Senna was not part of the team! OK.') Now Prost again: 'I was had. It's a lesson, that's all. At Monza he is due to have the spare car, at Estoril it's me. For the three other Grands Prix it will be decided by our positions in the Championship.' And in conclusion: 'We'll truly see whether we are put on an equal footing or not. If they want to advantage Senna they have that possibility.'

Ominous . . .

A question to Senna: Is friendship possible in Formula One? 'Evidently it is, but terribly difficult because we all come from different horizons, with different educations, different cultures.' Another question: Will you ever speak to Prost again? 'I know that you must never say "never" but in this case I can't see what could make me change my mind. In ten years one might be able to exchange a few banalities but we won't be sincere. There will never again be any complicity between us, it's finished.'

And they came to Monza. We must start with the statistics, and they are these:

Friday	Free practice	Qualifying
Senna	1:25.979	1:25.021
Prost	1:26.135	1:25.872
Saturday		
Senna	1:26.243	1:23.720
Prost	1:27.444	1:25.510

Prost now said: 'Nothing working properly – car or engine. I just don't know what to say. Sometimes the car feels good, sometimes not. This morning with a low fuel load the chassis was not bad but the engine in qualifying was

impossible low down the rev range. Very disappointing.'
His hair shaggy as a mane, his face mournful, Prost began
to make louder and louder noises about equal treatment
and word of it spread like high voltage through the paddock; Ron Dennis was moved to hold an impromptu press
conference to deny this vehemently, pointing out that each
driver's car is prepared after lengthy and complex calcula-
tions. He also said: 'I think that was certainly the best pole
position of Ayrton's career to date. The conditions were still
very difficult and the track was still not completely dry
round the back of the circuit. This is his pole, not ours.'

There was, then, a troubled backdrop to Monza and
– although this was only an impression – a sense of
something beginning to work its way towards a climax;
not necessarily here, but surely soon. The forces in play
were too strong, too entrenched for anything else.

As it happened Senna led the race for 44 laps and the
engine blew up, letting Prost in. Senna summed it up like
this: 'From the start I had not needed to rev the engine as
high as it could have gone and about five laps before my
retirement the oil pressure warning light began flashing
intermittently. Then it began flashing more and more so
I reduced the revs slightly but there was nothing I could
really do. The engine broke coming down to Parabolica so
I switched it off and coasted into the corner when I spun
on my own oil.'

On the podium Prost deliberately lowered the trophy
into the adoring crowd below (he was joining Ferrari,
don't forget) and that gesture signalled the end of the
relationship with McLaren. Dennis, measuring his words
as carefully as Senna does, was speaking from the heart
when he said: 'We had a relationship that was based on
slow, progressive mutual respect for each other. Something
took place in the Italian Grand Prix that broke that relationship. He gave to the crowd the trophy for winning

the race, something which was not even his.' Then, again like Senna, he became another person as he added: 'When something breaks a relationship you have to become very professional and look after the values of the company.'

Prost had been making even louder noises about equal treatment. 'I want to race and I want to compete with Ayrton with the same equipment and I think the engine was not good at all ... the engine was very bad ... I am still a bit unhappy but that is normal because in the next four races I don't know what is going to happen ... I was complaining about the engine the whole weekend and it did not improve at all. It's very easy to say luck is on my side, luck is not on his side. You have to understand they don't make engines like this for Ayrton. The chassis was not bad at all. Sure, I don't feel very confident that is the problem ...'

These words wounded McLaren and by Portugal a statement had been drafted. It read: 'As a result of the consequences of press statements at the Italian Grand Prix, Alain Prost, Honda and McLaren have had extensive discussions and wish to put on record their intentions for creating the best possible working environment for the driver and the team for the remainder of the season. Honda and McLaren have again reassured Alain, to his satisfaction, of their commitment to equality and will continue the policy regardless of Alain's move to another team for the 1990 season.

'Alain deeply regrets the adverse publicity and the resulting embarrassment that has been caused by his actions. Honda and McLaren have accepted that these resulted from Alain's perception of his treatment by the team and were not made with malicious intent. He has agreed that in future any doubts that he might have about the parity of performance of his car will be discussed with the relevant engineers prior to comments being made to the press. The team also expresses its disdain and dissatisfaction over the inaccurate, unqualified and damaging statements made by third parties subsequent to Monza.'

At Portugal Senna said: 'If you have God on your side, everything becomes clear: white becomes white again, and black becomes black, and you realize what is really important in life.' The references to God would henceforth be made more and more often and with increasing intensity. The other Senna said: 'I'm obviously very satisfied with another pole position although I had a slight gear selection problem during the morning which recurred again in the afternoon. Going down into fourth gear at the end of the startline straight was where I encountered the problem, but the car went well.'

Now a deeper chill settled across Grand Prix racing. On lap 39 Mansell came into the pits, overshot and reversed – a clear, unequivocal breach of the regulations. He came out of the pits in fourth place, Senna ahead of him, then Berger and (briefly) Pierluigi Martini. For three laps Mansell was black-flagged as he hounded Senna and Mansell strongly denied that he had seen the flag. 'Have you ever been on that part of the circuit at that time? I was trying to overtake Senna, the sun was in my eyes and I couldn't see anything.' Senna, directly in front of Mansell, could see the flag but 'I wasn't sure about anything. I wasn't worried much about it because the flag wasn't for me.'

On lap 49, as they reached on to the start-finish straight – in fact as they crossed the line itself – Mansell moved to the right to overtake. Turn One, a right-hander, was flowing hard at them. The two cars were abreast. Dennis realized that Senna didn't realize Mansell was out of the race and started to tell him on the radio link. 'Ayrton couldn't hear clearly so he pressed the button and said "Repeat". I was in the process of repeating it when . . .'

. . . when Mansell was hugging the inside at the very mouth of Turn One and Senna, fractionally ahead, moved on to the racing line. He was coming across Mansell. His right rear wheel struck Mansell's left front and the McLaren rotated away into the sand trap, that right rear cocked absurdly into the air, wobbling like a broken limb. For a long time Senna stood, hands resting on the rim of the tyre barrier. The Championship had almost certainly fled from him. 'I felt something incredible going through my head. I wanted to walk for a while, to relax, to get events in their right order once again.'

He did walk – back towards the pits . . .

And the storm broke.

That late afternoon he said pointedly: 'Why did Nigel stay out after he was disqualified? Everybody can see the television transmission of what happened. I really don't want to comment . . .'

The following morning, when things were, he felt, in their right order again, he was more expansive though equally pointed. 'In the last year and a half I have learned that in a heated situation it is best to keep quiet. Mansell was out of the race and he shouldn't have tried to overtake. Just a few instants before the accident Ron Dennis gave me the news via radio that Mansell was disqualified. He hadn't finished telling me when the accident happened.' As Mansell drew abreast 'I didn't alter my position. I was going straight ahead. I didn't intend to get involved in a mix-up. In the position he was in it was impossible for him to get round the bend, he was too far on the inside. He did it just for the sake of trying and bumped into me. I have seen it again on TV. Everything is clear but I think we miss the point completely. What happened could have had a terrible ending. A disastrous ending. Mansell put in danger the life of another person. When I went off the track I managed to stop after 200 metres. There was a barrier. I could have lost my life. That is why I say that what happened is very dangerous.'

Mansell and Ferrari were fined 50,000 dollars and Mansell excluded from the next race, Spain. He was so enraged he said he might leave the sport altogether. 'I'd swear on the Bible I never saw the black flag.'

Enter Ron Dennis, also enraged. 'I think Nigel did know he was disqualified. It's a driver's obligations to know the regulations. The moment Nigel selected reverse gear in the pit lane he disqualified himself. I just don't accept Nigel didn't know he was disqualified. I just don't buy that horse manure. He knew. End of story. In Italy, Ferrari team manager Cesare Fiorio said Nigel asked on the radio "Why do I have to come in?" Why ask the question when he has said he didn't see the flag? Maybe he didn't, but what about the pit board or radio?'

Mansell, who was due to appear before the FISA tribunal in Paris to appeal, called a press conference in Spain. 'When I left Estoril I was under the impression I would be fined. There was no talk of a ban whatsoever. My point is this: you can have a mass murderer with all the evidence you want, but he is tried and found guilty beyond reasonable doubt before being hanged. I would suggest that there is plenty of reasonable doubt as to whether I deliberately ignored the black flag. If they believe honestly that I saw it and ignored it, I will have to consider retiring sooner than later from Formula One.' (At the Paris meeting, three Grand Prix jurors postponed a decision until 27 October.) And of the overtaking: 'He saw perfectly well that I was starting to overtake. Senna even turned his head towards me but he still cut in on me.'

There was a bizarre twist. Senna was black-flagged on his flying lap during qualifying for the Spanish Grand Prix, didn't slow down at all and was fined 20,000 dollars. He said he didn't see the flags. 'I made a mistake and I must pay.' He won the race comfortably and now needed to win the last two, Suzuka and Adelaide.

Suzuka. Ah, Suzuka. 'I want Prost to win the Championship as much as I don't want Senna to win it. Alain is my team mate at Ferrari next year and for another thing I like him.' That was Mansell. Prost said: 'I don't care about it because it will always have a bitter taste.' Senna, who had spent the flight to Japan consuming religious writings, spoke of his 'faith' but to reports that as a consequence he could not be hurt in a racing car he retorts with vehemence that 'of course I can get hurt or killed as anybody can and this feeling – or this knowledge – is what keeps you together as self-preservation.' At Suzuka he did say: 'It's a blessing from Him. Other people may try to use me or destroy me but they will not succeed.' The other Senna said: 'In the car I don't even look at the rev counter because if you do that you must be a fraction less committed to your driving at that moment. So you change gear by sound. When I have finished a lap, I can recall it completely . . .' It was the same man who had astonished so many people along the way by doing just this, Ralph Firmin, Dennis Rushen, Dick Bennetts, Gerard Ducarouge, Steve Nichols . . .

He took pole, of course, his twelfth of the season. 'I have nothing to lose. I will drive as fast as I can to win. It is the way I like to drive. I like the challenge of racing to win. It is something that stimulates me.' It was the same man who had felt just this in karts, Formula Ford 1600, Formula Ford 2000, Formula Three . . .

Before the race Prost made a fateful declaration: 'A lot of times, if you remember, last year and this, I opened the door and if I did not open the door we would have crashed.' This time he did not intend to open the door. It was a chilling thought so deep into that first chilled autumn, even as Honda's ten thousand guests arrived to witness what could well be the Championship decided. Prost got away at the start and drove a race plucked purely

204

from all our memories, drove it the way he used to handle races, goddamned fast, a lovely sureness of touch, an all-pervading feel of control, as if certainty of movement had been conjured from all the uncertainties of a Formula One car. This, very suddenly, was the man who had once regularly outdriven Niki Lauda, who had taken a heap of pole positions, commanded and won races from the front.

At Suzuka he was quicker at the exits to each corner so that Senna, who had drawn up to him after a long chase, was squeezing himself hard to catch him again by the next corner and Senna had to overtake or the Championship was gone. On lap 47 they were both moving towards the chicane – a proper old-fashioned chicane which twisted right then left, tight as hell – and Senna lunged down the inside. Prost turned into him and, the cars locked together, they clattered on to the beginning of the escape road directly ahead. Prost got out, Senna got a push and rejoined down the escape road. Prost walked back and as he was on the grassy verge at the entrance to the pit-lane road he turned, saw Senna – the front of the car damaged – coming in for a new nose cone. Prost was certain Senna would be disqualified. Prost was certain he was World Champion for the third time. Senna had had a push, hadn't he? Everybody had seen that. Senna had not rejoined the track where he had left it but taken a short cut, hadn't he? Everybody had seen that, too. Senna 'won' the race – and there was another irony in that because he overtook Alessandro Nannini at the same chicane with the same move to do it. Nannini got smartly out of the way, so smartly that his tyres gave off white whiffs of smoke when he hit the brakes. Senna cites 'Nannini's own statement: he tried to avoid the overtaking manoeuvre by braking very late and it was normal the front wheels locked – his own words!'

And another storm broke. Senna was disqualified.

Emotionally, Prost felt himself drawn in several different directions at once. 'The stress has been unbelievable, it has been my worst year in Formula One. I felt very comfortable in the lead and I really didn't expect him to pass me then. A couple of times he had been much closer at that corner and yet he didn't try it. This time when I looked in my mirror he was a long way back but he just kept coming although I had the line for the corner.'

Senna also was being drawn in several different directions. 'The results as they stand provisionally do not reflect the truth of the race in either the sporting sense or the sense of the regulations. I see this result as temporary but the matter is now out of my hands. It was obvious I won the race on the track. The taste of victory was taken away.' He had judged that the chicane was 'the only place where I could overtake and somebody who shouldn't have been there just closed the door and that was that.' He would not mention Prost by name: it had gone as deep as that.

Prost had sensed what might happen with great clarity. 'I was absolutely sure I would win the race or have an accident like this. I knew that he wanted to win absolutely. The problem with Ayrton is that he can't accept not to win and he can't accept that someone will resist an overtaking move.' He was talking about the same man who had provoked the same sentiments in Rick Morris, Calvin Fish, Martin Brundle . . .

McLaren, who are slavishly conscious of their image, were deep into unfamiliar territory again, almost enemy territory. Would they protest Senna's disqualification? After all, their other man, Prost, had just won the Championship for them. If they did protest, and it was upheld, they might be taking that Championship from Prost (on the assumption that Senna won Adelaide). McLaren produced the perfect man to read out the perfect reply, Creighton Brown, a tall, co-operative, popular, approachable sort of chap who habitually thaws the ice which can surround the closed world of the McLaren motorhome. 'We feel it is important that you all know what is happening and why, so there can be no misinterpretation or misunderstanding. We think there is a possibility that Ayrton's disqualification is not consistent with some things that have happened during the rest of the year where people have missed chicanes without being disqualified. There are two things to note. It is our duty as a team to try to win every race if at all possible, and it is on that basis we have made this appeal. Also, there is absolutely no way we are doing this because we want to favour one driver against the other. We are very happy for either of them to win the Championship. We are trying to clarify the matter on the basis of finishing this race. We are only doing this to maximize our chances of winning this race.'

Senna was understandably circumspect. 'As to the appeal, I do not want to comment because it will be prepared very carefully on the basis of the regulations and on fact.'

What really happened at that chicane admits several interpretations, not least of which is that Senna had become so controversial that rational judgement about his conduct was extremely difficult for many people, among them Prost. It may well have been the wrong place to try and overtake but, as Senna says, it was the only place. He went to the inside, which was the only way to do it. If he counted on Prost opening the door (as Prost admits he had done before in both '88 and '89) he was wrong this time; he was ill advised to suggest that Prost should not have been there. Prost was leading the race and where else could Prost have been but angling his car to take the chicane in the normal way?

At Brazil, in the heat before the cold of autumn, Senna had been sandwiched between Berger and Patrese and had said the only free space available was 'up in the air'. He was now saying this about Prost; and his case was further weakened because he'd cut across Mansell in Portugal and wondered whatever Mansell was doing there. Now Prost had done the same to him and he wondered whatever Prost was doing there.

But you needed to look at it another way to be fair to Senna and what he did. Here was the crucial moment in the Championship and Senna would lose that Championship if he did not find a way past Prost, however difficult that might be, whatever inherent risks that would carry. He had rationalized the possibilities of overtaking to this one corner where he might, with all his fearsome courage and speed of reaction, get himself in the right place fast enough to do it. In the matter of late braking, he was supreme. He tried it. In retrospect the move recalled the memorable words of the general who surrendered Berlin to the Russians in 1945: 'There are no desperate situations, only desperate men.'

The chance of decisively beating Prost to the corner was remote because Prost was already close to the corner, but he knew he had no other chance and he did what a racer does, balanced the risk against the logistics of the moment and went for it. FISA called the risk dangerous and their phrase for that demands to be set down: 'one who endangers the safety of others'.

The storm did not abate.

At a press conference near Heathrow Airport, between Suzuka and Adelaide, Dennis made a detailed and eloquent defence of McLaren's position – and Senna's position, too: of how Senna had re-started, of how others (including Mansell at Spa) had missed chicanes. In direct answer to the accusation that Senna had carried out a 'dangerous manoeuvre' in trying to overtake at the chicane Dennis said: 'Senna overtook on Prost's right-hand side and it would appear that FISA regard this manoeuvre as dangerous. However Chapter IV paragraph (c) of the Sporting Code (page 313) expressly permits overtaking on the right. Senna was participating in a Formula One race.'

Dennis was angry, also, that FISA were suddenly making other accusations, six in all, about Senna's previous behaviour, with among them his crash with Schlesser at Monza, 1988, his crash with Berger, Rio 1989, his crash with Mansell at Portugal. It begged a question: why hadn't FISA done anything about these at the time? Why fling them at Senna retrospectively?

Nor did FISA relent. As Senna reached Adelaide he heard that he had been fined 100,000 dollars and given a six months suspended sentence. He was virtually in tears. 'I will drive here the way I have driven all my career. I am supposed to be a lunatic, a dangerous man breaking all the rules but people have the wrong impression. It is a question of justice, and what has happened in Suzuka and subsequently in Paris at the appeal court is totally unfair. I have spent enough time in Formula One to realize you make mistakes which compromise yourself and sometimes other people but that is inevitable and you won't find another driver who won't accept that. What happened at Suzuka reflects the political situation in the sport. I never caused the accident and I'm prepared to fight to the end for my values, for justice.'

And: 'When everything goes against you, you ask yourself why you need to carry on, particularly when you have not been fairly treated. I thought about stopping, about not coming to Australia, so many things have gone through my head.'

McLaren vowed to find that justice in the French courts, although Senna's Championship was now all but gone; and gone completely in a rain-riven Adelaide Grand Prix – itself a wild thing, Prost refusing to risk his life, Senna having to risk his life. Within a few laps Senna was almost half a minute in the lead, spun as if he was being borne on a carousel, caught it, set off again and somewhere in the walls of water did not see Martin Brundle's Brabham and struck it very hard indeed as he tried to lap it.

Brundle had an on-board camera pointing backwards and the pictures it gave seemed to capture the whole savage season: the churning ball of spray and from nowhere, glimpsed like a ghostly, frantic vision, the flickering red and white of the McLaren, a hammer striking an anvil, one instant invisible, the next instant plunging into the Brabham. It was the same Brundle who had known just this in 1983 . . .

Senna limped back to the pits on three wheels – travelling at quite a respectable speed, actually – and clambered out.

Prost? He said 1989 had been the worst of his life. It was a sentiment shared by many other players in the big game.

CHAPTER TWELVE

Equilibrium . . . ?

And then there was, we thought, another Ayrton Senna. This one was the child of the other Ayrton Sennas, unmistakably their progeny but The Face had softened, the eyes were no longer hunted and haunted; there was a calm about him, an ease about him, a looseness about him, a tangible, touchable tranquillity. But I wrote those words before Suzuka, 1990.

Silverstone, nearly mid-season, he leads the Championship but this is tyre testing and now during the lunch break he sits and speaks and nurses a bowl of what seems to be organic food. From time to time he feeds himself a mouthful although he is careful not to let this interrupt what he has to say. As each question is posed he hesitates, measuring his response exactly before he delivers it. Sometimes the hesitation is as long as seven seconds so that you are unsure whether he is going to answer the question at all; but he does, every time.

Question: Are you a more contented person? 'Other than winning there was not much else positive in the past [the Prost angst]. Under normal circumstances there's so much pressure, so much stress and if you have to add on top of it situations like that it is very difficult to handle. It takes away a lot of the happiness and joy of your profession. Gerhard Berger has been very easy-going and there's been no problem at all. We have shared some moments of fun, we've made some jokes and we spent some time together between Phoenix and Brazil [the first two Grands Prix] away from racing, enjoying the sun, sea and playing on

211

jet skis. With Elio de Angelis at Lotus I did this at the beginning but not with anyone else.'

He had found, as it seemed, equilibrium and that was a surprise in itself. When 1990 began we might have expected anything but that; the odours of '89 remained strong in the nostrils, the sense of frostbite still lingered. FISA said that if he did not retract his allegations about how the Championship had been settled and pay his 100,000 dollar fine by Thursday 15 February he would not be given a Superlicence.

Senna passed the close season with 'a completely open mind, just waiting. I was ready for anything. There was talk of continuing racing as well as talk of changing to America. I don't have much identification with racing other than driving so I wouldn't be a team manager. I don't think I'd be much good at it. I have come a long way fast and once you get to that level, just to throw it away is not an easy decision. I would have stopped but it would have let people down. For lots of fans we are a kind of dream, that's the way they see us. It is a different world for them and a different way of living – it is not a reality but a dream. You have some influence on the lives of those people, you get genuine enthusiasm from people you have never met. They see many positive things and it gives you a good feeling to see people like that.'

But now there was a deadline, there was Jean-Marie Balestre in one trench and across no-man's-land Senna in another, both strong-willed, both with positions to defend.

'I asked myself about continuing to race. I was perfectly calm and I discussed the matter with Honda and McLaren. I said to them that I was only a driver and that McLaren and Honda would continue after me. I said that I did not want to compromise their efforts and those of the people who work to run the cars. I asked Nobuhiko Kawamoto and Ron Dennis to decide in my place. I said I would completely respect their wishes, that I was ready to retire or fight on as they thought fit.'

Ron Dennis, not a man given to revealing his emotions, will never forget that close season. 'Both Ayrton and I were suffering. We were the two individuals who were exposed to the Superlicence issues and the two individuals who experienced the unpleasant — I must choose my words carefully, I can't use the right words because they will only get me into more aggravation, into opening the wound again . . . well, let's just say it was a very unpleasant experience with lots of people not keeping their words. It had a profound effect on me and a pretty significant one on him.'

But there was the deadline and it was approaching. Late February Balestre returned McLaren's entries for their two cars and implied that Dennis had the responsibility for making Senna retract. Early March: McLaren paid the 100,000 dollar fine and their two entries were granted, 'one for G. Berger amd the second for a driver who remains to be named'. What followed is frankly complicated, to put it mildly. Senna, through his promotions company, issued a statement saying that Balestre had respected his integrity, the Court of Appeal in Paris had removed the suspended sentence on his future conduct as a driver and that Dennis had 'interceded and assumed responsibility for the payment of the fine'. Surely all was well? It wasn't.

Balestre proclaimed himself 'stupefied' but quietly began negotiations with Dennis, the negotiations broke down and, that Thursday, with the FISA switchboard at the Place de la Concorde under siege by the world's press (and me) we got the one statement that nobody had expected: there would be no statement.

Overnight common sense prevailed, something we did expect. Senna did make a statement. 'During the meeting

213

of the FISA World Council which took place on 7 December 1989, I listened to statements and testimonies from various people and from these statements one must conclude that they provide proof that no pressure group or the President of the FISA influenced the decisions regarding the results of the FIA Formula One World Championship.' It was as near as a proud man would get to leaving his trench with his arms up.

Balestre did make a statement. 'We acknowledge receipt of your letter of 15 February and of your application to take part in the 1990 World Championship. We are sending you your Superlicence accordingly and wish you every success in a Championship which promises to provide us with a fine sporting season, where you will be able to give full expression to those champion qualities which nobody ever denied that you had.' It was as near as an autocrat would get to leaving his trench with a white flag.

Phoenix, Arizona and the world was back in place for the first race, 11 March. Senna reflects that 'other than being in the car driving, there was no motivation left for me. I had no feeling for the car, not even in the pit lane. In Phoenix I just couldn't understand the car or the engine. I lost all sensitivity. Even the win wasn't enough to motivate me.' The win was a good one, however much that was lost on Senna. He stalked Jean Alesi (Tyrrell), took him and instantly – it was the sort of moment Senna himself would appreciate – Alesi re-took him in a challenging thrust with no spare space at either side. After that Senna went by and finished nearly ten seconds ahead.

Dennis is candid. 'I think both of us knew that it wasn't going to be fixed in five minutes, but that's where being a real team manager starts. It's about understanding. When someone has a problem in any company, one of the functions of management is to support the weaknesses of people, not expose them to the world. If you're trying to get the best out of people, you identify their weaknesses and either assist them to come to terms with them themselves or educate themselves around the weaknesses, you position them in the organization with a support structure. That's the role of management in any company. In a more refined, highly-tuned situation such as the relationship between a racing driver and the management of the team that becomes a more sensitive and delicate operation. I go back to the Prost situation: there was no way, no matter what he said or the press said, that we would have ever retaliated [by entering a public debate], not under any circumstances, and it was a very painful experience. It would have been counter-productive to retaliate. When a driver like Ayrton is down you don't do things to make him further down, you don't question his ability to drive. You say: hey come on, let's talk about it, let's have a realistic approach — you don't say: drink this glass of medicine and it'll all be better. My motivation was a lot longer coming back than his. I don't want this to come out as a ham statement but we are very close as men now, meaning we have taken the time and the trouble to go very much into each other's thinking.'

The Brazilian race, where Balestre reportedly had an armed guard, was at São Paulo, a rebuilt circuit and for Senna a homecoming. 'I got my motivation back there. I had had two weeks to think about it and then I faced the challenge of driving at home and I saw the enthusiasm from all the people. That gave me the pleasure, the fire to get in the car again. It was only the people of Brazil and the positive thoughts they had for me which gave me the ingredients to re-start my career.' He took pole, was in the lead and then tried to lap Nakajima. 'I was up behind him for four or five corners, I went to overtake him uphill to the slow corner, he opened the door and when I was halfway inside he decided to come back.' Unfortunately Nakajima had run on to dust at the side of the track and could do nothing. Senna needed a new nose cone and finished third.

At Imola he took pole, was in the lead and a stone flew up, sheared the brakes. At Monaco he took pole and won it handsomely. And he went to Montreal where, quite by chance, a respected Canadian journalist called Gerald Donaldson asked him for an interview for his book *Grand Prix People* (MRP). Since what Senna said is so staggering – even by his standards – I repeat a tract of it, with kind permission.

'Sometimes I think I know some of the reasons why I do the things the way I do in the car and sometimes I think I don't know why. There are some moments that seem to be the natural instinct that is in me. Whether I have been born with it or whether this feeling has grown in me more than other people I don't know, but it is inside me and it takes over with a great amount of space and intensity.

'When I am competing against the watch and against other competitors, the feeling of expectation, of getting it done and doing the best I can gives me a kind of power that some moments when I am driving actually detaches me completely from anything else as I am doing it . . . corner after corner, lap after lap. I can give you a true example.

'Monte Carlo '88, the last qualifying session. I was already on pole and I was going faster and faster. One lap after the other, quicker and quicker and quicker. I was at one stage just on pole, then by half a second and then one second and I kept going. Suddenly I was nearly two seconds faster than anybody else, including my team mate with the same car. And I suddenly realized I was no longer driving the car consciously.

'I was kind of driving it by instinct, only I was in a different dimension. It was like I was in a tunnel. Not only the tunnel under the hotel but the whole circuit was a tunnel.

'I was just going and going, more and more and more and more. I was way over the limit but still able to find even more. Then suddenly something just kicked me. I kind of woke up and realized that I was in a different atmosphere than you normally are. My immediate reaction was to back off, slow down. I drove back slowly to the pits and I didn't want to go out any more that day. It frightened me because I realized I was well beyond my conscious understanding. It happens rarely but I keep these experiences very much alive in me because it is something that is important for self-preservation.'

I think that Monsieur Prost's assertion about Senna thinking God would not allow him to be harmed has been finally and totally refuted by the paragraph above, despite what would subsequently happen; and you notice, too, that at no stage did Senna refer to what happened at Monte Carlo as being a religious or quasi-religious experience. It was a man taking a machine and a machine taking a man into secret places, into the subliminal.

Oh, and he won Canada, led Mexico and had a puncture.

He didn't get pole at Paul Ricard and explained that across a whole qualifying lap if you 'lift your foot by one-eighth of the play on the throttle' once it can make all the difference. Think about that. His chances in the race were essentially destroyed by a 16-second pitstop for tyres and he finished third; Prost won it and seemed to have rediscovered the vigour of youth as well as the wisdom of experience; something which was confirmed at Silverstone when Senna spun and inherited third place while Prost scanned developments, made incisive moves and won again.

Evening at Silverstone, a cloying, clammy heat from the embers of a burning hot day. Mansell has announced his retirement, some of the motorhomes are already packed

217

up, some of the transporters are already lumbering into the traffic jam directly outside the circuit. At the McLaren motorhome Senna's sister and father sit chatting with friends; his sister is disarmingly like him, the set of the face, the roll of the eyes, even the position of the teeth when she smiles, which she does a lot.

Senna comes from the pits, autograph hunters closing in on him and trailing him like a pack, journalists pressing tape recorders at his mouth as he walks; and this is only the journey from the pits to the motorhome. How can he tolerate it? Imagine if every time you stepped out of your front door you were mobbed. He does not acknowledge sister and father because he doesn't need to. He senses their proximity.

He wears blue jeans of a careful casual cut, a white Boss shirt, trainers. A sexy Italian girl interviewer with her TV crew corners him, she uses her wide eyes to full effect and yes, he does a brief interview, moving across the lock-step of question and answer, although less than an hour before he had done the same thing three times at the official interviews (always the same questions), and then come to a press conference for the journalists, where he was asked – well, the same questions. In each case he gave the same answers, varying only the odd word as if he'd forgotten part of the script or he was amusing himself with variations on language to sustain his own interest. How can he tolerate it?

Well, he's getting paid 15 million dollars a year to tolerate it (which leads to a paradox. Normally when a human being is earning that he doesn't have to do anything he doesn't want to). And anyway, Senna puts money itself into this context: 'A lot of people say the money is not important and it's only important to win but I think very few of them really mean it: some because they like money and some because if they have got some already they want still more, but I have never needed it and that's even more true now, because since I have been successful I have the material things.'

Or, as he has recounted when told that Dennis had described him as the shrewdest negotiator he had ever met: 'I'm not that hard. If you think that a few years ago when I was negotiating to join McLaren we got to a difficult moment right at the end trying to arrive at a figure. Instead of going for it and pushing really hard – which I could have done had I really wanted – I took a chance just to let it happen whichever way it would. We spun a coin, heads or tails, I called wrong and it cost me one and a half million dollars . . .'

But now at Silverstone the TV interview is over, the sexy girl gone, a gaggle of journalists call out 'Ayrton, Ayrton' but he won't come over, he shrugs, he's emptied, he's talked enough. He makes a racing driver's calculation, the mind moving incisively over the territory to be covered: if he goes immediately to his right and through the gap at the end of the motorhome he'll be good and clear before the journalists can reach him again.

It works.

He won Germany, then – inevitably perhaps – did something to imply implicitly that he hadn't fully reached equilibrium yet. The Hungarian Grand Prix was in my judgement very special, one of those rarities where many threads come together and interconnect and you have a real race. Towards the end of it Thierry Boutsen was leading with an enormous impetus of pressure gathered behind him, Sandro Nannini, Senna, Berger, Mansell. They circled the tight unforgiving corners nose-to-tail, nose-to-tail. All it lacked was Prost, but he'd gone in an accident on lap 36.

If this quintet had simply kept on circling nose-to-tail – holding station, as they say – it would have been no more than an interesting procession. The one place you could authentically overtake was the long straight, and lap after lap along that their speeds were evenly matched. Someone whispered to me when there were a handful of laps left that there was no chance, no chance whatever, that people of that disposition would all actually finish the race, not Senna looking for the Championship and behind Nannini, not Berger looking to vindicate McLaren's faith in him and a real racer anyway, not Mansell who adores such a challenge, particularly in the corners where you can't authentically overtake, can you? They dived and darted and ducked, pushed and probed and prodded and the race gathered an impetus of its own. On lap 64 Mansell was past Berger, Senna still behind Nannini.

A right-hand corner, a short sharp rush to the next right-hander, an innocent back-marker up ahead but too far away to be a factor in the pressure. Boutsen hugs the brightly striped kerbing on the left, positioned to take the ordinary racing line through the right-hander, and Nannini a car's length behind him does the same. Just another corner among so many. Thirty, forty metres from the turn into the corner Senna pulls decisively out into the middle of the track. He points the snout of the McLaren at the apex but already Boutsen is turning in, Nannini is following and turning in. Boutsen threads through and still Nannini is turning in – across, of course, Senna.

Let us be clear: if you try and go inside someone at a corner and you haul yourself alongside you can justifiably claim the corner; if you are not yet alongside you lose the corner. This is a fine point and also, alas, a theoretical one. When the theory meets the reality of two racing cars contesting one portion of tarmac it is no longer a theory, it is a crash. Senna's front wheel struck Nannini's rear wheel. There is no escape from the conclusion that he was not alongside. He was substantially behind. Nannini went into the air – for an instant a long way into the air, pitched

220

at an angle towards the critical point where he might flip. He skimmed off the circuit when he landed on all four wheels. Astonishingly Senna's car was undamaged and he continued. While Senna tracked Boutsen, Herr Berger – you'd better believe it because it happened – tried the same move on Mansell at the same place nine laps later and Mansell went into the air. Boutsen won, Senna hounding him all the way to the line.

He came to speak afterwards and he looked, as he so often does, softened by the race, mellowed in contemplation of it as if mind and body are becalmed. A pretty and nervous Hungarian translator asked if he'd mind pausing after each answer so that she could render it into Hungarian. He smiled that deep, withdrawn, weary smile which isn't a smile at all but a mannerism and said no, really, I can't go through all that, please, I just want to speak. It was done politely but decisively. 'I was fortunate,' he said. 'Nannini closed the door and I don't think he saw me.' It was one explanation but it did not explain why he chose that corner to try it. In the motorhome Nannini had been crying but was now composed. He said little. There was little to say. Someone whispered 'good drive, anyway' and Nannini smiled his smile which wasn't a smile at all but a mannerism, accepting the compliment and concealing all the rest.

On the Friday before Spa Senna duly re-signed for McLaren for 1991 although (again) he said that Ron was a tough negotiator and (again) Ron said that he was a tough negotiation. He won Spa comfortably enough from Prost and the Championship was moving decisively towards him, 63 points against Prost's 50. It's a lot, the safety margin of the next race and perhaps the one after that.

Senna won Monza from Prost and Berger, and there is a very great emptiness after any race at Monza unless Ferrari win. Expectations have been constructed on a missionary level, the old legends have been restated and regurgitated, a full litany of phrases has been mouthed in quasi-religious language by journalists and TV commentators (Monza a sacred place, a shrine where pilgrims come and so forth). But it does leave an emptiness when the engines fade away unless, of course, Ferrari win in which case there is hysteria and then the emptiness.

Senna sits arranged to face the press with Berger in the middle and Prost on the other side of Berger. It is a comfortable arrangement. Senna and Prost have not exchanged a word for almost a calendar year and Berger is the logistical buffer. His role seems to be minor but in fact it is very major indeed. Berger goes subconsciously straight into race-speak, the car began to slide around, I chose A compound tyres and maybe that wasn't the right choice and so forth, he stands and leaves.

And then there were two . . .

The questioning moved through the lock-step of more race-speak and when that was exhausted (it didn't take long and I won't trouble you with it) someone did ask a real live question and it was addressed squarely to two men who were supreme in their art – for different reasons – and who now sat within reach of each other. The question was: how much longer before you at least reach an accommodation with each other?

For a long moment Prost said nothing. It was a hell of a question and it might have involved retreat, surrender, submission, the negation of his integrity.

Prost: 'I tried to shake hands with Ayrton at the first race of the season at Phoenix. Ask him.' It was a hard point to make.

Senna: 'I did not think he was entirely sincere about it. If I had I would have shaken his hand. It is not easy to forget what happened between us last season. However, although we don't have many things in common, we share the same passion for Formula One and this is very important for us. When he is able to say he is sincere in front of everyone I will accept it. I don't have a problem with that.'

Prost: 'Yes, this is very important. Ayrton is right about that. He has his ideas about what happened last year and I have my ideas. Whatever happened, I would like to forget it. We do have the same passion for the sport. I believe I have changed a lot since last year and perhaps I understand some things more clearly than I did. I think it would be good for our sport if today as we go into the last four races we could somehow go together. So if Ayrton agrees . . .'

It had gone beyond words because at this extremely moving juncture (or more properly conjunction) concrete gestures were needed, too. They shook hands, there was instinctive applause and almost as if a Berlin Wall had come down, emotion – or release, or understandable over-reaction – seized these two men and they began to slap each other on the back, and within it Ayrton Senna began to acquire stature as well as status. Prost had always had stature. It was a good moment as good moments go and even some pressmen caught the emotion, and I mention this only because they abstract themselves from it more than drivers, even. It was a cleansing moment, it was the sort of moment when human beings rediscover the common sense of humanity, and the beauty was that it was executed with maturity, no retreat, no submission, no surrender. There was another truth: drivers who spend their waking hours combating time to the most tiny, flickering fraction of a second discover that time heals if you have enough of it. But I wrote these words before Suzuka . . .

Senna 72 points, Prost 56.

Mansell won Estoril from Senna, Prost third after a frightener at the very start when Mansell veered at Prost and Prost had to hug the pit-lane wall so closely that his wheels brushed against it. Afterwards Prost rounded on the

223

Ferrari management, rounded on their lack of organization, said they didn't deserve the Championship and implied that he might walk away from the whole thing. It was a hard point to make.

On the rostrum, where you can see exhibited before your very eyes the shifting patterns of relationships which constantly evolve and dissolve, generally expressed by whether the drivers actually look at each other or away from each other, or the gestures they make towards each other (a hug can mean reconciliation, a handshake can mean cohabitation), Mansell put an arm round Senna (excuse me, didn't they dislike each other?) but didn't put an arm round Prost (excuse me, weren't they bosom buddies as well as team mates?) Ah, well. It was only evolving and dissolving the way it does.

Senna 78, Prost 60.

Jerez and the Spanish Grand Prix were a week away, Prost conceded the Championship and if you followed Senna you were worried about that. Excuse me, but hadn't Prost conceded it only the season before and won it? In the background to all this Senna had been taking pole after pole and he was now on 49. Jim Clark, as we have seen, had 33 and that had stood since 1968 until Senna beat it at Phoenix in 1989. Senna needed only one more special, squeezed lap and he had the round fifty, quite possibly beyond the reach of any man who would come after him.

At 1.52 on the Friday qualifying session of the Spanish Grand Prix Martin Donnelly (Lotus) struck a barrier virtually head-on at 147 mph. What remained of the car looked like something which had been savagely torn to pieces and, worse, Donnelly lay in the middle of the track. The Spanish television camera remained on him a long time, lingered there, and the first impression was that he could not have survived it. Professor Sid Watkins, the British doctor who goes to every race, was there within two minutes.

In the air hung the chords of memory and the associations of memory. At Zolder in 1982 Gilles Villeneuve had been killed in qualifying. The time: 1.52.

Senna was told of Donnelly and he was close to tears. He walked to where Donnelly still lay and remained there a long time. He was not required to go, no protocol demanded that he go; but he went, and he stood, and he returned to the motorhome and he asked everyone else to leave it. 'I wanted to be alone with my thoughts. They were private moments and I doubt that I will ever be able to express what I felt.'

Donnelly lay on the track for twenty minutes before Professor Watkins judged that he could be safely moved to the track's hospital. The qualifying session was resumed, Senna didn't want to drive and then he made a fundamental decision: he would take the McLaren to its limit or he wouldn't get in it at all. No compromise between the two positions. He went a full second quicker than he had done before the accident.

Why did Senna go to where Donnelly lay? In part because, I believe, his religious convictions took him there to face it, in part because he was now becoming a seigneur in Grand Prix racing, very possibly a potential spokesman for safety — as Lauda had been, as Prost was — and he felt he should have been there; in part because he cared very deeply about the consequences of human actions — which is another way of saying humanity again. Later that evening he visited Donnelly in hospital and Donnelly recognized him and that was a moment, that was.

The following day he took the fiftieth pole although on the lap he met a vision and a spectre which both disturbed and angered him. He had an on-board camera and what it portrayed was so fluid, something happening so fast that he seemed to skim the whole circuit, gloved hands pump-pump-pumping the steering wheel, G-forces

225

jud-jud-juddering the helmet, wheels fleeing across kerbing in almost brutal ferocity, corner after corner melting
and rushing, melting and rushing in a sustained surge. He
rounded a corner and halfway down a straight, were two
cars going very slowly indeed. One instant they were shapes
in the distance – evidently arguing about who'd done what
to whom – and as the Honda engine pumped in the speed
he was on them fast as you can blink your eye. The sheer
compression of time between Senna rounding the corner and
reaching them was damn nearly beyond comprehension.

One car was full to the left, the other behind it and
outside it. Two-thirds of the width of the circuit was
completely filled and this by cars doing what Senna esti-
mated at 120mph less than he was. He lifted his foot off
the throttle a fraction as he placed the McLaren to the
right and they vanished somewhere into the blur and the
engine's shriek and the next corner were already coming,
coming, coming.

He completed the lap, completed the fifty pole positions
and was greeted by the mechanics in euphoria, had a
touching moment with Ron Dennis, got a cake with 50 on
it but those eyes were close to tears again. He spoke of what
lifting from the throttle had cost in time lost, said of course
that it wasn't a perfect lap; but that wasn't the point. Still
Donnelly's crash was utterly vivid in the memory, it had
only been the day before and here you have two cars
meandering along and, Senna said, what if I'd hit one? I'd
have been airborne for sure, what are these people, crazy?
He'd have landed outside the circuit. And he rationalized
it: something like that happens, it gets into you, it gets into
your blood, you want to react but you know that reacting
is intrinsically crazy in itself – these speeds, these cars – so
you find mechanisms inside yourself to ignore it, complete
the lap, draw into the pits, examine what your next course
of action will be. You don't give anybody a brake test if

they do that to you, don't draw alongside them and trade insults.

It flawed the occasion, flawed the celebration of that lap of 1 minute 18.387 seconds.

Something happened in the Spanish Grand Prix, too, and it was (again we thought) another clue about the equilibrium. Senna took the lead but he sensed that Prost was quicker and after the pit stops for tyres he came out entirely by chance at a very ripe moment. Mansell was moving aside to let Prost through into the lead (bosom buddies again, OK?) That was down the start-finish straight and Senna was travelling hard from the pit-lane exit and Mansell had gone wide and Senna nipped into the gap just as Mansell turned in to take the corner. 'It was,' Mansell said, deadpan as you like, 'an interesting moment.' Yes, and Senna's corner, too.

Ultimately a stone punctured Senna's radiator, water boiled and bubbled back and he swerved once, twice, as it smeared a tyre, naturally thought it a puncture, pitted for tyres again, retired. He clambered from the car and bent over it looking for the cause, was satisfied, went to the wall nearby and sat on it. He was lost in contemplation. You don't sit on the wall, you get over the wall to safety. He sat for a long time and some say he was in tears again. He turned his back on the track and talked to the people who wanted to talk to him and he remained on the action side of the wall. He was in another dimension: he couldn't have seen any spinning car which might have come at him, any errant car cavorting. In his mind he wasn't really there, he was somewhere else.

He walked back sucking liquid from a bottle someone had given him and he made his way along the side of the track. He scoured the sweat from his neck with a sponge. He looked loose, easy in himself now, returning to normal, and step by step he was tracked by the inevitable TV crew

227

– which was normality itself, the familiar backdrop to years of his life. It wasn't exactly an invasion of privacy, I know, but what did they want of him, pictures, pictures, pictures, then more pictures, pictures, pictures?

Senna 78, Prost 69.

During this season of 1990 he would say: 'Time shows us, as we progress, different perspectives of life. A few years ago I had no time for anything or anybody other than racing. Today I not only have the time but I need the time for my family, my friends and particularly my girlfriend. I organize myself to strike the right balance between my private and professional lives because only that way, having the equilibrium between both sides of myself, can I perform to my best.' This was the man who, also during the season of 1990, was giving an interview when a fan approached him and offered him some little gifts. One of those gifts was a piece of ceramic with his name on it. Another was a cake from the fan's wife. 'It makes me feel embarrassed and humble. It shows how much you can touch people without knowing or even speaking to them and as much as you try to give those people something, it is nothing compared to what they live in their own minds, in their dreams for you.'

And now it was autumn again, now it was October. They went to Suzuka. On the Thursday Prost jogged round the track and paused at the chicane, as if by standing before it he could assess its dimensions slowly, the way you never can in a racing car. His thoughts no doubt were of '89. The entrance to the chicane, he concluded, really was too narrow to be a passing point. Later Senna was asked about that and tacitly agreed. Some observers took this as, well, something approaching a suggestion of culpability about '89 . . .

The mathematics had become (relatively) straightforward. Senna had the 78 points, Prost 69 and both had filled their quota of eleven finishes-in-the-points. This margin-ally favoured Prost who would only have to drop a fifth, then a fourth place. Senna had been no lower than third all season so that only victories or second places were of any material benefit to him. Anything less would be automatically discarded. The permutations were also (rela-tively) straightforward. If Prost won Suzuka and Adelaide he could count 82 points and if Senna was second behind him both times he, too, could count 82 but he would lose it on the number of wins, Prost gathering a total of seven, Senna six. If Prost won Suzuka and Senna was lower than second, and if Prost was himself second at Adelaide with Senna behind him, Prost was Champion on 79 points. In that scenario the most Senna could get was 78.

In reality Senna remained clear favourite. If he won Suzuka he was Champion there and then, and even if he came second behind anybody but Prost he was Champion there and then, too. Adelaide would be irrelevant.

Prost confessed that he felt the same sort of relief he had at Adelaide in 1986 against Mansell and Piquet, when the niceties and permutations of the mathematics could be completely ignored. He'd had to go for the win then and see what happened. All the rest was outside his control. Suzuka '90 was the same in all its essentials. There was another factor and it began to loom larger and larger. The respective situations of Senna and Prost were exactly reversed from Suzuka '89; then it was Senna who had to ignore the mathematics and go for the win or he was bust. So what would happen when they re-reached the chicane? It might well be that Prost would be the desperate man there this time round and as someone at McLaren pointed out, Ayrton hasn't forgotten, Ayrton hasn't forgotten. The only calming thought was that they were friends now. Weren't they?

Pole position seemed crucial. If either man reached that

unfolding right-hand corner at the end of the start-finish straight first they could win the race from there; the other man would find it extremely difficult to overtake elsewhere, not forgetting the chicane . . .

This was compounded by the sure and certain knowledge that the Ferrari was now a very potent piece of machinery indeed and in it Prost had been decisively quicker at Jerez. Senna simply could not afford to let Prost get away from him at Suzuka. If he did he might not see him again until the podium. It was further compounded by the knowledge that Prost was driving as well as he had done in his life, expressed through a beautiful balancing of racecraft, calculation and prudence; and from all that Prost drew great speed. In the matter of minimizing risk and maximizing the machinery Prost was unsurpassed.

In the first grid session Berger was quickest, Senna third behind Prost. 'This morning [in the untimed session] I made a mistake on the slippery track surface and spun off,' Senna said. 'This afternoon my car was OK but it bottomed out badly at one point just as I was changing from fourth to fifth and I got a little sideways – I was glancing at the rev counter at the time. I feel quite satisfied with my performance as a whole.'

In the second session he took the fifty-first pole position of his career although it was taut and tight. He and Prost lay in wait for each other until the last five minutes before they made their final, decisive gestures. Senna, a master of the mechanisms of knowing how long to wait, sensed that he needed a clear road. 'I was determined that I was going to get out on the circuit in front of Prost. The Ferrari pit was near ours and when I heard them fire his engine up I immediately gave the signal to my mechanics to do the same.' The two men circled the emptied circuit, warmed their tyres, went hard for it.

Senna 1: 36.996

Prost 1: 37.228

'The whole team,' Senna said, 'really contributed to my performance, men and machine working extremely well but tomorrow's race is a long one and anything can happen. I'm sure it will be the most exciting race of the season. We and Ferrari are very close now but despite the pressure I am under I feel really fit. Naturally I am thinking of the Championship and this one would mean more to me than 1988.' You can read into these words what you like, although retrospectively you cannot escape the irony of . . . long race . . . anything can happen.

This Saturday something unusual was happening. The placing of the pole position car was on the right of the straight, but the track was 'dirty' there, and Senna argued that that negated the legitimate advantage bestowed by pole. (Remember we are talking about merest fractions of difference, but they assume major proportions at this level.) Prost, while geometrically behind Senna because of the grid's traditional stagger, had the advantage of a clean segment of track. Senna's arguments were not accepted.

Sunday 21 October, the clock moved towards one o'clock, the parade lap had been completed, the official on the rim of the track waved his flag now that all the cars had come to rest, the red light flicked to green. Prost did take the lead, Senna did try to take it from him and inside ten seconds two damaged racing cars were wreathed in a pall of dust, were buried into the surface of the run-off area as if it had become a graveyard; and that was another chilling image from another cold autumn. Senna clambered out and moved towards the track itself, plucking his driving gloves off as he went. Only once did he glance back and that seemed to be at his car, not Prost who lingered a brief moment beside the tyre-wall and he, too, was plucking his gloves off. Then he began to jog towards the track.

Questions arose clamorously. Would the race be stopped and re-started? The cars were in a potentially danger-ous position because anyone else going off there might strike them. Japanese efficiency solved that. Both cars were promptly hoisted away. Would Ferrari protest? Even if they did and the protest was upheld it would not help Prost. He could scarcely be awarded the race by default and so he would still have no points from it, was still nine points behind Senna and even if he did win Adelaide and Senna didn't finish the race there, he'd be punished by having to drop two points, the two he got from Canada in June.

Immediately the reverberations started. The Ferrari team manager Cesare Fiorio confirmed that no protest would be made but he did say it was a 'scandal' not to have stopped the race with the two cars in the positions they were in the run-off area. He added – and here was the nub, here was the sharpest of sharp edges to it – 'Prost was in front and had the right to turn into the corner.'

Balestre was not there but had seen it all on television. 'It was a scandal that the World Championship should be decided on such a collision. I leave everyone to be their own judge of who is to blame. I am sure all motor racing supporters throughout the world will feel as frustrated as I do after such an appalling end to the World Champion-ship.' He was asked a poignant question: will Senna be disqualified? 'I am the FISA President, not a judge. Last year race stewards disqualified Senna because he cut short in the chicane. This time I am told there were no elements to allow Senna's disqualification.'

Not that it mattered now. Disqualifying a man who had only reached the first corner of a race could hardly be con-strued as punishment, particularly since it could have no material effect on the Championship either way, and what

232

do you fine a man whose father is rich and who himself is earning fifteen million dollars a year?

There was understandably not the sort of euphoria at McLaren you normally get when a Championship has been won, although Senna did give Dennis a bear-hug when he returned to the pits. 'I had been asking the officials to move pole position to the other side of the track all weekend,' Senna said, 'and their refusal to do it created so many problems that I suppose this accident was likely to happen. But that's motor racing and a Championship title is the result of a whole season's work. This title is particularly satisfying to me as the competition from other teams has been much closer than when I won in 1988. As for the accident, it was just one of those things. I certainly wanted to win this race as much as any this season.'

The friendship with Prost had proved very fragile indeed. Prost said: 'Anyone who understands motor racing does not have to ask what happened. He did it on purpose because he saw that I had a good start, that my car was better and he had no chance to win. So he just pushed me out. What he did was more than unsporting, it was disgusting. I have no problems with losing the World Championship, I have lost many – but not this way. Can you imagine what young drivers think when they see things like that in Formula One? They'll think they can get away with anything.' And the fragile friendship? 'It is all over. I do not like people who show one thing but are different inside. Everything that has happened here has shown his real face. I hate this kind of situation. He has completely destroyed everything. For him it is much more important to win the Championship than it is for me. It is the only thing he has in life. He is completely screwed up.'

Nor was Prost finished yet. 'Senna is completely the opposite in character to what he wants people to believe. Technically I believe we won the World Championship.

We were not even side by side. If you accept Senna's behaviour then perhaps we will get to a situation where people will start entering a team with one car specifically intended to push off the opposition to enable the other guy to win. This man has no value.'

'I don't give a damn what he says,' Senna responded. 'He took a chance going into the first corner when he couldn't afford to. He knew I was going to come down the inside. He made the biggest mistake by closing the door. He knows I always go for the gap. It has turned things upside down from last year. I cannot be responsible for Prost's actions. I know what I can do and I am happy inside.'

Ron Dennis was more pragmatic. 'This would never have happened if the officials had agreed to move pole position to the other side of the track.'

Prost's words are eminently understandable but difficult to digest. Surely he knew Senna by now, he of all people? Surely he can't have been surprised by what happened at the first corner of the Japanese Grand Prix? Surely he had worked out the importance of it? Surely he did know Senna always went for the gap, always had gone for the gap? He'd had the most direct circumstantial evidence of that at the chicane at Suzuka, '89. And the phrase comes back like an echo: there are no desperate situations, only desperate men. Was Senna right? It's difficult to mount a defence because he was not yet alongside Prost and convention demands – absolutely demands – that you can only claim the corner if you are, unless of course the other guy moves out of your way. Surely Senna knew Prost wasn't going to do that, not here, not now?

Of course armchair critics (like me) can play judge, jury and executioner as long as they like, replay their video recordings of an incident, then replay them in slow-mo, then use the freeze-frame button to see exactly where one car was in relation to another and pronounce sentence. Courtesy of on-board cameras we have been treated to what it's really like for the driver and it all looks different from the cockpit. The angles which your slow-mo reveals so clearly are fluid fractions from there and everything is coming at you impossibly fast, fast, fast. In a milli-second Senna would have been alongside and the whole story altered but even Senna can't deal in milli-seconds, plus or minus. This is not to make excuses, not to exculpate anything – getting it right is what a driver should be able to do in whatever time is available to him – but it might perhaps help a little understanding.

There was, too, fall-out. The week after, Ferrari's chairman Piero Fuscaro wrote to FISA with a straightforward request that something be done so that in future this wouldn't happen again with 'more serious and sad consequences. Everything leads one to assume that, through lack of firmness on the part of officials, certain drivers believe that crashes are now an acceptable tactic.' And now the fall-out was becoming more intense. Fiat own Ferrari and Cesare Romiti, Fiat's managing director, said: 'We are not prepared to put in so much capital and man-hours building better cars just to see them shunted off the track.' The implication was clear and enormous: Ferrari were prepared to leave Formula One altogether.

It had come to this: Prost might or might not have taken the corner but Senna took the Championship.

The fall-out continued to fall all over the place. Ron Dennis returned from Japan and appeared on a BBC television programme, *Sportsnight*, where he was interviewed by Steve Rider. Dennis: 'We are a team steeped in commitment to doing it well and there is nothing that tarnishes our success more than that the Championship should be decided on an incident like this.'

Rider: 'Perhaps an ingredient was that there were two very highly motivated men on the front row?'

Dennis: 'It certainly didn't help.'

Rider: 'Let's take another look at that start and get your views on it. It did seem that Prost certainly got the better start. He gets a car's length pretty early on, doesn't he?' (A re-run of the start is now being played.)

Dennis: 'That's quite right. The grip on that side of the circuit is superior to the right-hand side. It's just here where Prost moves to the left of Senna and opens the door, Senna just makes a total commitment to the corner. As regards the pre-race strategy, we had everything to lose by not winning the race. The organizers had laid down some conditions limiting the places where it would be possible to overtake, and who emerged from that corner pretty much would have won the race. Therefore, with Ayrton needing to win, Alain needing to win, there was a lot of pressure to come out of that first corner first.'

Rider: 'Shall we have another look at it and perhaps explain a bit more about that little gap Senna saw because when Senna sees a gap every driver in the field knows he goes for it.' (The re-run is being re-run.)

Dennis: 'You can see here where Prost is clearly ahead and it's just coming up now, he moves to the left, opens the gap and Senna goes for it and then it's closed again. In our briefing before the event we were actually of the opinion that Prost – knowing he had to finish the next two races in good positions – would never close the door because the resulting consequences would have lost him the World Championship, he'd leave it open – and he didn't.'

Rider: 'In general do you think rivalries in the sport are getting a bit too intense and maybe becoming a danger during the course of races?'

Dennis: 'The problem with motor sport at the moment is that there is such a shortfall in the supply of top drivers. The drivers who are recognized as being la crème de la crème struggle to come to terms with being number two and it's

236

my view – and one shared by most people in motor sport – that Ayrton Senna is the best driver that motor sport has ever seen and therefore he becomes the subject of much criticism about his total commitment to the sport.'

In Paris FISA formally announced that a Special Commission of Inquiry for Safety was being formed to cast a careful eye over 'incidents' during the season. It would have extensive powers enabling it to amass evidence from whichever quarter it chose and that embraced all officials (including race stewards) as well as any documents. There was a telling, almost icy phrase that 'some of the participants' – drivers – had damaged the image of Formula One and that the image had 'deteriorated'. There was a telling, almost icy sting: the granting of Superlicences for the 1991 season would depend on the findings of this Commission.

A British Sunday newspaper trawled deep among its records and propped up a long article with the information that since the beginning of season 1987 Senna had been disqualified three times and involved in eleven crashes whilst winning twenty-two races; Prost had not been disqualified at all, had crashed only three times (two of them with Senna at Suzuka) and won nineteen races. I mention the article not because of the statistics, interesting though they are, but because it occupied a whole page, complete with diagrams of the crash of '90: Senna v Prost had now become a matter of international sporting importance and well worth the whole page in a British paper, although neither of them was remotely British. The matter had grown vastly, perhaps monstrously too big for parochialism.

Senna arrived in Adelaide trenchant and unrepentant in his logic. He spoke of the Commission thus: 'This is about a lot of drivers in a lot of races. A lot of incidents have occurred this year because of the intensity of competition between cars and drivers which was not present in 1988

237

and 1989. It is not directed at me. It just happened that this was announced shortly after Japan.'

He spoke of Prost thus: 'He made the better start and went towards the first corner just ahead of me. He moved to the inside but I knew my engine had better acceleration than his so I was not concerned. I knew there was a possibility to do it at the first corner so I chased him and as we came to the corner he moved to the outside and I went for the space. As I did so he came back at me. I was surprised because it was totally unexpected for a driver of his knowledge and experience to make such a move. Under the circumstances a crash was unavoidable. We hit each other side by side. You can see from the television cameras that it is a fact. If I had been leading under the same circumstances I would not have left room on the inside and if I had left room I would not under any circumstances have closed the door for a second time so I think it was a major tactical mistake by him. It was really pathetic to hear him say the race should have been stopped. I don't think anyone can dispute that our cars were in a safe position.

'In the end he makes me laugh because he is the guy that complains so much and not just this year but ever since we first raced as team mates in 1988. He complained a lot about me, then about Honda, then the following year he complained about me and Honda again, he complained about the team, and it was the team for which he won three Championships. Then he goes to a new team, Ferrari, and he criticizes a tyre company for supplying us with different tyres. Then he moves on and criticizes Berger, then Alesi, then his own team and management, then he ends up criticizing Mansell and finishes up criticizing me again so it comes as no surprise that he criticizes me over the Suzuka affair. I am used to it.

'This whole controversy has been going round a single man. If anybody gets near to him and something goes wrong he has something to say.' Senna added that the Championship had been won – and lost – during the whole season, not Suzuka, and Prost 'does a good job diverting people from thinking about that. His complaints in Japan were designed to ignore the other races in which we beat him. I find it amazing that an organization like Fiat and Ferrari is manipulated by one man.'

He appeared on television under interrogation by Jackie Stewart who in his crisp Scottish way said he (Senna) had been involved in more coming-togethers on circuits than any World Champion before him. For once Senna betrayed anger, a momentous lapse, shifted forward on his chair, used a cocked finger to stab an accompaniment to his defence. Stewart was prepared for – nay, anticipated – that Senna would walk out. He did not, of course.

By now Prost had had enough of being pursued by media men with microphones 'stuck up my nose' trying to goad him into fuelling it all again. He did say he had been misquoted about threatening to retire and 'if I don't speak now I can't be misquoted again'.

The first day of qualifying produced a situation uncanny enough to be haunting. Senna was quickest (1 minute 15.671) but Prost next (1 minute 16.635), and if it remained so, if that was the front row of the grid, what would happen from the green light when they moved down the start-finish straight and reached the S-shaped corner where there would be only room for one car? Even the contemplation of it was extremely uncomfortable. At one level Adelaide no longer carried the currency of a live Championship because that was decided, and in theory nobody needed to take particular risks. At the other level, the personal level, who knew?

Senna did get pole on the Saturday although his best time (1 minute 15.693) didn't improve on Friday. He had a tilt right at the end of the session 'just for the pure pleasure of driving and to please the spectators'. He judged that he felt 'too relaxed' to beat his own time. Berger and Mansell stole past Prost, who was off the pace with 1 minute 17.021. His Friday time placed him on the second row of the grid. That militated against Prost meeting Senna at the S and so it proved. Senna moved cleanly and incisively clear at the green, shook off Mansell and deep into the race – with Prost completely off the pace – had a lead of nearly twenty seconds. He went off into a tyre barrier. 'I couldn't get second gear, it was stuck in neutral.' He climbed out and walked away from 1990.

CHAPTER THIRTEEN

The Hall of Fame

'He's got his way of relaxing but when he's racing he's serious. We've had drivers worse than him in terms of intensity – without mentioning names – but he has an ability to concentrate and that's when he didn't like mixing with people. He puts his blinkers on, as I call it, and he was condemned because he didn't speak to people in the pit lane. You don't have to, you're there as a racing driver. People accuse me of the same, but I'm not there as a journalist, I'm not there to talk, I'm there to do a job. We had a couple of parties and the boys invited him round, a group of twelve, maybe fourteen and he'd love it, you know, a good Kiwi-style barbecue. If it was a bigger party, thirty, maybe forty, he would still be there but he wouldn't sit down and relax. My view is that he doesn't like too many people around, but that of course is his decision.' – Dick Bennetts.

'Sometimes I try to beat other people's achievements but on many occasions I find it's better to beat my own achievements. That can give me more satisfaction. I don't feel happy if I am comfortable. Something inside me pushes me when I get comfortable. It makes me go further and want to keep pushing.' – Ayrton Senna.

'I have to establish for myself my own limits. When I have reached those limits I want to beat them and establish new ones. I still don't know how far I can go. I have an understanding of what I am doing, but I don't know how far it will take me.' – Ayrton Senna.

*

Reginaldo Leme: 'I don't feel Senna is a happy man.'

Paulo Casseb: 'He's very lonely, very lonely. When he gets back to his hotel room he feels really lonely.'

Reginaldo: 'Every time, he is alone.'

Paulo: 'Why? Because at least twenty-four hours most days he concentrates on races and when he comes back to himself as a human being he feels around himself emptiness. Once he's finished at the track he goes back to the hotel and nothing happens.'

Reginaldo: 'He likes the races so much that it's very difficult when he becomes a human being again. I want to talk, go out to dinner, smile, he – no. He doesn't need this.'

Paulo: 'He does need that but from Friday onwards he just takes care about his sleeping time, his food, he's talking a little bit with people but he's always concentrating on the race. That's the reason I think he performs so well.'

'My girlfriend is even more famous than me in Brazil because she's in a very popular television series. When we go to the cinema and the lights go down, it's something more accessible to us – to be incognito.' – Ayrton Senna.

'On the plane back from Foz do Iguacu in 1981 was the last time I had a talk to him as a friend. Since then we have met in England, in Formula One and everything but we've never had the time to talk as friends. We say "Hello, good morning, how are you, how is the family?" and that's it. That's how it can happen, you get pulled apart by the pressures, I think so. He put all his effort into his career but outside motor racing he is an unhappy person. It's what you have to pay for a life like that. If you gain something you have to lose something. If he meets the woman of his life tomorrow and she gives him happiness outside motor racing he'll just stop, finish, that will be it. Because we are always concentrating on what we are doing we forget what the world is about. We don't know what's going on outside of our own lives. For us to keep going we have to go deeper and deeper into what we're doing. And that's what happened with him.' – Maurizio Sala.

'If I am obsessive it is in a positive way. I have a strong natural push but it is not unhealthy, not a disease.' – Ayrton Senna.

'A lot of it depends on the cars. You take a McLaren or a Ferrari which is going two seconds faster than the rest and their tyres look beautiful. The driver has to be able to set up the car balance so there is proper weight distribution, no understeer, no oversteer. A well-balanced car will go fast and be easy on tyres. That is a Senna hallmark, yes it is, although it's not his monopoly. I mean, he's fast at it. Senna and McLaren are one of the three easiest teams on tyres. His hallmark is to be able to understand the tyres and the car and be able to get the maximum out of them. So when the qualifiers don't work for many people they do for him. He gets more time out of them, he is able to know when he has to push hard on corners or not push too hard, he's able to scrub them in fast or, if he needs to, make them last an extra warm-up lap. He can always get time out of the qualifiers and many, many other people can't. That's a gift, absolutely, it's a God-given gift. I used to be a jet fighter pilot, a lot of people do dangerous things and they've got big balls but they don't think while they're doing them. The adrenalin starts, they'll go fast as hell but they don't know what happens in between. He knows exactly what happened in between. We talk to him all the time. I don't know that we've discussed how tyres are made. What we discuss is which tyres need scrubbing with sandpaper, for consistency. He wants to know what he should use and what he can expect. Certainly he is intense.' – Lee Gaug of Goodyear Tyres.

'Humanly, there's nobody out there at the moment who can push him. He has a reservoir that goes so much deeper than people imagine. He can pull it out and he does pull it out whenever he needs to. If it came to a last lap shoot-out, nobody should take him on. [Chuckle]. He's an enigma, he's not something that anybody is going to handle or understand. I can only say that I was part of his growing up and I don't think he's remotely the guy that we knew. He has proved, I am sure, so many things to himself.' – Alex Hawkridge.

'I am able to experience God's presence on earth. If I go to church I go on my own and I like to be there alone. I find more peace that way.' – Ayrton Senna.

'He wanted Formula One so much and yet he never got big-headed about it. For example, when he did get in and it was one of the first European races – Imola, I think – I said I want to come into the paddock. He just took off his FOCA pass and said "There you are." It never meant anything to him, it was no big deal. It was always his right to be in Formula One. Most people let Formula One go to their heads, don't they? "I'm a superstar." He doesn't. It never enters his mind that anyone is better than him. Obviously the pressure is getting to him now [Spa 1989], enormous pressure. He's quite capable of walking past here at this moment, giving me his FOCA pass and leaving the whole thing. He could do that. "I don't want this any more." At the end of the day, all he wants is to be home, doesn't he? He misses Brazil a lot, he always has done.' – Dennis Rushen.

'My determination, my dedication and the desire I have to be number one, that is my strength. I have the desire to go faster, to do it better. If I have become number one it means that I am better than anyone else, therefore if I go even better it should mean I am able to stay number one. I know how hard it is to become number one and now I know how hard it is to stay number one.' – Ayrton Senna.

'Ayrton is a driver who can channel his skills into well-defined periods of time. It can be for an entire race, as it normally is during the season, and it can also be for a pole lap. He is capable of weighing up far more options than me in how he approaches this. He takes into account the weather, the temperature of the tyres, the number of people out on the lap at any one time, he has a huge awareness of what other people are doing by virtue of his interpretation of the Longines monitor. He is able to take from the car the maximum in all the car's parameters which go towards fulfilling its performance. In other words he will extract the maximum from the brakes, from the tyres, from the engine, from the gearbox, every single part. He will consider each and all of these separately to find where his limit is and where he can extend it. Then he combines them all for the lap he does. For me, when he was with us, it was a privilege working with him, just seeing it done and being part of the team which helped him to do it.' – Steve Hallam.

'Harry was a good friend. I mean, he's still a friend. When I see him he speaks to me, he doesn't forget old friends. You get a lot of drivers who move up to Formula One and haven't got the time of day for you any more. I can remember when he was at Lotus, it was a press interview or something, photographers were taking pictures. I was walking by and he suddenly waved me over. I stood back. "No, no, come over." It's not just that I like him, I'm a fan.' – Malcolm Pullen.

'Physically I can do it for many, many years. I am in good physical condition. It depends on the limits of my mind. Once I am not extending those limits it will be time to go. I won't go on when I know I am past my best and all I can do is run in the middle of the field. I will not allow myself to do that.' – Ayrton Senna.

'I'm sure that he runs the McLaren team but they don't know it. I'm sure he does. I am sure he's created the real direction and the real controlling influence within that team without them knowing it's happening – and Ron would argue that "it couldn't happen in my team". Ayrton would influence the aerodynamic way the car performs, he'd influence the tyre manufacturer and the way they're going, he'd influence everybody because they all know that at the end of the day he delivers.' – Alex Hawkridge.

'We were testing at Zandvoort and Senna was driving for Toleman then. About seven o'clock in the evening everybody else had long gone except the mechanics. I was sitting there and I noticed Senna. He was just about to leave. He gets in his hire car, gets out again, goes over and stands for about twenty minutes looking at all the tyres he has gone through in the day. He was looking at whether the front left was grained, what this tyre was like, what that tyre was like. Then he disappeared to his hotel. I was so fascinated I went over and looked at all these tyres to see what the hell he was looking at.' – Steve Nichols.

*

'You know, between Mauricio Gugelmin and me it's truly friendship with a capital F. Only, it's true, we live differently today because we see each other very little. At the circuits we haven't the time. Before, we shared the same house in England and we were interested in the same things, we had so much in common. Now I live in Monaco when I am in Europe and I don't see Mauricio except at the circuits but deep down nothing has changed.' – Ayrton Senna.

'He means a lot to us. I want to see him quit before he kills himself. That's always a fear I have – that he'll kill himself. You can want it too much on just that one lap and you know it happens, doesn't it? He wants it more than anyone else, doesn't he? There's a little bit of Villeneuve in him and you never know in this business, do you? Your luck runs out one day. He has an intensity. You watch him, he is the best, he knows he is the best, but you can want something too much. He's unhealthy at the moment, isn't he? It's crowding him, that's right. He's very lonely, isn't he?' – Dennis Rushen.

'Once you sit in a racing car you know you are taking risks. We never think we are going to have an accident or get hurt but it is always at the back of the mind. It is that knowledge which determines the limit you establish for yourself. It is very important because it helps you to stay together and not go beyond your limit. You can be guided by self-preservation without losing your commitment.' – Ayrton Senna.

These quotations are set down in no particular order. I have selected them because they are perhaps the final fragments of the mirror and I hope that by now all the distortions are gone and we are seeing a clear image of the man. Piquet called him 'the São Paulo taxi driver'. As I write these words Piquet has won twenty-two Grand Prix races from 188 starts, Senna twenty-six from 110. It was a very silly thing to say and, paradoxically, leads us to the question we have only hinted at so far: how good is Senna in the broader historical sense? This evidently does not concern him. When he was asked if he ever compared himself with the great drivers of the past he replied 'No, I don't.' It does not prevent us from doing so, and in this matter all roads lead to Jim Clark.

Derek Bell was woken at five that morning. From the road outside the Hotel Luxhof in Speyer, near Hockenheim, he heard the cough and churn of an engine with a misfire being laboriously driven up and down. It was 7 April 1968.

'Stirling Moss was basically my hero but Jimmy Clark became my idol and I'd always used Jimmy as – what's the word? – my yardstick because he'd raced for years and never broken the skin on his body. Everybody told me motor racing was dangerous. I'd counter it with Jimmy Clark this and Jimmy Clark that.

'The day before, we were all soaked because it had been raining all afternoon and we went back to the hotel for tea. It was only my second race in what you might call the big time. Anyway, there we were having tea and Jimmy said: "When you come up to lap me don't get too close." I thought that is the former World Champion telling me to watch out when I come up to lap him. I said: "You must be joking. What's the trouble?" He said: "Oh, I've got this misfire."

'So the next morning I was woken by the sound of his car being driven by his mechanic. He was running this damn car up and down the public road outside the hotel trying to get this misfire going (so he could cure it) but of

248

course you don't get it unless you're really cracking on. I couldn't get back to sleep. I had breakfast with Jimmy and Graham Hill. The mechanics used to work on the cars in lock-ups underneath the hotel and the cars had gone to the track. Jimmy said: "OK, let's go." There I was in the back of the hire car, my eyes wide open. Graham drove, Jimmy in the passenger seat. I didn't say anything, just listened, and when we got to the track they stopped at my pit. The rain was pouring down. Jimmy said: "Goodbye, have a good race."

'The race started and I was lying fourth and I came round and there was the accident. I don't think I could even see the car. It was where the first chicane is now. It was flat – even in the rain it was flat two abreast, so he must have gone off of his own accord . . .'

Jim Clark, driving a Lotus in a Formula Two race, was killed. Mystery still surrounds it and will always do so. He was thirty-two. He had driven only 72 Grand Prix races, had been on pole 33 times, had won 25 times. The number of pole positions was an absolute record and stood until 3 June 1989 when Ayrton Senna took a Marlboro McLaren Honda round 2.36 miles of street roads at Phoenix, Arizona, in 1 minute 30.710 seconds.

All comparisons are dangerous and the more so when you are comparing men from different eras because you have to pluck them from their own contexts and who knows where that leaves them? This is more pointed in motor racing than any other sport: a car is subject to a rate of improvement without known horizons. Engine designer Brian Hart says 'the bottom line is that there is so much you can do now that all the engines are electrically managed. If it was mechanically limited, you'd be knackered. But it isn't. Nobody can see limits to the frontier of electronics.'

A runner is constrained by his own body and can't change it for a new one each season. If he takes drugs he finds a new constraint: what the drugs can enable his body to do – and no more. A footballer kicks a ball. His fitness may be better than his father's, his tactics more refined, his boots of better material, the ball of better material, but these are only, so to speak, creature comforts. He is still kicking a ball well or badly, just the way his father and grandfather did.

The racing driver is handling a machine utterly remote from anything even a generation before. You only have to glance casually at photographs to know that. The pace of progress, often measured by months – and supercharged at sporadic intervals by complete innovation – creates world after world, and when this is magnified across twenty years (I am writing in 1990; Clark died in 1968) the gulf is so vast that the worlds seem related only in that one somehow spawned the other.

This is why when arguments begin they are instinctively confined to eras. Is Senna better than Prost or Mansell? You can pore over that one endlessly, but at least you have some sort of direct form guide on which to base evidence. Was Fangio better than Ascari and Moss? Was Clark better than Stewart and Rindt?

The problem is that the eras virtually never overlap. Of the three groups above, there is only one example. Moss raced against Clark eleven times and even then, of course, Moss was at the end of a career, Clark at the beginning. Or, putting it more starkly, Fangio retired in 1958, two years before Senna was born.

There is another immediate problem. Up to and including Clark, drivers drove whatever they fancied wherever they fancied many weekends of their lives. The Formula One contract precluding everything but Formula One – and even regulating what pastimes a driver can pursue – did not exist and would have been unacceptable. It would have violated the spirit of the times. (Senna, however: 'I absolutely refuse to do sports in which I could break a leg or an arm.') And driving a variety of cars? This was how Moss won the Mille Miglia and Clark found himself, while he was trying to become World Champion Formula One champion again, in a Formula Two race in Hockenheim (he'd gone there in preference to driving a Ford sportscar in a 500-mile race at Brands Hatch). Both he and Graham Hill took part in the RAC Rally. Hill contested Le Mans, so did Moss, so did Clark. He won Indianapolis. To take a random year, 1962, Clark drove a Lotus 21 at Cape Town, a Lotus Elite at Daytona, the Lotus 24 in the Grand Prix races, and an Aston Martin at Silverstone.

'It was the only chance to see how good a young driver was, to compete against Clark and Hill and Stewart in Formula Two races,' Bell says. 'Then Jimmy would be in a Lotus Cortina afterwards and that was when he'd be something to watch . . . the way he drove that Cortina. One time he was literally on the RAC Rally with a bloody Lotus Cortina! It was certainly much more friendly but the guys who wanted to make it could. It was a bit intense. I remember seeing a lot of white-faced drivers. One was Trevor Taylor and he always lived on the white-knuckle-ride, he always walked up to you with this stance: "Christ, I've survived another moment in practice, it's a miracle . . ."'

This does not negate the basic premise that it was more friendly then, more relaxed out of the cars; the drivers were approachable, Clark (by nature shy) was just a man in a crowd. Bell retains a flavour of the man: 'He was such a nice bloke, he was so calm. Obviously the atmosphere in racing has changed considerably since. He talked to everybody, he didn't really keep himself to himself, he would chat if people wanted to. He was such an idol of everybody that maybe they didn't dare to talk to him that much. He was most easy-going. I was amazed at how easy-going, and of course for a young bloke like me I hung on every word he said.'

So we have the gulf: Fangio competing all over the place, like Ascari, and Moss, and Clark; while in contrast Senna is held a captive of the Formula One contract, like the others of his generation.

We have already seen that at Oulton Park in 1982 Senna won the celebrity Talbot Ti race easily. We have already seen that he won another celebrity race at the Nürburgring in 1984 in a Mercedes 190E, and that, two months later at the same circuit, he did a fast lap in a Porsche 956 in a round of the World Sportscar Championship when he hadn't handled anything like it before. All this does not amount to much – three races – but you cannot escape the conclusion, particularly when it is balanced against what he had done in karts and a variety of single-seater cars, that he can drive anything fast. Would he have been fast in a Lotus Cortina? You bet your life. (Gugelmin once said, when I asked him how good Senna was: 'Well, put it this way, if you took twenty-six double-decker buses and put twenty-six Grand Prix drivers in them and raced around Silverstone, we know who'd win, don't we?' Point taken.)

In the early autumn of 1986 a van crawled up a tree-lined 'road' in mid-Wales, hit a tree and brought it down. Among the passengers was a Ford and rally sport dealer called Mike Hill. 'We had to go and get a hand saw from a local farmer to cut it into pieces. Guess who was up there on the bonnet doing it? Ayrton Senna. We'd been told he was miserable and arrogant. Nonsense. He was a hell of a nice guy . . .'

Russell Bulgin had had a most original idea: why don't we see what Senna can do in a rally car or, to be precise, several rally cars? It was an idea Senna liked a lot and when Bulgin rang him he opened his diary, found two free days and said 'whichever day you want'. So they went to what Hill describes as 'a rally stage which was no longer used as that, but typical mid-Wales, gravel, bends, hills'.

Senna took the wheel of a Ford Cosworth Sierra Turbo – a 300bhp turbo-charged rally car. 'The first corner he flung the car in and went off into a ditch,' Hill says, 'but he didn't do that again. He seemed so natural, he learnt so quickly.'

That car was the treasured property of Phil Collins, who had been rallying since 1978. 'I'd never met the guy before,' Collins says. 'It was a week before the final round of the Sierra Challenge – which I needed to win – so I was a bit nervous about anything going wrong. We strapped him in the passenger seat. I gave him a ride to show him what it was about. He was scared witless, he was letting out gasps, the usual stuff from someone in a rally car for the first time. He took over and I was the passenger. I talked to him about the difference between tarmac and the loose stuff. I gave him as much simple theory as I could.

'The first corner was a fast right-hander, almost square, and he did everything wrong, he approached it from the outside, he had understeer, we went into the ditch and bounced along over a row of saplings. "I'm sorry, I'm not thinking, now I know what you meant." There wasn't a mark on the car. Away we went again. Being the nice guy he is he was careful not to damage the car but gradually over two runs he became far more professional at it.'

He drove a Metro Clubman, insisting on having Bulgin in the passenger seat. Bulgin: 'What you notice most is his right foot. It is never still. Senna is literally tapping the throttle through its half-inch of travel. Continuously. The rev counter doesn't flicker, but he's dancing on the accelerator with tiny movements. This car is getting very sideways. Then you tumble it. He's using the throttle to keep the front end working, to give him some – as he puts it – bite.'

He was fast in the Metro, fast in a four-wheel Escort, fast in a Nova. Senna would say that 'here it's much more natural because you have to improvise all the time, you have to have a lot of judgement. There is no room for error. Otherwise you go off the road.'

Collins was spectating: 'I could see he was enjoying it, attacking corners sideways, there was a bigger plume of dust being carried behind the cars – and then he said: "I would like to drive your car again . . ."'

Collins demurred.

'Come on, let me.' Collins finally did what a good man would do and agreed. 'Senna was brilliant. He was braking with his left foot, bringing the power in at exactly the right place, throwing it, and I felt totally safe. And that Sierra was not an easy car to get the most out of, a wide power band, turbo lag. "Perfect," I said, and when I got out I said "This boy is something else." There was nothing to add to that.'

Bulgin, not a man given to being awestruck, wrote this: 'Senna's last try in the Cosworth is wonderful. He takes the final left-hander in three jolts of oversteer, running the car up the shale piled on the track edge to straighten its exit. The engine note doesn't waver, the hands pummelling the steering wheel. He looks like a rally driver: a brave rally driver.'

Hill remembers Senna saying 'he was very surprised at how much traction the Cosworth had on different surfaces and amazed at how much grip the Metro had. He just got better and better at it. I formed the impression that, given a couple of events, he'd be right up there.'

'We didn't have a budget from the magazine for the job and if Senna had asked for £1,000 for the day I don't know

254

what we would have done,' Bulgin says. 'I asked him what he did want and he replied "I don't want anything. I came here to learn." I said "Well, at least let me fill your Mercedes up with petrol." He said "No, no, nothing thank you."'

And a last memory of mid-Wales. Collins: 'When it was over I said "Now you have driven my Cosworth let me come and have a go in your Formula One car." He said "It is not a problem for me ... [pause, slow smile] ... but it is not my car ..."'

In comparisons, statistics mean very little. You need to know a great deal more, like how good the other drivers were, how hard (or easy) the cars were to handle, who had the best cars, and even perhaps how high the overall standard was in any particular era.

'I drove the Cooper Maserati, which was an absolutely diabolical thing, like driving a big tractor,' Bell says. 'If you happened to be in a Cosworth Lotus, like Jimmy, I guess it was rather nice. They were big cars then, they were fast, but of course there was no great wham of power coming in. They had pretty wide tyres. My first Grand Prix (Monza 1968) was also the first time we had wings, which went up and down as you accelerated. You could throw the cars round, oh yes. The Ferrari was the car I got used to. You could actually chuck it at corners because you had bottom end power pulling; but you never had great power, it didn't come in like the Cosworth, it was just a nice, typical Ferrari V12. It was purring away from no revs to top revs, you know, no trouble. But they were chuckable, all right. I've got some pictures of me in that first Grand Prix, complete opposite lock, lovely stuff ...' Search photographic libraries and you won't find a picture of Senna doing this sort of thing. The cars he drove simply wouldn't do it.

This brings us back to Clark. 'He always looked smooth,

that was the amazing thing. He was so smooth, well within control, he seemed always to drive so much in control. He was such a neat driver, he was a bit like Jackie Stewart, I mean he wasn't tail-out-over-the-kerbs like Jochen Rindt.'

Now – the statistics:

Juan Manuel Fangio (1950–58): 51 races for four teams, 28 pole positions, 24 wins, five World Championships.

Alberto Ascari (1950–55): 32 races for three teams, 14 pole positions, 13 wins, two World Championships.

Stirling Moss (1951–61): 66 races for nine teams, 16 pole positions, 16 wins, never World Champion.

Jim Clark (1960–68): 72 races for one team, 33 pole positions, 25 wins, two World Championships.

Jackie Stewart (1965–73): 99 races for three teams, 17 pole positions, 27 wins, three World Championships.

Jochen Rindt (1964–70): 60 races for three teams, 10 pole positions, 6 wins, one World Championship.

Alain Prost (1980–90): 169 races for three teams, 20 pole positions, 44 wins, three World Championships.

Nigel Mansell (1980–90): 149 races for three teams, 15 pole positions, 16 wins, no World Championship.

Ayrton Senna (1984–90): 110 races for three teams, 52 pole positions, 26 wins, two World Championships.

Such statistics prove little, except that all these drivers were very good, but notice Senna's striking rate and his totals after only six years compared to, say, the six years of Rindt. As Alex Hawkridge has said: 'I believe in the merit system . . .'

'In my opinion there is no-one in the modern era like Jimmy – Jimmy wasn't the tiger that Senna is,' Bell says. 'We've said for some time that Senna lives dangerously, but Formula One is much more competitive so I suppose you have to. In that sense it really is another era. Senna is developing into being the consummate driver but Jimmy was that all the time. He didn't have to develop. He never looked as though he was stretched. I think he had it in him to go quicker although Senna too is driving within himself, yes he is . . .'

Jackie Stewart is sitting outside the Ford motorhome at Monza, 1989 – the day before the Prost-McLaren eruption. Since Stewart is a central character in this discussion, let him speak:

'I don't think the time has come for Senna to be on the same page of history as people like Fangio or Clark or Niki Lauda. Every time there is a brilliant new driver coming along everybody says he's probably the greatest driver ever. It happened to me, it happened to Niki, it happened to Prost. What you have to do is stay longer than Senna has and establish yourself. At the moment it's really unfair competition [McLaren verus the rest] and it has been now for two years. He's going to have to consolidate his position over three or four years before he gets on that particular page of history.

'To start proclaiming it at this early stage is unfair on him. They said the same about Alain and Alain is now growing into that mantle – not because he's won more Grands Prix than Fangio or me or Jimmy or anybody else, but because he has consolidated into being the skill that everybody accepts. Of course it is possible that Senna can become this.

'In America in the Football Hall of Fame, why do they not give them their positions until they have really shown themselves to be the great people that the Hall of Fame represents? Senna has had a good season [1989] like Jim Clark had in 1963, but Jim Clark drove for another five years.

'Driving styles? Clark was even smoother than Senna. You watch Senna go round a corner, he's on and off the throttle a lot. Clark didn't do that and Prost doesn't do it either, so I'd put Prost more towards the Clark style.

'Senna I respect enormously as a very rapid driver but there is a mental element missing. Why did he have an accident on the first lap of the Brazilian Grand Prix? Why did he have that coming together with Mansell at Spa in 1987? It was Mansell's fault – and also Senna's fault. Why did he have a crash here in 1988 when he was going for the Championship? Why did he go off at Monte Carlo? He's had two incredible seasons of racing with an advantage that Fangio and Clark never had over the rest. I mean, how can you compensate for fifty horsepower difference? If I had nine horsepower of an advantage I'd have thought they'd given me a Christmas present. [This does not explain how Prost, with the same fifty horsepower, was blown away.]

'Senna would have driven my Tyrrell just as well as I did or Jimmy would have done . . . or Fangio . . . or Nuvolari . . . because when you get skill of that level people just can. Clark would have driven Nuvolari's Alfa as well as Nuvolari . . .'

These are wise and pragmatic words (though not really an answer to the big question); if we project them forward, say, over another couple of years we discover that, assuming Senna maintains his present striking rate, he will have taken around seventy pole positions and won around forty races. Senna: 'In my spirit, I still have numerous years in Formula One left in front of me. It won't please certain people.'

We shall never establish who, of all these great drivers, is 'the best', but I have a feeling that Senna's stature will grow when he retires and that he – not Clark – will become the yardstick and the touchstone. This may take years, but in the historical context time will always be on his side. His career will be too monumental for anything else and a question will remain. Who, of all of them, would you have risked your life savings on to beat him? Hawkridge: 'Nobody out there should take him on . . .'

So what have we? A selfish man (professionally) in a selfish sport. A man who has taken a long and deliberate route towards a solitary exploitation of himself and is now close to authentic greatness measured against all comers past, present and future, if indeed he has not reached it already. A man who invited misunderstanding because he chose to remain safe behind The Face. He did not reply to Prost's accusations over Imola 1989 for six months and when he did he began (reluctantly) with these words: 'It didn't serve any purpose to talk about it. I took the stance of keeping it to myself. What do you want to stir all that up for . . . ?'

A man who has a talent bordering on the mysterious. You simply cannot clamber into unfamiliar cars as he has done – FF 1600, FF 2000, Talbot, Porsche, Mercedes, Ford Cosworth, Metro, Nova, F3, F1 turbo and normally-aspirated – and make them go fast first time out without real natural talent.

This is what designer Steve Nichols says of his time with Senna at McLaren in the turbo, watch-your-fuel-consumption era: 'He was always storing up all kinds of information and he came back and regurgitated it to me – what the car was doing at the entry of every corner, what it was doing at the exit and what it was doing in the middle of the corner. Even several hours later he could tell it all to me or write notes which would be good for the next testing at that circuit. In addition to that he remembered exactly what the engine was doing and related that to the whole thing. He'd say he was doing such-and-such a time and I'd ask him what sort of fuel economy he got. He could tell me to three decimal places [on the cockpit read-out which altered all the while]. "When I did a 1 minute 29 seconds lap I got this fuel economy, when I did a 1 minute 39 seconds lap I got this fuel economy." In the car he had a knob which controlled the boost and a knob that controlled various other circuits on the engine, the so-called mixture settings, but it was more complicated than that: it controlled air temperature, fuel mixture, ignition settings so there were various combinations. He remembered all those combinations, what position he had had the knobs in, which one had what effect on fuel economy. To sum it up, he had two knobs, one with eight positions and one with five positions, and he remembered all the combinations and what effect they had – and all that while he was driving the car very, very fast.'

It takes a very special talent to do that and the words we have heard so often before – intensity, dedication, concentration – simply do not explain it fully. Could Fangio or Clark or Stewart himself have given the fuel read-out to three decimal places each lap at the end of testing, and how each tyre behaved at each corner?

Beneath it all there remains the elusive prey. Even those who were close to him along the way, those who shared the anxieties, prepared the cars, lived through it all with him and saw him when his guard was down are still faced with unanswered questions. Nigel Stepney: 'It takes a long time to get to know him and I don't know him fully.' Alex Hawkridge: 'Would he have retired? I never know with Ayrton. He's a self-assured, confident negotiator and I'm sure it's the same dilemma for anybody that he deals with. You just don't know how far he'll go, how far he believes what he says. I don't doubt him.' Funny how they both used the same phrase – 'don't know'.

It is odd that Senna has given us so many superb motor racing moments and yet so few rejoice in them. People speak of Villeneuve with misty eyes. They will never do this of Senna, although he could be daring enough, heat your blood, drive like a real racer, perennially going for it. Observers castigate him for taking risks; but when Villeneuve took them, the same observers rejoiced. A story illustrates it nicely: Villeneuve in an uncompetitive Ferrari at Zandvoort back down the grid and the team begged him to drive a percentage race, just get to the finish, see if you can pick up a point or two. Villeneuve crashed on the first corner trying to get into the lead. Wonderful vignette of the man, eh? Yes. Good old Villeneuve, the right stuff, eh? Yes. If Senna had done exactly the same thing the vilification would have begun instantly.

This has to be due entirely to other people's perception of the man, not the man himself, and probably that's to do with The Face and the silences and the distances between you and him. He never did find a method of communicating with the public and they responded by sometimes jeering and taunting him when the car broke down or he crashed. Press rooms would do the same – an amazing sight. Why? Because he was unco-operative? Because he was always locked into himself or locked in the McLaren motorhome? Because everybody liked Prost and wanted him to win? Maybe. I think it was something else, built upon those things: ordinary people simply could not relate to one man with a total obsession, it was utterly unfamiliar to them, they instinctively distrusted it. They never saw the warmth at all and consequently concluded that the warmth didn't exist. Curious, too, that Senna should seek to say the obsession was not 'unhealthy' – a strong and revealing word.

It is almost inhuman that he could isolate himself to the degree that he has and, as it would seem, remain impervious to whatever others thought of him – or if he was hurt by it, choose not to defend himself until he was absolutely ready. This is mental discipline of a mercilessly high order, whether you approve of it or not, and it instantly separates him from the mainstream of Formula One drivers, never mind mere mortals like you or me.

It has led to a ridiculous situation. There is a very real danger that the magnitude of what he has achieved will in some way be obscured by an external perception of him; that he will have to force his way into the Hall of Racing Fame rather than be embraced with open arms; that the precious moments of absolute artistry will be forgotten because somehow there was something about the man which did not encourage remembrance of them – especially after the autumn chills of 1989 and 1990.

Or perhaps this is completely wrong. Perhaps it is because he won races so easily, picked off pole after pole so easily, piled up points into such a mountain that nobody is surprised by anything he does. Senna on pole again, and they'll shrug, mutter 'what did you expect?' and talk about something else. And the splendour of the lap, the construction of the lap, the fleeting, transient nuances of the lap, the lonely moves made out there on the far side of the circuit are obscured.

Or perhaps it is all just too awesome to find a sensible context in which to fit Senna's achievement. Of the thirty-two Grand Prix races in 1988 and 1989 he was only beaten six times when the car was still running at the end. On every other occasion he crashed, the car failed or he won. Those are the statistics. In 1989 only one man actually overtook him – Mansell.

Memory holds him at Spa in 1989 in the heavy rain. The start was delayed and the murmur was that it was crazy to race, truly crazy. Sure, they raced. You need to know Spa to savour Senna, need to know the steepness of the descent to Eau Rouge, the strange ferocity of the left-right kink at the bottom of Eau Rouge, the mountain-climb up the other side; and you need to know that running water is slipping, grey and ghostly, across the track in rivers and no driver can be sure where; you need to know that Eau Rouge is taken at high speed, balls to the wall . . .

He seized the lead and moved away from the pack at a controlled pace. Through his own spray you could glimpse him on the descent, the yellow helmet rigid. You could see the certainty of control through Eau Rouge, hear the blip of a rumbling, grumbling engine working itself up to a shriek; and he did this fifty-three times, each one the same. No mistake. No deviation. No suggestion that he was on the equivalent of sheet ice. It was a train ride through a storm, just following the rails. For him, of course, it wasn't like that at all, it was nervy, dangerous, every moment an uncertainty; the trick – he made it look easy.

Memory holds that, too: a man where he has always been, alone in a car, and the car where it has so often been, alone on a racing circuit because all the others are back there somewhere struggling and jostling, playing their percentages, urging what they can out of their cars, but in a completely different race.

Standing there on the press room platform with the rain spitting in the eyes and the crowd spread like a mushroom field of umbrellas, one of those silly subconscious things happened. A line of a song stirred within me almost as if it had chosen itself; it was being delivered by the sharp-smooth voice of Carly Simon and the line went on and on as Ayrton Senna da Silva went on and on, down that descent, down into the dripping mouth of Eau Rouge.

Nobody does it better . . .

P = pole position; Fl = fastest lap; R = retired; Dns = did not start; Dis = disqualified.

1973	1 Jul First kart race Interlagos	1
1977	S. American championships	1
1978	S. American champion, Brazilian championships	1
	13–17 Sep World Karts, Le Mans	6
1979	Brazilian championships	1
	18–23 Sep World Karts, Estoril	2
1980	Brazilian championships	1
	17–21 Sep World Karts, Nivelles, Belgium	2
1981	Brazilian championships	1

Formula Ford 1600 (Van Diemen)
(P & O = P & O Ferries; TT = Townsend Thoresen)

Date	Sponsor	Circuit	Car	Pos.	Title
1 Mar	P & O	Brands Hatch	Van Diemen RF80-Ford	5	
8 Mar	TT	Thruxton	Van Diemen RF81-Ford	3	
15 Mar	TT	Brands Hatch	Van Diemen RF81-Ford	1	
22 Mar	TT	Mallory	Van Diemen RF81-Ford	2	P
5 Apr	TT	Mallory	Van Diemen RF81-Ford	2	
3 May	TT	Snetterton	Van Diemen RF81-Ford	2	P
24 May	RAC	Oulton Park	Van Diemen RF81-Ford	1	F1
25 May	TT	Mallory	Van Diemen RF81-Ford	1	
7 June	TT	Snetterton	Van Diemen RF81-Ford	1	F1
21 June	RAC	Silverstone	Van Diemen RF81-Ford	2	
27 June	TT	Oulton Park	Van Diemen RF81-Ford	1	F1
4 Jul	RAC	Donington	Van Diemen RF81-Ford	1	F1
12 Jul	RAC	Brands Hatch	Van Diemen RF81-Ford	4	F1
25 Jul	TT	Oulton	Van Diemen RF81-Ford	1	F1
26 Jul	RAC	Mallory	Van Diemen RF81-Ford	1	F1
2 Aug	TT	Brands Hatch	Van Diemen RF81-Ford	1	
9 Aug	RAC	Snetterton	Van Diemen RF81-Ford	1	F1
15 Aug	TT	Donington	Van Diemen RF81-Ford	1	

31 Aug	Thruxton	TT	Van Diemen RF81-Ford	1	P/F1
16–20 Sep	World Karts		Parma	4	
29 Sep	Brands Hatch	TT	Van Diemen RF81-Ford	2	F1

1982 Formula Ford 2000 (Rushen Green Racing)

(PB = Pace British FF 2000; EFDA = European 2000)

7 Mar	Brands Hatch	PB	Van Diemen RF82-Ford	1	P/F1
27 Mar	Oulton	PB	Van Diemen RF82-Ford	1	P/F1
28 Mar	Silverstone	PB	Van Diemen RF82-Ford	1	P/F1
4 Apr	Donington	PB	Van Diemen RF82-Ford	1	P/F1
9 Apr	Snetterton	PB	Van Diemen RF82-Ford	1	P/F1
12 Apr	Silverstone	PB	Van Diemen RF82-Ford	1	P/F1
18 Apr	Zolder	EFDA	Van Diemen RF82-Ford		P/R
2 May	Donington	EFDA	Van Diemen RF82-Ford	1	P/F1
3 May	Mallory	PB	Van Diemen RF82-Ford	1	F1
9 May	Zolder	EFDA	Van Diemen RF82-Ford		P/F1/R
30 May	Oulton	PB	Van Diemen RF82-Ford		R
30 May	Oulton	Celebrity	Sunbeam Talbot T1	1	F1
31 May	Brands Hatch	PB	Van Diemen RF82-Ford	1	F1

6 June	PB	Mallory	Van Diemen RF82-Ford	1	F1
13 June	PB	Brands Hatch	Van Diemen RF82-Ford	1	F1
20 June	EFDA	Hockenheim	Van Diemen RF82-Ford		P/R
26 June	PB	Oulton	Van Diemen RF82-Ford	1	F1
3 Jul	EFDA	Zandvoort	Van Diemen RF82-Ford	1	P
4 Jul	PB	Snetterton	Van Diemen RF82-Ford	2	
10 Jul	PB	Castle Combe	Van Diemen RF82-Ford	1	P/F1
1 Aug	PB	Snetterton	Van Diemen RF82-Ford	1	F1
8 Aug	EFDA	Hockenheim	Van Diemen RF82-Ford	1	P/F1
15 Aug	EFDA	Österreichring	Van Diemen RF82-Ford	1	P/F1
22 Aug	EFDA	Jyllandsring	Van Diemen RF82-Ford	1	P/F1
30 Aug	PB	Thruxton	Van Diemen RF82-Ford	1	F1
5 Sep	PB	Silverstone	Van Diemen RF82-Ford	1	F1
12 Sep	EFDA	Mondello Park	Van Diemen RF82-Ford	1	F1
15–19 Sep	World Karts	Kalmar, Sweden		14	
26 Sep	PB	Brands Hatch	Van Diemen RF82-Ford	2	F1
13 Nov	Formula 3	Thruxton	Ralt RT3-Toyota	1	P/F1

1983 Marlboro British Formula 3 Championship (West Surrey Racing except Macau when Senna drove for Marlboro/Teddy Yip)

Date	Team	Circuit	Car	Pos	Result
6 Mar	MB	Silverstone	Ralt RT3-Toyota	1	F1
13 Mar	MB	Thruxton	Ralt RT3-Toyota	1	P
20 Mar	MB	Silverstone	Ralt RT3-Toyota	1	P/F1
27 Mar	MB	Donington	Ralt RT3-Toyota	1	P/F1
4 Apr	MB	Thruxton	Ralt RT3-Toyota	1	P
24 Apr	MB	Silverstone	Ralt RT3-Toyota	1	P/F1
2 May	MB	Thruxton	Ralt RT3-Toyota	1	P/F1
8 May	MB	Brands Hatch	Ralt RT3-Toyota	1	P/F1
30 May	MB	Silverstone	Ralt RT3-Toyota	1	P/F1
12 June	MB	Silverstone	Ralt RT3-Toyota		R
19 June	MB	Cadwell Park	Ralt RT3-Toyota		P/Dns
3 Jul	MB	Snetterton	Ralt RT3-Toyota		F1/R
16 Jul	MB	Silverstone	Ralt RT3-Toyota	1	P/F1
24 Jul	MB	Donington	Ralt RT3-Toyota	2	P/F1
6 Aug	MB	Oulton	Ralt RT3-Toyota		F1/R
29 Aug	MB	Silverstone	Ralt RT3-Toyota	1	P
11 Sep	MB	Oulton	Ralt RT3-Toyota		R
18 Sep	MB	Thruxton	Ralt RT3-Toyota		P/R

2 Oct	MB	Silverstone	Ralt RT3-Toyota	2	P/Fl
20 Oct	Macau GP	Macau	Ralt RT3-Toyota	1	P/Fl
23 Oct	MB	Thruxton	Ralt RT3-Toyota	1	P/Fl

1984 *Formula One* (Toleman Group Motorsport except 12 May, Nürburgring, Daimler Benz AG and 15 July, Nürburgring, Joest Racing Porsche 956)

25 Mar	Brazilian GP	Rio	Toleman TG183B-Hart		R
7 Apr	S. African GP	Kyalami	Toleman TG183B-Hart	6	
29 Apr	Belgian GP	Zolder	Toleman TG183B-Hart	6	R
6 May	San Marino GP	Imola	Toleman TH183B-Hart		R
12 May	Inaugural SCR	Nürburgring	Mercedes Benz 190E	1	
20 May	French GP	Dijon	Toleman TG184-Hart		R
3 June	Monaco GP	Monte Carlo	Toleman TG184-Hart	2	Fl
17 June	Canadian GP	Montreal	Toleman TG184-Hart	7	
24 June	Detroit GP	Detroit	Toleman TG184-Hart		R
8 July	Dallas GP	Dallas	Toleman TG184-Hart		R
15 July	Nürburgring				
22 July	1000 KMS	Nürburgring	Porsche 956	8	
	British GP	Brands Hatch	Toleman TG184-Hart	3	

Date	GP	Circuit	Car	Grid	Result
5 Aug	German GP	Hockenheim	Toleman TG184-Hart		R
19 Aug	Austrian GP	Österreichring	Toleman TG184-Hart		R
26 Aug	Dutch GP	Zandvoort	Toleman TG184-Hart		R
9 Sep	Italian GP	Monza	Toleman TG184-Hart		Dns
7 Oct	European GP	Nürburgring	Toleman TG184-Hart		R
21 Oct	Portuguese GP	Estoril	Toleman TG184-Hart	3	R

1985

Date	GP	Circuit	Car	Grid	Result
7 Apr	Brazilian GP	Rio	Lotus 97T-Renault		R
21 Apr	Portuguese GP	Estoril	Lotus 97T-Renault	1	P/Fl
5 May	San Marino GP	Imola	Lotus 97T-Renault	7	P
19 May	Monaco GP	Monte Carlo	Lotus 97T-Renault		P/R
16 June	Canadian GP	Montreal	Lotus 97T-Renault	16	Fl
23 June	Detroit GP	Detroit	Lotus 97T-Renault		P/Fl/R
7 Jul	French GP	Paul Ricard	Lotus 97T-Renault		R
21 Jul	British GP	Silverstone	Lotus 97T-Renault	10	
4 Aug	German GP	Nürburgring	Lotus 97T-Renault		R
18 Aug	Austrian GP	Österreichring	Lotus 97T-Renault	2	
25 Aug	Dutch GP	Zandvoort	Lotus 97T-Renault	3	
8 Sep	Italian GP	Monza	Lotus 97T-Renault	3	P

[271]

Date	GP	Circuit	Car	Pos	P/R
15 Sep	Belgian GP	Spa	Lotus 97T-Renault	1	
6 Oct	European GP	Brands Hatch	Lotus 97T-Renault	2	P
19 Oct	S. African GP	Kyalami	Lotus 97T-Renault		R
3 Nov	Australian GP	Adelaide	Lotus 97T-Renault		P/R

1986

Date	GP	Circuit	Car	Pos	P/R
23 Mar	Brazilian GP	Rio	Lotus 98T-Renault	2	P
13 Apr	Spanish GP	Jerez	Lotus 98T-Renault	1	P
27 Apr	San Marino GP	Imola	Lotus 98T-Renault		P/R
11 May	Monaco GP	Monte Carlo	Lotus 98T-Renault	3	
25 May	Belgian GP	Spa	Lotus 98T-Renault	2	
15 June	Canadian GP	Montreal	Lotus 98T-Renault	5	
22 June	Detroit GP	Detroit	Lotus 98T-Renault	1	P
6 Jul	French GP	Paul Ricard	Lotus 98T-Renault		P/R
13 Jul	British GP	Brands Hatch	Lotus 98T-Renault		R
27 Jul	German GP	Hockenheim	Lotus 98T-Renault	2	
10 Aug	Hungarian GP	Hungaroring	Lotus 98T-Renault	2	P
17 Aug	Austrian GP	Österreichring	Lotus 98T-Renault		R
7 Sep	Italian GP	Monza	Lotus 98T-Renault		R
21 Sep	Portuguese GP	Estoril	Lotus 98T-Renault	4	P

12 Oct	Mexican GP	Mexico City	Lotus 98T-Renault	3	P
26 Oct	Australian GP	Adelaide	Lotus 98T-Renault		R

1987

12 Apr	Brazilian GP	Rio	Lotus 99T-Honda		R
3 May	San Marino GP	Imola	Lotus 99T-Honda	2	P
17 May	Belgian GP	Spa	Lotus 99T-Honda		R
31 May	Monaco GP	Monte Carlo	Lotus 99T-Honda	1	Fl
21 June	Detroit GP	Detroit	Lotus 99T-Honda	1	Fl
5 Jul	French GP	Paul Ricard	Lotus 99T-Honda	4	
12 Jul	British GP	Silverstone	Lotus 99T-Honda	3	
26 Jul	German GP	Hockenheim	Lotus 99T-Honda	3	
9 Aug	Hungarian GP	Hungaroring	Lotus 99T-Honda	2	
16 Aug	Austrian GP	Österreichring	Lotus 99T-Honda	5	Fl
6 Sep	Italian GP	Monza	Lotus 99T-Honda	2	
20 Sep	Portuguese GP	Estoril	Lotus 99T-Honda	7	
27 Sep	Spanish GP	Jerez	Lotus 99T-Honda	5	
18 Oct	Mexican GP	Mexico City	Lotus 99T-Honda		R
1 Nov	Japanese GP	Suzuka	Lotus 99T-Honda	2	
15 Nov	Australian GP	Adelaide	Lotus 99T-Honda		R

1988

3 Apr	Brazilian GP	Rio	McLaren MP4/4 Honda		P/Dis
1 May	San Marino GP	Imola	McLaren MP4/4 Honda	1	P
15 May	Monaco GP	Monte Carlo	McLaren MP4/4 Honda		P/F1/R
29 May	Mexican GP	Mexico City	McLaren MP4/4 Honda	2	P
12 June	Canadian GP	Montreal	McLaren MP4/4 Honda	1	P/F1
19 June	Detroit GP	Detroit	McLaren MP4/4 Honda	1	P
3 Jul	French GP	Paul Ricard	McLaren MP4/4 Honda	2	
10 Jul	British GP	Silverstone	McLaren MP4/4 Honda	1	
24 Jul	German GP	Hockenheim	McLaren MP4/4 Honda	1	P
8 Aug	Hungarian GP	Hungaroring	McLaren MP4/4 Honda	1	P
28 Aug	Belgian GP	Spa	McLaren MP4/4 Honda	1	P
11 Sep	Italian GP	Monza	McLaren MP4/4 Honda		P/R
25 Sep	Portuguese GP	Estoril	McLaren MP4/4 Honda	6	
2 Oct	Spanish GP	Jerez	McLaren MP4/4 Honda	4	P
30 Oct	Japanese GP	Suzuka	McLaren MP4/4 Honda	1	P/F1
13 Nov	Australian GP	Adelaide	McLaren MP4/4 Honda	2	P

1989

26 Mar	Brazilian GP	Rio	McLaren MP4/5 Honda	11	P

23 Apr	San Marino GP	Imola	McLaren MP4/5 Honda	1	P
7 May	Monaco GP	Monte Carlo	McLaren MP4/5 Honda	1	P
28 May	Mexican GP	Mexico City	McLaren MP4/5 Honda	1	P
4 June	American GP	Phoenix	McLaren MP4/5 Honda		P/F1/R
18 June	Canadian GP	Montreal	McLaren MP4/5 Honda		R
9 Jul	French GP	Paul Ricard	McLaren MP4/5 Honda		R
16 Jul	British GP	Silverstone	McLaren MP4/5 Honda		P/R
30 Jul	German GP	Hockenheim	McLaren MP4/5 Honda	1	P/F1
13 Aug	Hungarian GP	Hungaroring	McLaren MP4/5 Honda	2	
27 Aug	Belgian GP	Spa	McLaren MP4/5 Honda	1	P
10 Sep	Italian GP	Monza	McLaren MP4/5 Honda		P/R
24 Sep	Portuguese GP	Estoril	McLaren MP4/5 Honda		P/R
1 Oct	Spanish GP	Jerez	McLaren MP4/5 Honda		P/F1
22 Oct	Japanese GP	Suzuka	McLaren MP4/5 Honda	1	P/F1/Dis
5 Nov	Australian GP	Adelaide	McLaren MP4/5 Honda		P/R

1990

11 Mar	American GP	Phoenix	McLaren MP4/5B Honda	1	
25 Mar	Brazilian GP	Interlagos	McLaren MP4/5B Honda	3	P
13 May	San Marino GP	Imola	McLaren MP4/5B Honda		P/R

Date	Race	Circuit	Car	No.	Result
27 May	Monaco GP	Monte Carlo	McLaren MP4/5B Honda	1	P/F1
10 June	Canadian GP	Montreal	McLaren MP4/5B Honda	1	P
24 June	Mexican GP	Mexico City	McLaren MP4/5B Honda		R
8 Jul	French GP	Paul Ricard	McLaren MP4/5B Honda	3	
15 Jul	British GP	Silverstone	McLaren MP4/5B Honda	3	
29 Jul	German GP	Hockenheim	McLaren MP4/5B Honda	1	P
12 Aug	Hungarian GP	Hungaroring	McLaren MP4/5B Honda	2	
25 Aug	Belgian GP	Spa	McLaren MP4/5B Honda	1	P
9 Sep	Italian GP	Monza	McLaren MP4/5B Honda	1	P/F1
23 Sep	Portuguese GP	Estoril	McLaren MP4/5B Honda	2	P
30 Sep	Spanish GP	Jerez	McLaren MP4/5B Honda		P/R
21 Oct	Japanese GP	Suzuka	McLaren MP4/5B Honda		P/R
4 Nov	Australian GP	Adelaide	McLaren MP4/5B Honda		P/R

INDEX

278

279

280